Sports Chaplaincy

'This book is a much needed contribution towards the development of scholarly thought in the under-researched area of sports chaplaincy. Addressing wide-ranging topics including anecdotal and historical narratives of sports chaplaincy, Christian theological reflection on the role of the sports chaplain, and analyses of the relationship between sports chaplains and psychologists, this interdisciplinary collection will be sure to generate responses from diverse voices and open up scholarly discussion about the increasingly provocative field of sports chaplaincy.'

Tracy J. Trothen, Queen's University, Canada

'Written by those at the front lines of sports ministry, this is a must read, not only for those engaged in sports ministry but also for anyone studying the evolving relationship between sport and religion in the modern age.'

Shirl James Hoffman, University of North Carolina at Greensboro, USA

'When theology rightly meets praxis, a fruitful result is a book like this. Because the sport-Christianity relationship is tricky, what we do not need is another book that unwittingly gorges on sports culture like a glutton. Discernment about how matters of faith relate to and in the contested world of sports is a prerequisite. This book critically and constructively provides a way forward for how sports chaplains and others might meaningfully interpret and inhabit sports and pastorally care for sportspersons. The blend of academician with practitioner coupled with specific geographical and cultural contexts allow for different perspectives. I look forward to seeing others' responses especially from my former world of professional sports.'

Joe Ehrmann, Coach for America

This ground-breaking book provides an in-depth analysis of the theory and practice of sports chaplaincy in a global context. Written in an accessible style, yet based on academic evidence and theory, the contributors include those leading major national chaplaincy organisations located in the UK, US, Australia and Continental Europe, as well as chaplains and sport psychologists working in elite and amateur sport and those involved in teaching pastoral theology. Providing a rich and informative source of knowledge and inspiration for practitioners, athletes, academics and those interested in the general relationship between sport and faith, contributors also address the provision of sports chaplaincy at sporting mega-events, including the Olympic Games.

This much needed overview of chaplaincy provision in sport across a range of national and international contexts and settings, including both catholic and protestant perspectives, is the first collection of its kind to bring together leading scholars in sports chaplaincy with a view to providing professional accreditation and training amidst the fast-emerging field of sports theology.

Andrew Parker is Professor of Sport and Christian Outreach and Director of the Centre for Sport, Spirituality and Religion (CSSR) in the Faculty of Applied Sciences at the University of Gloucestershire, UK. Andrew's research interests include sport and spirituality, sport and social identity, and physical activity and schooling. Published outputs reflect these interests and have appeared in periodicals such as the *Sociology of Sport Journal*, and the *International Review for the Sociology of Sport*. He is co-author (with Nick J. Watson) of *Sports and Christianity: Historical and Contemporary Perspectives*, *Sport and the Christian Religion: A Systematic Review of Literature* and *Sport, Religion and Disability*. Andrew has served on the editorial boards of the *Sociology of Sport Journal* (2005–2008), *Qualitative Research* (2001–present), and was co-editor of the *International Journal of Religion and Sport* between 2010–2012.

Nick J. Watson is Senior Lecturer in Sport, Culture and Religion and head of pastoral care for sports students at York St John University (YSJU), UK. He is the Co-Director (with Andrew Parker) of the *Centre for Sport, Spirituality and Religion* (CSSR) at the University of Gloucestershire, UK, has coached soccer in England and America and was the Founding Head Coach of La Manga Junior Football Academy, Spain (2001–2006). Nick is a Founder member of the *Sport and Christianity Group*, a collection of scholars and practitioners who developed 'The Declaration on Sport and the Christian Life'. He is the co-author/editor of seven books that address sports and the Christian faith, most recently, *Sport, Religion and Disability* and *Sport and the Christian Religion: A Systematic Review of Literature*, both with Andrew Parker. Nick is the convener for the *Inaugural Global Congress on Sports and Christianity*, YSJU, UK, 2016.

John B. White is Assistant Professor and holder of the Harold and Dottie Riley Professorship in Practical Theology and Director of the Sport Chaplaincy Program at Baylor University: George W. Truett Theological Seminary, USA. John has edited and/or published a range of scholarly articles and books on theology, ethics, religion and sport including: Deardorff, D. and White, J. B. (eds), *The Image of God in the Human Body: Essays on Christianity and Sports*; and White, J. B. and White, C., *Game Day Glory*. Prior to his academic post, John worked in sports ministry and as a sports chaplain which comprised serving and ministering in churches on various NCAA Division 1, 2 and 3 university campuses, at the Olympic Training Center and in Eastern and Western Europe.

Sports Chaplaincy

Trends, issues and debates

Edited by
**Andrew Parker, Nick J. Watson
and John B. White**

Routledge
Taylor & Francis Group

LONDON AND NEW YORK

First published 2016
by Routledge
2 Park Square, Milton Park, Abingdon, Oxon OX14 4RN

and by Routledge
711 Third Avenue, New York, NY 10017

Routledge is an imprint of the Taylor & Francis Group, an informa business

British Library Cataloguing in Publication Data
A catalogue record for this book is available from the British Library

Library of Congress Cataloging-in-Publication Data
Names: Parker, Andrew, 1965– editor. | Watson, Nick J., editor. | White, John B.,
    1967– editor.
Title: Sports chaplaincy : trends, issues and debates / edited by Andrew Parker,
    Nick J. Watson and John B. White.
Description: Surrey, UK, England ; Burlington, VT : Ashgate Publishing Limited,
    [2016] | Includes index.
Identifiers: LCCN 2015026615 | ISBN 9781472414038 (hardcover) |
    ISBN 9781472414045 (pbk)
Subjects: LCSH: Sports—Religious aspects—Christianity. | Athletes—Religious
    life. | Pastoral theology.
Classification: LCC GV706.42. S678 2016 | DDC 796.01—dc23
LC record available at http://lccn.loc.gov/2015026615

ISBN: 9781472414038 (hbk)
ISBN: 9781472414045 (pbk)
ISBN: 9781315610450 (ebk)

Typeset in Bembo
by Apex CoVantage, LLC

In memory of Mike Collins (AP)

To Mark Ellis (Ello), my best mate and best man (NJW)

For chaplain Charles Dupree, a mentor and friend who modelled pastoral care as witnessed in Holy Scripture (JBW)

Contents

Contributors

James H. Bemiller is Associate Professor at the University of Tennessee where he teaches graduate level courses in sports law, organizational behaviour and leadership. His primary research interests include elite performance, risk management and constitutional issues in sport. He lectures nationally and internationally on legal issues in sport and elite performance in sport. Previous publications have appeared in the *Journal of Intercollegiate Sport, Scholastic Coach and Athletic Director, Michigan State University Sport and Entertainment Law Journal* and *Journal of Physical Education Recreation and Dance*. James has also negotiated endorsement and marketing opportunities for professional athletes, including Olympic and World Champions in track and field.

John Boyers began professional life as a schoolteacher before being called to train for Christian ministry. His sports chaplaincy work began in 1977 at Watford Football Club whilst minister at a local church. Some years later his denominational leaders asked him to leave local church ministry to pioneer the development of sports chaplaincy interdenominationally, in the United Kingdom. This became a full-time focus for 20 years under the auspices of the organisation SCORE, now Sports Chaplaincy UK. John has been involved in over 14 major sports event chaplaincies, has served Manchester United Football Club as their official chaplain since 1992, and has spoken and taught extensively on sports chaplaincy. He and his wife Anne live in Sale, south Manchester. They have two grown up boys, each married with two children.

Cameron Butler is national director (CEO) of Sports Chaplaincy Australia where he is strategically involved in developing sports chaplaincy networks for sports communities throughout Australia and internationally. A former youth and assistant church pastor and chaplain to the Melbourne Football Club (1998–2013), he is a member of the Life Saving Chaplaincy Australia Board and is Australia's representative on the International Sports Coalition Council. Cameron lives in Melbourne with his wife Merryl and they have four children.

Harold Cottom has been in ministry for over 30 years and is pastor of Daytonview Church of the Nazarene in Dayton, Ohio. He is a fitness consultant for General Nutrition Center, a personal trainer, competitive body builder and has been involved with sports chaplaincy for nearly 25 years. He works closely with youth, high school, college and professional athletes. Harold is an adjunct faculty in pastoral theology at United Theological Seminary, Dayton, Ohio where he also co-directs the Doctor of Ministry degree cohort in sports chaplaincy. His research interests include pastoral theology in sport, spiritual renewal of clergy, including sports chaplains, and holistic care for athletes.

Lars Dzikus is Associate Professor at the University of Tennessee where he teaches undergraduate and graduate courses in the socio-cultural aspects of sport and leisure. His research interests include sport and globalization (for example, the diffusion of American football to Europe); sport and religion (for example, collegiate sports chaplains) and sport and violence (for example, sexual abuse in youth sport). Previous publications have featured in scholarly journals such as *Athletic Insight, The Sport Psychologist, International Journal of Sport and Ethics, Journal of Contemporary Athletics, Journal of Sport History* and *Journal of Issues in Intercollegiate Athletics*.

Trevor J. Egli is Assistant Professor of sport and fitness leadership at Johnson University, Knoxville. He recently received his doctorate in sport psychology and motor behaviour from the University of Tennessee, Knoxville where his dissertation focused on understanding the role of spirituality within sport psychology consulting relationships. Trevor has also completed research on the exercise motivation of college students and has published in the *Journal of American College Health* and the *Journal of Psychology and Christianity*. He has provided sport psychology consultation to teams and individuals in the United States, Europe and the Caribbean. He is currently working towards certification through the Association for Applied Sport Psychology (AASP).

Leslee A. Fisher is Associate Professor of sport psychology at the University of Tennessee. A former track-and-field and volleyball athlete, she has two Master's degrees (counsellor education and adult fitness) and a doctorate in sport psychology and is the author of numerous academic and applied publications and national and international presentations. Her research focuses on the integration of cultural studies and sport studies, particularly the newly emerging field of cultural sport psychology. Previous publications have appeared in the *Journal of Sport and Exercise Psychology, Sport Psychologist*, the *International Journal of Sport and Exercise Psychology*, the *International Journal of Sport Psychology, Women in Sport and Physical Activity* and *Athletic Insight*. She has served as Secretary/Treasurer of the Association for Applied Sport Psychology (AASP). She is also an AASP fellow, an AASP-certified sport psychology consultant, a National Board Certified Counsellor and a limited licensed professional counsellor.

Richard Gamble is International Development Director for Sports Chaplaincy UK having been Chief Executive Officer of the charity between 2012 and 2014. Prior to this he was chaplain to Leicester City Football Club and has 10 years' experience as a business entrepreneur. His current role focuses on the training and equipping of sports chaplains at the global level and this is informed by his on-going research into the sports chaplaincy–sport psychology interface.

Duncan Green originally qualified as an engineer and was ordained in the Church of England in 1984 following a successful career in the agricultural industry. After serving his curacy in Sussex, he was appointed diocesan youth officer in the Chelmsford Diocese. He later served as team rector and area dean in Saffron Walden, Essex. He was appointed as the Church of England Olympic and Paralympic coordinator in 2007 and seconded to the London Organising Committee for the Olympic Games where he served first as their faith advisor then as head of multi-faith chaplaincy services leading a team of 162 multi-faith chaplains at the 2012 Olympic and Paralympic Games. In 2013 he was appointed Archdeacon of Northolt in the London diocese. Duncan is married to Janet. They have three grown up children and one granddaughter. His interests are youth work, sailing, car restoration (he has a 1931 Morris), rugby and DIY.

Robin L. Hardin is Professor in the sport management programme at the University of Tennessee where he teaches in the areas of intercollegiate athletics, sport communication and sport and religion. His research interests are in the area of intercollegiate athletics especially consumer behaviour, governance, sport communication and the holistic care of collegiate student-athletes. He is author of over 50 academic publications and numerous scholarly presentations. Previous publications have appeared in the *Journal of Applied Sport Management*, the *Journal of Sports Media*, the *International Journal of Sport Management*, the *International Journal of Sport Communication*, the *Journal of Intercollegiate Sport*, *Sport Management Education Journal* and *Sport Marketing Quarterly*. He has served on the editorial boards of the *Journal of Applied Sport Management*, the *International Journal of Sport Communication* and *Sport Management Education Journal*.

Denise M. Hill is Senior Lecturer in sport and exercise psychology in the Faculty of Applied Sciences at the University of Gloucestershire. Her area of research specialism lies within performance psychology, although she has a broad range of academic interests that include exercise and mental health, athletic well-being, and performance failure under pressure. Denise is an accredited sport and exercise scientist with the British Association of Sport and Exercise Science (BASES) offering mental skills support to a number of elite athletes. She currently offers psychological training to a number of professional golfers on the Ladies European Golf Tour and provides mental skills support to a range of athletes within rugby union, hockey, swimming, equestrian and professional snooker.

Greg Linville has served as a professional and college sports chaplain for over 20 years. He is Executive Director of the Association of Church Sports and Recreation Ministers (CSRM) and a licensed Christian worker with the Evangelical Friends Church. He has taught at four different seminaries and universities in three different countries most recently as faculty specialist at Malone University, Canton, Ohio. Awarded the world's first Honorary Doctorate in Sports Ministry (DDiv) from Briercrest Seminary his other degrees include DMin, MDiv Equivalency, MA from Ashland Seminary, BA from Malone College with additional course work at both Reformed and Fuller Seminaries. He is the author of *Christmanship: A Theology of Competition and Sport* (Oliver House Publishers, 2014) and his wider writings include the insert for the official 2002 Salt Lake City (Winter) Olympics Bible, a weekly blog on sports outreach, and a regular column in *Sport Spectrum*.

Anthony M.J. Maranise is a research scholar in the Department of Religion and Philosophy affiliated with the Master of Arts in Catholic Studies Programme at Christian Brothers University in Memphis, Tennessee. He is an oblate of the Order of St Benedict in the Roman Catholic Church, having dedicated his life to academic research and instruction with specializations in the intersection of sport, spirituality and religion; Catholic spirituality; and Benedictine monasticism. As a certified sports lifestyle coach (recognized through the International Sports Professionals Association), he serves student-athletes as a sports chaplain at various institutions throughout the southern United States and is the author of *Sport and the Spiritual Life: The Integration of Playing & Praying* (Amazon Press, 2013).

Noel Mitaxa is an Australian Baptist pastor, author and columnist. He first saw the strategic pastoral and cultural potential of sports ministry in 1989, and his involvement has since included summer speedway and winter football chaplaincies. Sports outreach has also been a major focus through coordinating youth clinics and dinners and the production of publications and short media broadcasts featuring high-profile Christian sports figures. He and his wife Judy live near Ballarat, Australia and have four adult children and four grandchildren.

Mark Nesti is Reader in sport psychology at Liverpool John Moores University, UK where he is also head of the Master of Science in Sport Psychology. Current research interests focus on existential phenomenological psychology, identity, meaning and critical moments in sport. Mark was formerly the consultant counselling sport psychologist to the first team at Bolton Wanderers FC (2003–7), Newcastle United FC (2007–8) and Hull City AFC (2008–10) in the English Premier League. His most recent book *Psychology in Football* (Routledge, 2010) is based on over 15 years' involvement in the sport at Premier League level. A BASES accredited sport psychologist and British Psychological Society chartered psychologist, he has been involved in applied work with many sports during the past 25 years. He is the former Executive Director of the Centre for the Study of Sport and Spirituality at York St John University and is research and scholarship lead for the Saint John Paul II Foundation for Sport.

Ashley Null is a DFG research fellow with the Thomas Cranmer Project, Humboldt-Universitaet zu Berlin, and a three-time Summer Olympic Chaplain. Since 2006, he has also chaired the International Sports Coalition's Major Event Chaplaincy Commission which recommends international Protestant chaplains to global and major regional sporting events. His previous publications include *Real Joy: Freedom to be Your Best* (Haenssler, 2004).

Andrew Parker is Professor of Sport and Christian Outreach and co-director (with Nick Watson) of the Centre for Sport, Spirituality and Religion (CSSR) in the Faculty of Applied Sciences at the University of Gloucestershire. Andrew's research interests include sport and spirituality, sport and social identity, and physical activity and schooling. He has served on the editorial boards of the *Sociology of Sport Journal* (2005–8), *Qualitative Research* (2001–present) and is a former co-editor of the *International Journal of Religion and Sport* (2010–12).

Ed Uszynski (PhD, Bowling Green State University) has been working with collegiate and professional athletes in various roles with Athletes in Action since 1992. He speaks across the US to college students, churches and men's groups on biblical Christianity. He also co-hosts a weekly podcast called *Under Review*, a show dedicated to the examination of ethical, social and theological issues arising from sport culture. He has previously contributed to the four-volume *C.S. Lewis: Life, Works, and Legacy* (edited by Bruce Edwards) and his recent research examines the implicitly religious nature of professional sport fandom through a bar-room ethnography of Cleveland sport fans. He and his wife Amy also speak nationally at the Weekend to Remember Conference with Family Life Ministry and together they have four children.

Steven N. Waller is Associate Professor in the sport management programme at the University of Tennessee where he teaches graduate level courses in research methods, personnel management, organizational behaviour, sport finance and sport and religion. His research interests include religion and sport and barriers to carrier mobility for under-represented groups in sports organizations. He has a particular interest in holistic and pastoral care for athletes and the professional certification of sports chaplains. Steven has published numerous refereed articles in journals such as the *Journal of Religion and Popular Culture*, *Managing Leisure*, *Sport Science Review*, *Therapeutic Recreation Journal*, *Leisure Studies*, *Journal of Contemporary Athletics* and the *Journal of Sport and Social Issues*. He has also contributed to the *Encyclopedia of Sports Management and Marketing*

(Sage, 2011), the *Handbook of Human Resource Management and Workplace Policy* (Praeger, 2007) and the *Dictionary of the Bible and Western Culture* (Phoenix, 2012).

Nick J. Watson is Senior Lecturer in Sport, Culture and Religion and head of pastoral care for sports students at York St John University (YSJU). He has coached soccer in the USA and UK and was founding head coach of La Manga Junior Football Academy, Spain (2001–6). He is co-director (with Andrew Parker) of the Centre for Sport, Spirituality and Religion (CSSR) at the University of Gloucestershire and is convener of the Inaugural Global Congress on Sports and Christianity, 2016 at YSJU. His doctoral work examined the sports–Christianity interface and he has published a number of books on this topic, most recently, *Sport and the Christian Religion: A Systematic Review of Literature* (Cambridge Scholars Publishing, 2014) and *Sports, Religion and Disability* (Routledge, 2015), both with Andrew Parker. He also has a part-time church leadership role in his home town of York.

J. Stuart Weir has been in full-time Christian ministry to sport for 25 years. He is currently director of Verite Sport, a registered charity which exists to promote a Christian presence in sport. As a sports writer he has been to football World Cups, Olympic and Paralympic Games and several sporting world championships. At the 2012 Olympics he served as attaché for Togo. He also writes on sport and Christianity. He is married to Lynne, has two grown-up children and lives in Oxford.

John B. White (PhD, University of Edinburgh) is Assistant Professor and holder of the Harold and Dottie Riley Professorship in Practical Theology and director of the Sport Chaplaincy/Ministry Program at George W. Truett Theological Seminary of Baylor University. He is the Principal Investigator and Faculty Director of the newly established Youth Spirituality and Sports Institute: *Running the Race Well* at Baylor University, which is funded by a grant from Lilly Endowment, Inc. He served for 17 years with Athletes in Action as a campus and sports chaplain, ministering to Olympic and collegiate athletes both in the United States and in western and eastern Europe. His research interests are primarily in theology, Christian ethics and sport and Christianity. His publications have appeared in *Sport, Ethics and Philosophy*, *Implicit Religion*, *Studies in Christian Ethics*, *Practical Theology*, and *The Oxford Encyclopedia of Bible and Ethics* (Oxford, 2014). He is co-editor (with Bracy Hill) of *God, Nimrod, and the World: Exploring Christian Perspectives on Sport Hunting* (Mercer University Press, 2017).

Acknowledgements

Writing projects of this kind are always collective ventures and ones which often take longer than we might first imagine. We wish to record our grateful thanks to those who have helped us to produce this volume. We are especially indebted to our contributors: for agreeing to be involved in the first place, for their attention to detail on editorial queries, and for their patience concerning final publication. We are also grateful to friends and colleagues who have offered encouragements and support along the way and who have endured our endless deliberations and questions. Likewise, we are extremely grateful to Sarah Lloyd at Ashgate for her help and advice and to others who provided insightful comments on earlier drafts. Last, but by no means least, we would like to thank our wives, Beckie, Kate and Cindy, for their love, patience and support and for taking care of all the things that we should have been doing whilst we were working on what follows. Needless to say, the inadequacies and inconsistencies found herein are entirely our own.

Preface

Chaplaincy is burgeoning throughout the western world. Everywhere we look we find chaplains: in the supermarket, at the airport, in the train station, within industry and business. It seems that chaplaincy has become necessary right across our social strata. Precisely why this is the case is unclear. Does the rise of chaplaincy mirror the general rise of a broad and open spirituality which seems to be on the increase in the West? Are chaplains called to be the heart of organizations which otherwise can appear cold, clinical and deeply materialistic in orientation? Whatever the reason, chaplaincy seems to matter.

But what exactly do chaplains do? Some years ago my colleague Harriet Mowat and I were commissioned by the Scottish government to do some research into the nature of chaplaincy in Scotland. The Scottish government had extended its spiritual care policy to make it compulsory for each healthcare trust to have a 'Centre for Spiritual Care'. Once upon a time it would have been called a 'chaplaincy centre', but, within a spiritual environment wherein spirituality was becoming more and more pluralistic, the idea of 'spiritual care' was perceived as a more inclusive concept. However, having implemented this policy, people realized that no one had done any research into exactly what it was that healthcare chaplains do. So the task that we were given was to try to find an answer to the question 'What do chaplains do?' Chaplaincy, we observed, was in an interesting and transient phase. In its original form it was a task that was done by ordained ministers. The qualification for chaplaincy was ordination. Now that was changing and opening up. The actual practices of chaplaincy were becoming as diverse as the modes of spirituality that they were called to encounter. What we discovered was that chaplains did not necessarily do anything different from other healthcare professionals: caring presence, listening, counselling, grief work and so forth. The originality of what they did emerged from the ways in which they configured these different pastoral skills around the task of meeting people spiritually. It was this reconfiguration that gave them their depth, healing potential and a place within the complexities of a modern healthcare context. Chaplaincy provided for the soul of healthcare. We concluded that what chaplains do, is to bring the system and all who work within it back to issues of the heart.

Within the Christian tradition the heart is the seat of our affectivity. It relates to that dimension within us that is not driven by materialistic goals but rather finds its focus in the desire to relate, to love, to be in communion with that which is beyond, be it temporal or divine. Jean Vanier suggests:

> The heart is capable of receiving and giving love, of living in communion with another person and with God, capable of being a source of life for others. In the designs of God, it is the heart, which is meant to inspire all human activities.[1]

To bring us back to issues of the heart is to enable us to live out our humanness wherever we are called to be. Chaplains are always and inevitably people of the heart.

What is true of healthcare chaplains is surely true of sports chaplains. In a world that can at times be quite heartless, sports chaplains are called to become people of the heart who help others to re-imagine sport as a practice of the heart as well as the body. The contributors to this book begin to open up the question of what it is that sports chaplains do. Each of the chapters provides different facets that, taken together, outline the meaning of sports chaplaincy. As we read them as a whole, rather like the different facets of a diamond, we are moved to see the deep significance of chaplaincy for those engaging in the competitive and sometimes difficult world of sport. In a world that is driven by the desire to win, to beat your neighbour rather than to love your neighbour, the role of the chaplain who brings the gentle, peaceful and democratizing power of the gospel into that context is not always obvious. How can the virtues of gentleness, patience, kindness, humility, respectfulness and unfailing love for one's brother and sister, find any kind of meaningful place within a world of sport that seems to be driven by the desire to overcome and to overpower the other? Such an environment can easily militate against the purposes of the heart.

Sports chaplains strive to bring practical answers to such questions. It is not necessary to set an antithesis between the goals of competitive sport and the goals of heartfelt communion, but it does take a particular kind of culture broker to bring the two together. A culture broker is someone who bridges the gap between two quite different cultures, someone who has a foot in both camps, someone who knows and understands the language of competition and who is fluent in the language of the heart. That person is the chaplain. The chaplain embodies the communion of the heart and seeks to draw the practices of competitiveness into their proper place. Competitiveness finds its true direction only when it realizes the significance of the heart. The task of the chaplain is to create contexts where hospitable conversations between these two quite different worlds can be opened up and brought to fruitful conclusions.

This book is a fascinating and important contribution both to chaplaincy and to the world of sport. It deserves to be taken seriously. In a world that looks as though it has lost its sense of communion, reclaiming the significance of the heart is a powerful contribution to the type of transformation that sits at the heart of the gospel. Sports chaplaincy is one way in which such transformation can find embodiment.

Professor John Swinton
Chair in Divinity and Religious Studies
University of Aberdeen, UK

Note

1 J.Vanier (2007). *Man and Woman, God Made Them*, Mahwah, NJ: Paulist Press, 36.

Introduction

Trends, issues and debates in sports chaplaincy

Andrew Parker, Nick J. Watson and John B. White

Over the past 30 to 40 years, there has been a steady growth in the academic literature concerning sport and religion. Within this genre, authors have explored a variety of topics and issues. There are books about sport and faith, sport and spirituality, sport and religious ethics. This is a book about sports chaplaincy and, more specifically, the major trends, issues and debates that have shaped (and continue to shape) the public outworking of Christian chaplaincy in sporting contexts. One of the things that stands out in the more recent academic literature on sport and religion is the way in which the specific relationship between sport and Christianity has developed over time, not simply because scholars have had the compulsion to delve deeper into the similarities between these two cultural entities but also because of the fact that the Church was one social institution among many which historically found itself caught up in the momentum surrounding the wider popularization of sport. Since then the relationship has ebbed and flowed, characterized on the one hand by a more general (and growing) Christian acceptance of sport as a 'useful' and 'acceptable' physical, moral and emotional practice, and on the other by an increasingly commercialized sporting world the values of which, as time goes on, appear to sit less and less easily with formal religion of any kind.

Of course, what all of this illustrates is that sport does not exist in a social vacuum. On the contrary, it evolves and develops in accordance with a variety of broader factors and forces whilst at the same time embedding itself further into the very fabric of everyday life. Modern-day sport looks like it does, because it has been (and continues to be) shaped and formed in line with the turbulence of social existence (politics, economics, culture etc.) which, in turn, makes it what it is. The sport–Christianity relationship is no different. This too is a reflection of the way in which sport has had an increasing impact upon wider society and has progressed from being a marginal social pastime to an established feature of daily living. It is neither the intention nor the remit of this book to debate the pros and cons of such matters, but what the following chapters do illustrate is the way in which this relationship has developed in specific social and cultural contexts and how we might think further about the connections between sport and the Christian faith in and through the work of sports chaplains.

So, why this particular book and why now? Amidst the growth of publications on the relationship between sport and Christianity, this volume is born out of a sense of momentum, a momentum which has gathered pace as a consequence of the expansion of sports chaplaincy globally and the growing interest amongst practitioners and scholars alike in analysing and interrogating what it is that sports chaplains do and how they might critically assess the processes and practices of their everyday work. The genesis of the book is rooted in three main aims: (1) to build upon and extend the personalized accounts of sports chaplaincy which already exist; (2) to further the establishment of a body of scholarly literature in this, as yet, under-researched and under-reported field; and (3) to uncover more fully what the role of the sports chaplain looks like within specific geographical and cultural contexts. The overall objective is to provide an academic resource from which students, scholars and lay readers may gain both a flavour and an overview of the variety and quality of previous and on-going work in this area. What transpires is a series of essays produced by a selection of writers who bring with them a wide range of experience in and around related fields and who, as a result, provide a series of informed and challenging essays in their particular areas of expertise. To this end, the book is divided into three parts which encapsulate the specific interests of the featured authors: Part I, international perspectives on sports chaplaincy (Weir; Boyers; Linville; Butler and Mitaxa; Green); Part II, conceptualizing sports chaplaincy (Watson; Uszynski; Waller and Cottom; White; Null) and Part III, sports chaplaincy: practice and praxis (Maranise; Waller et al.; Nesti; Egli and Fisher; Gamble, Parker and Hill).

Much has been said and written about sports ministry per se but little about the specifics of chaplaincy within sporting contexts, and kicking-off proceedings in Chapter 1 is someone who has a significant degree of oversight and influence across the sport–Christianity landscape as a practitioner, J. Stuart Weir. By charting a range of contexts within which sports chaplains operate, Weir's portrayal of the evolution of sports chaplaincy globally serves to set the scene for the remaining contributors. Reflecting his extensive knowledge and experience in this area, Weir tracks the evolution of sports chaplaincy at the elite sports level in relation both to individual sports and major sporting events. Accordingly, what Weir provides is a mapping of the global landscape upon which sports chaplaincy sits and the diversity of events and contexts which it serves.

Building upon the global picture put forward by Weir, in Chapter 2 John Boyers provides the first of four personal reflections on sports chaplaincy in different geographical regions and settings. Armed with over 35 years of experience of working as an official sports chaplain at Watford Football Club from 1977 to 1992 and Manchester United Football Club from 1992 to the present and at over a dozen major sporting events, Boyers outlines the main historical and conceptual developments in the evolution of sports chaplaincy in the UK from the mid-1970s to the present day. In detailing this history, Boyers discusses some of the pioneers of UK sports chaplaincy and the contributions which they made to the evolution of that movement.

One of the things that both Weir and Boyers acknowledge is that North America has long been a hive of activity with regards to sports chaplaincy. That said, relatively few writers have explored either the denominational complexities or the broader evangelical nuances of the US sports chaplaincy model. Addressing all of these objectives, Greg Linville's work in Chapter 3 seeks to uncover some of the characteristics of chaplaincy provision to US sports whilst at the same time mounting a critique of its generic methodology. Linville argues that the cultural and institutional conditions under which elite sports chaplaincy functions in the US often militates against its overall effectiveness and efficiency as a form of ministry. Emphasizing the need for a greater sense of connection between sports chaplaincy, sport-related para-ministries and the local church, Linville puts forward a series of propositions as to how the US model might be re-envisioned in line with specific theological and philosophical principles.

Common to anecdotal and practitioner accounts of the sport–Christianity nexus is the sense that the 1970s and 1980s were a time when chaplaincy began to gain momentum across a range of sporting locales, and what Cameron Butler and Noel Mitaxa present in Chapter 4 confirms that Australia was no exception in this respect. Charting the birth and subsequent expansion of Sports Chaplaincy Australia, Butler and Mitaxa argue that as the pastoral needs of sporting communities have increased in Australia over the past 30 years so too have the opportunities for sports chaplains to serve and minister to unchurched groups. Demonstrating the practical application of some of the arguments put forward by Linville, Butler and Mitaxa articulate the way in which, in the face of unprecedented demand for pastoral care-givers in sports settings, the work of Sports Chaplaincy Australia seeks to empower the local church to release its members into ministry as chaplains in their local communities.

What these initial chapters clearly articulate is that by the late 1980s individuals working in and around the broader orbits of sports ministry had come to identify major sporting events as an important setting for chaplaincy provision. As Weir observes, formalized accounts of how mega-event chaplaincy is planned and organized are few and far between and so who better to provide an in-depth commentary on how such provision takes shape than the person responsible for fulfilling this role at the London 2012 Olympics and Paralympics, Reverend Canon Duncan Green. In Chapter 5, Green maps his involvement in the bringing together of various faith communities to create the infrastructure for what he describes as a 'radical and innovative chaplaincy programme' at London 2012. Beginning with his appointment as the Church of England Olympics Executive Coordinator in November 2007, Green provides a fly-on-the-wall account of the practical and political nuances of his role and how chaplaincy services were ultimately delivered at the Games.

Part II takes a slightly different tack and focuses on theological conceptualizations of sports chaplaincy amidst the complex realities of modern life. Countering the dearth of academic literature addressing the specific impact of family breakdown on sport, in Chapter 6, Nick J. Watson demonstrates how sports chaplaincy might address the cultural phenomenon of 'fatherlessness'. Examining the pandemic of fatherlessness in modern Western culture, Watson argues that the mystery and beauty of servant-hearted sports chaplaincy is its ability to reveal the heart of the Father to players (and staff) who are in a state of crisis or transition, experiencing failure, grief or stress or who are simply in need of a non-judgemental friend or mentor whom they can trust. Watson reflects upon the socio-cultural and spiritual context in which sports chaplains currently operate and offers a series of suggestions as to how they might recognise and deal with fatherlessness as and when it arises as an underlying issue in the course of their everyday work.

Discussions of the socio-cultural realities of modern life necessarily bring with them images of a move away from collective religious experience towards more individualized notions of spirituality, and, in Chapter 7, Ed Uszynski considers the implications of such a shift for sports chaplains. Uszynski argues that those who seek to minister within contemporary culture must contend with and understand this new social reality. Sports chaplains are tasked with stepping fully into this cultural moment prepared to act as a guide, a conductor equipped not only to understand the default spiritual mentality of the typical modern-day athlete but also to escort them toward an understanding of how the gospel intersects with their personal journey to shape their lives and identities.

Picking up on the offerings of both Uszynski and Butler and Mitaxa, in Chapter 8 Harold Cottom and Steven N. Waller further advance our broader conceptualizations by exploring the 'shepherding' responsibilities of the modern-day sports chaplain. Locating their discussion within the specific context of US sports chaplaincy, Cottom and Waller examine the biblical and theological aspects of pastoral or 'shepherding' ministry whilst exploring some of the challenges facing exponents of such roles (that is, chaplains) within and across sporting locales. Cottom and Waller conclude that the presence of a coherent pastoral theology is an essential underpinning to the potential contribution which sports chaplains can make across the world.

Furthering considerations of the specific nature of sports chaplaincy amidst the vagaries of the contemporary sporting life, in Chapter, 9 John B. White poses two main questions: how are the convictions of the gospel fundamental to Christian sports chaplaincy and how should the good news inform and transform the way in which sports chaplains serve? White's central claim is that the modern-day culture of sport requires sports chaplains to be shaped by the whole gospel and to view this both as a theological task and personal responsibility. Arguing the case for the prophetic voice of sports chaplaincy, White concludes that the gospel calls chaplains back to the work of Christ as definitive for how they care for the people of sport and that when sportspersons reflect and practise a distorted identity, chaplains must graciously speak in word and deed God's perspective on sport and life.

Our concluding sojourn into the conceptualization of sports chaplaincy is provided, in Chapter 10, by Ashley Null who, drawing on many years of experience as an Olympic chaplain, raises the question: what should be the chaplain's approach to ministry to the sporting elite? Through examples and anecdotes of his work at this level, Null depicts the highs and the lows of athletic life positing the gospel as the antidote to the 'shame culture' of the world of elite sport. Reiterating the sentiments of Uszynski and White, Null counters the personal identity problems experienced by many high-profile athletes with the gospel truth of unconditional love. The task of any chaplain in such circumstances, Null argues, is to help athletes learn to separate their personal identity from their athletic performance and to make them aware that only love (and not sporting achievement) has the power to make human beings feel truly significant and to make them emotionally whole.

And finally to Part III, which discusses the practicalities of sports chaplaincy and investigates emerging connections with wider academic disciplines and discourse. First up is Anthony M.J. Maranise, who, in Chapter 11, draws on his expertise as a chaplain within the Catholic faith to discuss six primary responsibilities and practices common to all sports chaplains, regardless of their country of origin or nature of service. Contemplating the civil and moral threat posed by the 'win-at-all-costs' nature of elite sports participation and media reportage of the lives and lifestyles of modern sports stars, Maranise locates chaplains as 'first responders' to personal and moral emergencies in the sporting world. This discussion leads to the conclusion that sports chaplains provide a valuable resource – both to athletes and to the people whom they regularly encounter – by assisting in the holistic growth and development of those entrusted to their care and that the greater role of the sports chaplain is the implementation and continual maintenance of an 'ethical mentality' in sport.

Recent years have witnessed an increasing amount of discussion around how best to facilitate and organize the training and accreditation of sports chaplains thereby bringing a sense of standardization to the role and suitable preparatory (and on-going) support to those who are called to undertake its duties. Several key individuals have progressed such debate, none of which have been more influential than Steven N. Waller, Robin L. Hardin, Lars Dzikus and James H. Bemiller at the University of Tennessee, Knoxville. In Chapter 12, Waller and colleagues provide a comprehensive overview of their thinking on this topic that ultimately comprises a framework within which the 'professionalization' of sports chaplaincy can be situated. These authors argue that such debates are important not least because there is no single organization that serves to credentialize sports chaplains globally and, moreover, because in a world where certification and accreditation are the hallmarks of occupational identity, a myriad of administrative, theological, ethical and legal risks emerge.

Taking on board the disciplinary principles outlined by Waller and colleagues, the final three chapters of the book provide in-depth considerations of the possibilities and potential offered by the relationship between sports chaplaincy and sport psychology. In Chapter 13, established academic Mark Nesti presents his experiences of working as a consultant sport psychologist in the English (football) Premier League and examines the stereotypes and viewpoints attached to both psychologists and chaplains within this setting. What Nesti argues is that sport psychologists operating inside elite football have much to gain from developing their professional relationships with club chaplains. That is not to say that sport psychologists should be asked to provide religious or spiritual support to their clients, rather that collaboration between the two has the potential to assist sport psychologists in their broader understanding of the people with whom they work, whilst also allowing them to reflect more deeply on their own philosophy of practice.

Progressing the work of Nesti one step further, in Chapter 14, Trevor J. Egli and Leslee A. Fisher investigate how sport psychologists might engage with faith and spirituality issues during consultation. Beginning with an exploration of how the field of applied sport psychology has traditionally engaged with notions of faith, spirituality and religion, Egli and Fisher go on to present a series of practical steps that sport psychology consultants might consider before working with athletes who express an interest in (and affinity for) faith and spirituality issues. The authors conclude by putting forward suggestions as to how sport psychology consultants and sports chaplains might work together to better facilitate the needs of athletes who consider spirituality a salient component of their identity.

All of which leads nicely to Chapter 15, where Richard Gamble, Andrew Parker and Denise M. Hill provide an empirical depiction of the way in which the relationship between sports chaplaincy and sport psychology might work in practice. Drawing upon the findings of a small-scale, qualitative research study into the potential connections between those inhabiting these two distinct practitioner disciplines in English Premier League football, the chapter reveals a significant degree of overlap between the work of psychologists and chaplains, whilst at the same time identifying a number of barriers that may restrict the kinds of support which they collectively offer the players with whom they work.

In sum, *Sports Chaplaincy: Trends, Issues and Debates* aims not only to reflect on the ways in which the underpinning principles of the Christian faith might allow us to consider and challenge the values and practices of modern-day sport, but also how they might enhance the way in which we see the future of sport both in terms of its participatory and structural formation. We believe that it is by way of such reflection that our understandings of the role of the sports chaplain can continue to thrive and that the desire for on-going scholarship in this area will be stimulated and encouraged. Needless to say, we trust that this book will be both a stimulus and an encouragement to our readership.

Part I

International perspectives

1 Sports chaplaincy

A global overview

J. Stuart Weir[1]

Introduction

Sports chaplaincy should not be regarded as a homogenous entity. On the contrary, there are a range of models, frameworks, approaches and practices which fall under this generic heading. In turn, a variety of related roles have evolved over time, these include chaplains being associated with local sports clubs or teams, chaplains working with national teams, sports chaplains in colleges and universities, chaplains to particular sports (nationally or internationally) or sporting 'tours' (for example, a golf or tennis tour) and chaplains at major sports events.

The *modus operandi* of a sports chaplain can vary considerably from conducting pre-game chapel services – a mainly North American activity – to a less high profile pastoral role involving one-to-one support. One chaplain may stress the evangelistic nature of the role; another may see their primary function as that of Bible teacher. Others may speak of being a 'pastoral safety net' while others still may use the term 'sports mentor' (Lipe, 2006). For some, conducting weddings and funerals can be a significant part of the job and a means of establishing credibility through practical acts of service in a sporting environment. Most chaplains serve as volunteers, but some are paid. Since the origins of sports chaplaincy, chapel services or team Bible studies have been a significant part of the role, particularly in North America. The justification for chapel services is clear. With players travelling a great deal to compete nationally and internationally, they cannot be part of a local church every Sunday. Chapel is about bringing Church to the players.

Moreover, the way that sports chaplaincy has developed in the US or in Australia is not the same as in the UK. In this chapter I uncover the origins of sports chaplaincy and examine the different models which have emerged over the last 40 years. At the same time, I identify some of the key issues which have arisen from the development of sports chaplaincy as a practitioner field. The individuals mentioned in this chapter are to be considered pioneers in this field in that there was no existing model of sports chaplaincy for them to draw upon and replicate. For them it was a case of adopting and adapting existing practice from church, military and hospital chaplaincy (which had existed since the eighteenth century) to see what worked (Tyndall, 2004).

North American models of sports chaplaincy

The acknowledged pioneer of American professional sports chapel services was Ira 'Doc' Eshleman, who in 1950 was founding pastor of Bibletown Church, Boca Raton, Florida, now known as Boca Raton Community Church. As a sports fan, Eshleman was struck by the fame and potential influence as role models of NFL players, whose pictures he had seen on breakfast cereal packets and whose profiles he recognized as 'an untapped reservoir of spiritual witness' (Fisher, 1969: 44). Eshleman asked himself a simple question: Could these football players be reached for Christ? While Eshleman was not the pioneer of Christian ministry to NFL players, he was the first to do it in a systematic way, building on the earlier work of Bill Glass of the Cleveland Browns, Buddy Dial of the Pittsburgh Steelers and Norm Evans of the Miami Dolphins all of whom held Sunday morning chapel services for teammates in the early and mid-1960s (see Glass, 1971, 1974, 1981; Ladd and Mathisen, 1999).

Eshleman began to work with these teams and approached others. In 1968 he found himself 'on the road' for 18 weeks, travelling 100,000 miles and speaking at NFL chapels on consecutive Sundays. According to Fisher, Eshleman had a clear spiritual and evangelistic purpose: 'My mission to the pro is to help him establish a personal and meaningful relationship between himself and God, and then urge him to share his faith with others' (cited in Fisher, 1969: 54). At the same time he began to take on a pastoral and counselling role as players, learning to trust him, sought his advice on personal and family issues. He believed that a player could not 'be at his best on the field, if he goes out there worrying about an unfaithful wife, a rebellious child, or if he holds a grudge against one of his team mates' (cited ibid.). Yet Eshleman appeared to have a great sensitivity in ministry, realizing that players were 'quick to detect those who move among them for personal or selfish reasons' (cited ibid. 63). Without intention and unbeknown to himself, he created a blueprint for sports chaplaincy which others would follow.

The pattern in baseball was similar to that in American football. Bobby Richardson, who played for the New York Yankees (1955–66), started Sunday services for teammates in the mid-1960s at a time when chapel services were also taking place for the Minnesota Twins and Chicago Cubs (see Richardson, 2012). These informal gatherings of a few players reading the Bible and praying together at a team hotel or venue moved to more formal arrangements through an initiative by Watson Spoelstra, a Detroit sportswriter, who in 1973 approached baseball commissioner, Bowie Kuhn, with the idea of organizing a chapel programme for every major league baseball team. Kuhn granted approval and Baseball Chapel was created. By 1975 all of the major league baseball teams had a chapel programme.

In his professional ice-hockey playing days, Don Liesemer had a real passion to reach his teammates with the gospel. While playing for the Muskegon Mohawks, he enlisted the help of his church pastor, Bill Dondit, whose friendship was appreciated by the players. When Liesemer retired from professional ice-hockey in 1975 he worked as a school teacher and undertook NFL football chaplaincy while maintaining contact with hockey players that he knew. In 1977 he felt called to resign as a teacher and founded Hockey Ministries International (HMI) in order to encourage and meet the spiritual needs of the hockey world.

John Tolson, who had played basketball for Arizona State College and William Carey College in the 1960s, was one of the men who pioneered chapel services in the NBA starting with the Houston Rockets in 1978. Tolson initially went to a Rockets practice session, introduced himself to some of the players and enquired as to whether they ever prayed before games. On learning that such things were non-existent in the NBA, he offered to pray with players before the next game. The practice became established and chaplaincy had started. Tolson then contacted ministers he knew in other cities where there were NBA teams and encouraged them to become chaplains. In 1979 Joel Freeman became chaplain to the Washington Bullets (now the Washington Wizards), and in 1981 Bill Alexson became chaplain to the Boston Celtics where he served for 20 years. Alexson also travelled to other cities to meet players and teams and to introduce chaplaincy to them. In 1983 Pro-Basketball Fellowship was established to coordinate NBA chaplaincy and to network existing chaplains.

As part of his critique of North American sports chaplaincy, Krattenmaker (2010) raises two key concerns. First, he berates the commissioners and the management of the major leagues and the teams themselves for allowing 'one-sided' chapel services which are conducted in a way that 'denigrates legitimate religious alternatives' (p.103). He goes on to argue that chaplaincy should reflect the religious diversity of society rather than simply the leanings of evangelical Christianity. While the predominance of evangelical Protestant chaplains in North American sport may be seen to reflect the more pro-active organization of evangelicals with regard to an engagement with sport, there are questions to be answered here as to whether a proselytizing style of chaplaincy is appropriate within this context. Krattenmaker's second concern – echoing that of Deford (1976a, 1976b, 1976c) – is that, as one observes modern-day North American sport it is easy to see the vagaries of commercial excess – obsession with winning, racial and gender discrimination, unprecedented wealth, gratuitous violence, serious injury and the exploitation of sex – yet it is rare to hear a chaplain speak out prophetically against such 'evils and injustices' (see also Hoffman, 2010; Watson and White, 2007). Krattenmaker accepts that chaplains may be reluctant to jeopardize their position by criticizing their team or sport and, to this end, may choose to 'turn a blind eye' to such moral issues in order to preserve their status (p.103). All of which raises a series of further questions about the responsibilities of the chaplain within this environment, the expectations underpinning this role, and the kinds of tensions and dilemmas which may arise when sports chaplains are contractually bound and financially remunerated.

UK models of sports chaplaincy

The first chaplain to be officially appointed to an English professional football club was John Jackson in March 1962. The appointment came about when Jackson, who was minister of Harehills Methodist Church in Leeds at the time, met the Leeds United general manager, Cyril Williamson, and suggested that the club might consider appointing a chaplain. Initially Jackson was asked by the team manager, Don Revie, to concentrate on helping the junior players at the club to adapt to life in the 'big city'. In an article for the Methodist Home Mission, Jackson described his role as one through which he was simply able to be of service: 'I do not go to the ground to take Christ there since I remember that he is there before me. I just go in case he needs an errand boy' (1984: 34).

Michael Chantry became chaplain to Hertford College, Oxford in 1961. Shortly after Oxford United were promoted to the Football League in 1962, Chantry was invited to be their club chaplain, a position he held until his death in September 2003. The club may have chosen Chantry because of his experience of chaplaincy in his university post. Mike Pusey became chaplain to Aldershot in 1973. When Pusey came to speak at St James Road Baptist Church in Watford in 1977, he shared his passion for football chaplaincy with the then student minister, John Boyers. Boyers, who became chaplain to Watford FC in 1977, went on to play a leading role in the development of football chaplaincy, organizing the first English football chaplains conference in the UK under the auspices of Christians in Sport in the mid-1980s. In 1991 Boyers founded SCORE (Sports Chaplaincy Offering Resources and Encouragement, later Sports Chaplaincy UK) and worked full-time in sports chaplaincy through SCORE until his retirement in 2014. Currently 59 of the 92 English Premier League and Football League clubs have a chaplain, a small number of whom have documented the everyday nuances of the UK sports chaplaincy model (Boyers, 2000, 2011; Heskins and Baker, 2006; Rushworth-Smith, 1985; Wood, 2011).

The traditional pattern of chaplaincy in English professional football has been for a local minister to contact a club with a request to act as team chaplain, often assisted in this approach by SCORE/Sports Chaplaincy UK. In the North American context, the chaplain will seek to organize and speak at a team chapel service. Andrew Wingfield Digby's role as spiritual advisor to the England cricket team represents a totally different model for a number of reasons. Firstly, his appointment was at the invitation of the Test and County Cricket Board (renamed the England and Wales Cricket Board in 1997). Secondly, it was an appointment to a national team and not to an individual club. Thirdly, there was no formal religious aspect to the role. Wingfield Digby a Minor Counties (semi-professional) player and director of Christians in Sport, was a regular on the professional cricket scene and known to a significant number of professional players. Ted Dexter, Chairman of the England cricket selectors invited Wingfield Digby to be involved with the England team in the early 1990s. Dexter had been a contemporary of the Reverend David Sheppard in the England team in the late 1950s and had found it helpful to have a Christian influence around the dressing room.

Wingfield Digby, who was appointed in June 1991 and served until 2000, saw his role as offering spiritual support to anyone who sought it. The current England team do not have a chaplain, but players have access to sport psychologists. An important difference here is that a chaplain is independent of the team hierarchy while sport psychologists often report directly to management on issues relating to player welfare and performance.

Tour chaplaincy

Being a chaplain to a club or team which is based in one location or city for at least half of its games is one thing, but providing spiritual support to a group of sportsmen or women who are rarely, if ever, in the same place – perhaps not even in the same country — for more than a short amount of time is another matter altogether. Fritz Glaus, who had been a college tennis player and then coach, served as chaplain to the men's tennis tour for 12 years (1980–92), spending ten months a year travelling and watching an estimated 21,000 tennis matches in that time. However, he was not the pioneer of tennis ministry. Ramsey Earnhardt and Eddie Waxer (arguably the godfather of Christian ministry to sport), had previously travelled to a small number of tennis tournaments and led some chapel services for players. For some of the 12 years that Glaus was active, Jenny Geddes and Carol Fullerton carried out a parallel ministry among women tennis players. According to Glaus (2012: 17), the job involved (amongst other things) 'conducting twice-weekly Bible studies, meeting one-on-one with players, forming friendships in the locker rooms . . . [and] organizing housing for players with Christian families'. Given the early stage of the development of sports chaplaincy Glaus started his work with a remarkably clear job description which he and Waxer drew up in 1980. Glaus was to disciple existing Christian players on the men's tour, follow up new Christians on the tour, make himself available to a growing number of players who expressed an interest in spiritual matters, cultivate relationships with non-Christian players, identify key Christian leaders in the international tennis community who could speak to players about Christ in their mother tongue, recognize the broader spiritual needs of players, and explore ministry opportunities worldwide. The work was entirely unofficial with no recognition from the tennis authorities. Glaus (2012: 72) was sensitive to possible charges of what some might call inappropriate evangelism: 'The last thing I wanted to do was push my beliefs on anybody. Ask anyone who was in the men's tour in the 1980s, and they'll tell you I was out there to be a friend to them'.

Professional golf in the US has always been one of the most Christian of sports, with up to 60 players attending a weekly Bible study on the men's PGA Tour and 30 women involved in similar gatherings on the LPGA tour. Tournaments run from Thursday to Sunday, making conventional church attendance impossible, so the players 'do Church' on Wednesday evenings. The first PGA

Tour Bible study was held in 1965 with golfer Jim Hiskey the main instigator. In 1981 Hiskey invited Larry Moody who had been running chapel services for the Baltimore Colts NFL team since 1978 to be the PGA Bible study leader. Moody started in 1981 and at the time of writing is still serving in the role. Originally he went to around 10 tournaments a year but over time that increased to more than 30. As provider of chaplaincy to the travelling golf community, Moody aimed to be all the things that a minister would be in a local church – pastor, counsellor, Bible study leader and encourager – but in a different city each week.

Cris Stevens offers an equivalent ministry in women's professional golf. She attended the US Open in 1980 as a spectator and over the next two years got to know some of the players. She was invited to become their Bible study leader in 1982. Travelling to 30 tournaments per year, Stevens is there to help Christians on the tour to grow in their faith and to give other players the opportunity to think about the claims of Christianity. While she leads Bible studies and organizes events, she sees one-to-one relationships as the key to her work. Bruce Gillingham began chaplaincy to European Tour golf in 1989 before handing over some years later to Mark Pinney of Logos Golf. Liz Wilson supported players in European women's professional golf for a number of years. Gillingham, Wilson and Pinney largely followed the US golf chaplaincy model.

Like golf and tennis, athletics and motor sport bring with them large amounts of travel and transient lifestyles. In turn, they present a series of disparate and diverse tensions and pressures for those performing at the highest level. Mark McAllister worked as an unofficial chaplain to the British athletics team between 1989 and 2002, travelling to major sporting events – Olympics and World Championships – as well as five domestic events a year, this in addition to meeting athletes one-to-one out of season. At major championships daily Bible studies were not uncommon with McAllister estimating that about 60 British athletes attended at least one such event during that period.

Motor Racing Outreach (MRO) was founded in 1988 when Pastor Max Hilton met NASCAR driver Darrell Waltrip who told Hilton that he found it difficult racing on Sundays as this meant that he was unable to attend church. Hilton responded by resigning from his church in Los Angeles and moving his family to Charlotte, North Carolina, where the headquarters of NASCAR racing was situated and founding MRO. As the name suggests, MRO has an evangelistic emphasis but it also seeks to offer pastoral support to the racing community. In association with MRO, Alex Ribeiro, a former Formula One racing driver, spent three years (1999–2001) driving the medical car at F1 races in exchange for the opportunity to minister to the sport's wider community. He ran chapel services on race day and talked to racing people one-to-one.

Major event chaplaincy

Chaplaincy is an established feature of the Olympic and Paralympic Games and has become increasingly part and parcel of the Commonwealth Games,

Pan-American Games and World Athletics Championships. However, because 'local' organizing committees have a significant amount of autonomy over the formal structures around which these events are organized, the number of chaplains accredited, and the degree to which they are permitted access to competitors varies greatly. Lixey (2008) traces major event chaplaincy back to the early twentieth century. He argues that 'in the case of the Olympics, the pastoral care of the chaplains within the Olympic Village is subject to the specific norms of the International Olympic Committee which has made religious services a part of the Olympics since London 1908' (p.75). While it is true that Ethelbert Talbot, bishop of Central Pennsylvania, preached at a service on 19 July 1908 in St Paul's Cathedral to which athletes and Olympic officials were invited, there is no evidence of any chaplaincy until much later (Widund, 1994).

The first occasion on which an international team of chaplains ministered at the Olympic Games was in Seoul, South Korea in 1988, but there were a number of forerunners to this. Tyndall (2004: 118) reports that in Helsinki in 1952 'many Christian activities were organised' with Schäfer (2006) confirming that a German Lutheran pastor provided pastoral support for German speaking athletes and visitors in Helsinki. There is, however, no evidence of the local organizing committee running a chaplaincy programme in 1952. At the 1956 Melbourne Olympics, a ministry was exercised to Olympians through a team of chaplains within the Olympic Village (Tyndall, 2004). In turn, the Roman Catholic Church provided priests to hear confession and conduct Mass in the Village. There is no record of the number of chaplains involved, nor of the process of their appointment. As in Helsinki, a German Lutheran pastor was present to minister to the German speaking athletes and visitors at the games.

The 1972 Munich Olympics are remembered as much for their association with terrorism as for the sporting spectacle which they provided. On 5 September 1972 eight Palestinian terrorists belonging to the Black September group broke into the Olympic Village taking nine Israeli athletes, coaches and officials hostage. The incident resulted in the deaths of all nine Israelis, a West German policeman and five of the terrorists. During the Games there was some Christian ministry in the Athletes' Village and a German Lutheran sports pastor, Karl Zeiss, provided pastoral care for the German athletes. In Los Angeles in 1984, there was official chaplaincy, but this was limited. The organizing committee appointed local campus chaplains from the University of Southern California (USC) and University of California Los Angeles (UCLA) to serve as Olympic chaplains but they were confined to the religious services centre and did not have permission to circulate around the village. Unofficial reports suggest that 39 athletes attended chapel services in 1984 (Tyndall, 2004).

As noted above, the first modern Olympics to feature a formal chaplaincy programme with a team of international chaplains was Seoul in 1988 where 7,697 attended the chapel which was set aside in the Olympic Village for religious services. In total some 184 services were held in seven different languages with 2,046 individuals from 102 different nations counselled (Tyndall, 2004). The pattern of chaplaincy delivered in Seoul was largely replicated in 1992

(Barcelona), 1996 (Atlanta), 2000 (Sydney) and 2004 (Athens) although the number of chaplains, the balance between local and international personnel, and the level of access granted has varied from Games to Games. In Atlanta in 1996, 38 chaplains were accredited, all of whom emanated from the US (Tyndall, 2004). Of these 29 were Christian (25 Protestant and 4 Roman Catholic), 3 Muslim, 2 Buddhist, 2 Hindu, 1 Baha'i and 1 Jewish. The heavy bias towards Christianity may reflect both North America's Christian heritage and the fact that, at the time, sports chaplaincy was much more developed among Protestants than amongst other religious groups. While it is common for there to be a significant number of international Protestant sports chaplains at major events, this is not the case for other religions. There were a total of 88 chaplains at the 2000 Olympics in Sydney, 60 of whom were Christians (Tyndall, 2004). With regard to international Protestant chaplains, as far as can be ascertained (and in the absence of official records), the number of accredited international Protestant chaplains was 12 in 1988, six in 1992, seven in 2000, 21 in 2004 and 19 in 2012 – with none being recorded in 1996 and 2008.

The 2000 Sydney Olympic Organizing Committee provoked protests from Australian church and sports ministry leaders when it announced that it had decided to use the New South Wales Police Chaplaincy Service to 'exclusively' provide chaplaincy services to participants (Tyndall, 2004). The police chaplains understood chaplaincy but had no particular expertise in sport or major sports event chaplaincy. Eventually a compromise was reached and a number of Australian chaplains and seven international Protestant sports chaplains were added to the roster. Chaplaincy at the Sydney games could be deemed a success with 7,670 Olympians attending the chapel services. In terms of overall responsibilities, chaplains were required to work one day on and two days off which created a degree of frustration for a number of the international chaplains present who were left wondering about the value of travelling from such places as the US, India and England to work for only six hours every three days.

In 2008 in Beijing the religious centre was staffed entirely by Chinese chaplains with no international chaplains being accredited. The *Washington Post* ran a story concerning the disillusionment of some US athletes with the chaplaincy services provided (see Cha, 2008), to which the *China Daily* offered the riposte that the religious centre in Beijing was in great demand having already been visited by 665 athletes and officials from more than 50 countries, keeping the 69 'professional religious service volunteers' busy as a consequence of them 'holding services around the clock' (*China Daily*, 2008: 4). In addition to those officially accredited, some unofficial chaplains entered the Olympic Village on 'day pass' invitations from their respective national Olympic committees (Weir, 2008).

Chaplains have sometimes received accreditation through a National Olympic Committee. An early example is that of Fritz Pechtl, Roman Catholic chaplain to the Austrian team in Munich in 1972 (Maier, 2012). When the Austrian Olympic Committee accepted the offer of cooperation with the Church in

1972, it marked the start of a partnership which has continued for over 40 years. The reconstruction of German sport after the Second World War included consultation with the German Church. In 1952 Karl Zeiss led a service at a motor race at the Schottenring which signalled the Church's intention to get involved in high level sport. Starting with the 1952 Olympics the Lutheran (state) Church provided pastors for the care of competitors, coaches, administrators and spectators at major sports events though services, one-to-one conversations and a 'ministry of presence' (Schäfer, 2006).

Manfred Paas (2008), head of the German Roman Catholic Church and Sport Office, was a German chaplain at the 1988, 1992 and 1996 Olympics in an equivalent position for the Roman Catholic Church to that of Karl Zeiss for the Lutherans (see Paas, 2008). Kjell Marksett from Norway is another chaplain whose role is officially recognized at both national and international levels. While he has been an officially accredited International Olympic Committee chaplain since 1988 (including London 2012), he was accredited as part of the Norwegian delegation in 2002 in Salt Lake City.

FIFA does not accredit chaplains at the Football World Cup. However, a certain amount of unofficial chaplaincy has taken place at this event. In 2006 in Germany, chaplains worked with teams from the US, Brazil, Ivory Coast, Togo, Mexico, Netherlands and Poland. In South Africa in 2010, the Uruguayan, Brazilian, US and South African teams were helped by chaplains. Alex Ribeiro, who has served Brazil in five World Cups (1990–2006) has written of his experiences at the 1994 World Cup (Ribeiro, 1995). Likewise, Alfonso Lopez has also documented his experiences as chaplain to the Mexico team in 2006 (Lopez, 2008).

Many chaplains to major sports events come from overtly evangelistic parachurch backgrounds. Several US sports-based agencies also list evangelism as their aim. This has resulted in tensions and problems in chaplaincy at the Olympics and other major events. In his contribution to this volume, Linville asks if US chaplaincy as currently practised is an efficient outreach model, noting that chaplains' freedom to preach the gospel is often severely restricted. Tyndall asserts that one of the major aims of the evangelicals at 2000 Sydney Olympic Games was to distribute Christian material to all the athletes in the Olympic Village (Tyndall, 2004). Conversely, Wingfield Digby, operating from a UK perspective, has argued that sharing one's faith is generally not appropriate for chaplains. In view of all of this, one might understand the concerns aired by Olympic organizing committees about having too many evangelical chaplains involved. Indeed, such concerns have manifested themselves most clearly in the requirement (from 2000 onwards) for chaplains to sign an Olympic Village Religious Services Policy which includes the following statement: 'Religious Services personnel will not be permitted to use this ministry as a vehicle for conversion or proselytising'. This tension will need to be resolved if evangelical chaplains are to continue to play an important role in Olympic and major sports event chaplaincy (Tyndall, 2004).

Conclusions

Military, prison and hospital chaplaincy have existed for some time and in this sense the provision of chaplaincy services to specific areas of society is nothing new. For sports chaplaincy it was simply a case of adopting and adapting church practice, often by trial and error. Some have argued that the needs of the sick facing painful and sometimes terminal illness or of those in military contexts facing fear and danger are easy to recognize as being in need of spiritual and pastoral support. The need for chaplains to support multi-millionaire sports personnel whose greatest crisis may be coping with losing a basketball game is harder to justify (Hoffman, 2010). The counter-argument is that God's love extends to all humanity and there is therefore no reason why supporting athletes would be in any way less worthy than supporting others.

From small beginnings sports chaplaincy has become an accepted and integral part of the world of sport. We have noted that its evolution has witnessed the emergence of a number of models and frameworks and that a wide variety of approaches and practices make up its everyday outworking. Chaplaincy to a club or team requires a quite different approach to chaplaincy to a tour or disparate group of individuals. There is also a major difference between a chaplaincy model where the chaplain's primary function is to conduct a chapel service and a pastoral safety-net model devoid of public religious activities. It is interesting to note that these two models developed more or less simultaneously but quite independently of each other in the 1960s with North American chapels starting with 'chapel service' leaders and English football club chaplains serving in a more pastoral role, often without any overt need for chaplaincy services. Fifty years on since the early sports chaplains began to ply their trade, the complexion of elite level sport has changed considerably, and there are a number of ethical issues which sports chaplaincy may no longer be able to ignore. Key questions arise: is there a place for the prophetic ministry of the chaplain alongside the pastor/teacher role? If so, do chaplains have a responsibility to confront moral and ethical injustice when they come across it in their everyday work? Sports chaplaincy has come a long way and has demonstrated its value to athletes and teams across the spectrum of sport. Nonetheless, it is these kinds of ethical, theological and methodological issues which will shape the contours of sports chaplaincy in years to come.

Note

1   My grateful thanks to Patty Wilson, assistant librarian, United States Sports Academy for her help in finding several references for this chapter.

References

Boyers, J. (2000). *Beyond the Final Whistle*, London: Hodder & Stoughton.
—— (2011). 'Manchester United FC', in M. Threlfall-Holmes and M. Newitt (eds), *Being a Chaplain*, London: SPCK, 81–4.

Cha, A.E. (2008). 'Some Olympians Dissatisfied with Religious Center', *Washington Post*, 14 Aug. Available at <http://www.washingtonpost.com/wpdyn/content/article/2008/08/13/AR2008081303772.html>.

China Daily (2008). 'Religious Center Provides Succor', 16 Aug.: 4.

Deford, F. (1976a). 'Religion in Sport', *Sports Illustrated*, 44/16: 88–102.

—— (1976b). 'The Word According to Tom', *Sports Illustrated*, 44/17: 54–69.

—— (1976c). 'Reaching for the Stars', *Sports Illustrated*, 44/18: 42–60.

Fisher, L. (1969). *God's Voice to the Pro*, Boca Raton, FL: Sports World Chaplaincy.

Glass, B. (1971). *Get in the Game*, Waco, TX: Word Books.

—— (1974). *My Greatest Challenge*, Waco, TX: Word Books.

—— (1981). *Expect to Win*, Waco, TX: Word Books.

Glaus, F. (2012). *Love Game*, n.p.: Levita Media.

Heskins, J., and M. Baker (eds), (2006). *Footballing Lives: As Seen by Chaplains in the Beautiful Game*, Norwich: Canterbury Press.

Hoffman, S. (2010). *Good Game: Christianity and the Culture of Sports*, Waco, TX: Baylor University Press.

Jackson, J. (1984). 'A View of Chaplaincy', *Methodist Home Mission Report*, 128: 31–4.

Krattenmaker, T. (2010). *Onward Christian Athletes: Turning Ballparks into Pulpits and Players into Preachers*, Lanham, MD: Rowman & Littlefield.

Ladd, T. and J. Mathisen (1999). *Muscular Christianity*, Grand Rapids: Baker Books.

Lipe, R. (2006). *Transforming Lives in Sport: A Guide for Sport Chaplains and Sport Mentors*, Kearney, NE: Cross Training Publishing.

Lixey, K. (2008). 'Collaboration among Chaplains: Towards a Common Strategy at Major Sports Events', in *Sport: An Educational and Pastoral Challenge*, Vatican City: Liberia Editrice Vaticana, 69–80.

Lopez. A. (2008). 'The Presence of the Chaplain in the World of Sport', in *Sport: An Educational and Pastoral Challenge*, Vatican City: Liberia Editrice Vaticana, 122–6.

Maier, B. (2012). 'Sport as a Pastoral Opportunity: The Sports Chaplain', in K. Lixey et al. (eds), *Sport and Christianity (A Sign of the Times in the Light of Faith)*, Washington DC: Catholic University of America Press, 206–22.

Paas, M. (2008). 'The Presence of the Chaplain in the World of Sport', in *Sport: An Educational and Pastoral Challenge*, Vatican City, Liberia Editrice Vaticana, 61–8.

Ribeiro, A. (1995). *Who Won the '94 World Cup?*, Braunton, Devon: Rivers International.

Richardson, B. (2012). *Impact Player*, Carol Stream, IL: Tyndale House.

Rushworth-Smith, D. (1985). *Off the Ball*, Basingstoke: Marshall, Morgan & Scott.

Schäfer, C. (2006). 'Kirche im Spannungsfeld von Gesellschaft und Sport', Examensarbeit, Johannes: Gutenberg-Universität.

Tyndall, D. (2004). 'Evangelicalism, Sport and the Australian Olympics', PhD thesis, Macquarie University.

Watson, N.J., and J. White (2007). '"Winning at all Costs" in Modern Sport: Reflections on Pride and Humility in the Writings of C.S. Lewis', in J. Parry et al. (eds), *Sport and Spirituality: An Introduction*, London: Routledge, 61–79.

Weir, J.S. (2008). 'Soul Sadness: Olympic Competitors have Found the 2008 Games Tougher than Any to Date', *The Times*, 25 Aug.

Widund, T. (1994). 'Ethelbert Talbot: His Life and Place in Olympic History', in *Citius, Altius, Fortius: The International Society of Olympic History Journal*, 2/2: 7–14.

Wood, S. (2011). *Keeping Faith in the Team: The Chaplain's Story*, London: Longman, Dartman & Todd.

2 Sports chaplaincy in the United Kingdom

John Boyers[1]

Introduction

This chapter is a personal reflection on over 35 years of working as an official sports chaplain, at Watford Football Club (1977–92), Manchester United Football Club (1992–present), and over a dozen major sporting events. Much of that time has involved full-time work in sports chaplaincy development throughout the UK, and sometimes, beyond. First hand observations have been augmented by insights from related academic literature which has more recently emerged in the UK and the US (see Dzikus, Waller and Hardin, 2011; Gamble, Hill and Parker, 2013).

The aim of the chapter is to outline the major historical and conceptual developments in the evolution of sports chaplaincy in the UK from the mid-1970s to the present day. In detailing the history of this movement, inevitably I am unable to give due credit to all of the people who have helped bring sports chaplaincy to its present position. The fact that a particular chaplain is not mentioned by name is not to dismiss any one individual's work, for each has undoubtedly contributed in some small or significant manner. My first task is to briefly outline some of the pioneering chaplains who worked in sports contexts in the UK.

The early appointments

Reverend Mike Pusey

I was introduced to sports chaplaincy in September 1977 by Revd Mike Pusey who visited St James Road Baptist Church Watford, where I was working as student pastor. Noting the proximity of our church building to Watford Football Club's Vicarage Road ground, and describing his involvement with Aldershot Football Club, he urged me to consider chaplaincy work at Watford F.C. He explained the potential benefits that chaplaincy brought to Aldershot, and challenged me to think seriously about football club chaplaincy. Pusey was interested in sport and had attended games at Aldershot. He had also read about sports chaplaincy in the US. All of this prompted him to offer his services to the board of Aldershot F.C., who referred him to the manager, who, in turn, agreed to 'give it a go'. At the time of writing Pusey remains involved at Aldershot where he has served since 1973, though more recently he has shared his duties.

Eddie Waxer, an American with a vision to promote the Christian message across the world through sport, invited a group of Christians involved with sport in the UK (including Mike Pusey) to a Christian sports ministry conference in Orlando, Florida in 1976. That group returned with a plan to set up Christians in Sport (CIS) the evolution of which I return to in due course. The beginnings of CIS intersects with those of UK sports chaplaincy in two ways. First, the 1976 conference gave several of those within the UK Christian group the impetus to develop sports ministry, including chaplaincy, on home soil. Hence, for Mike Pusey, chaplaincy at Aldershot F.C. became not just an aspect of his local ministry but something that he could encourage others to consider. Second, and perhaps slightly more contentious, was the importing into UK thinking of a particular US ethos which saw sports chaplaincy primarily as an opportunity for evangelism (see Linville, 2014). This kind of approach was clearly acceptable in the US at that time (where there was a stronger Christian presence in sport than in the UK), but my early experiences of this kind of work indicated that English sports culture (especially professional football) was more attracted to a different style of chaplaincy – one which adopted a non-proselytizing approach (see Boyers, 2000). In short, coaches and managers in English professional football in the late 1970s appeared to be accepting of chaplaincy, providing that it prioritized player care and support. I quickly learned that within this world, proactive pastoral support and responsive spiritual input kept people at all levels appreciative of, trusting of, and accepting of chaplaincy. Overt evangelism was not welcomed.

As noted above, the group of UK Christians with whom Mike Pusey attended the 1976 Orlando conference returned to begin the work of CIS. One of these was an Anglican cricketing curate based at Cockfosters, North London, Revd Andrew Wingfield Digby, who went on to be appointed as 'spiritual advisor' to the England cricket team. Wingfield Digby heard about the Watford F.C. chaplaincy work and invited me and my wife to a 1978 pre-Wimbledon dinner organized by the embryonic CIS, which led to my involvement with the organization and my taking a lead role in their football club chaplaincy development. CIS became significant as a coordinator of a number of football club chaplains in the late 1980s, organizing bi-annual day conferences for this network in order to encourage chaplains in their endeavours. Indeed, the significant contribution of CIS to the development of UK sports chaplaincy should not be overlooked.

Though Mike Pusey was the first to introduce me to professional football club chaplaincy, there were other early pioneers of this work in the UK, one of whom was John Jackson.

Reverend John Jackson

In the *Methodist Church Home Mission Report* of 1984, Revd John Jackson tells of the origin and scope of his involvement in sports chaplaincy (Jackson, 1984). In early 1962, his church (Harehills Methodist Church in Leeds) held a 'Sportsmen's Service' and welcomed the general manager of Leeds United Football Club, Cyril Williamson, who was asked if the club would consider the benefits of having a chaplain. Williamson went one step further by taking the idea to the club's board of directors, who subsequently gave the go-ahead. In March 1962 an invitation was sent to Jackson asking him to become the club chaplain, which he accepted. He developed a pattern of weekly visits, spending the larger proportion of his time supporting younger players, but having access to employees at all levels within the club. His impact at Leeds might best be viewed through an assessment of ex-player Jack Charlton's policy of appointing chaplains when he went into management. 'Big Jack' (as he was known) initiated such appointments when team manager at Middlesbrough F.C. (1973–1977) and at Sheffield Wednesday F.C. (1977–1983), events which now lead me to describe the foundational work of the Revd (now Canon) Bill Hall.

Reverend Bill Hall

Canon Bill Hall, an Anglican clergyman in Durham diocese, worked as the Church of England chaplain to the arts and recreation in the north east. In the early part of 1973, when doing chaplaincy work in the Fiesta Club in Norton, he met Jack Charlton. They got on well, and spoke at length. Charlton revealed that he was about to become the new manager of Middlesbrough F.C. and suggested Hall could be his chaplain. Hall served the club for over 20 years using his diocesan role to seek other north eastern football club appointments. His work is worth noting as one of the early pioneers and propagators of UK sports chaplaincy. Hence, Revd John Jackson's influence at Leeds United was two-fold. He had a direct impact on the club itself, but he also he had an impact upon the development of wider football club chaplaincy as Leeds United players moved on to play and manage at other clubs. He was one of the earliest football club chaplains, as was Revd Michael Chantry.

Reverend Michael Chantry

Though close in chronology, there appears to be no link between the appointments of Revd John Jackson at Leeds United and Revd Michael Chantry at Oxford United. Chantry worked in academic chaplaincy, serving as the highly esteemed chaplain at Hertford College, Oxford, from 1961 to 2001 and at Oxford United for 41 years until his death in 2003. His appointment to the old Manor Ground, Oxford, probably arose from his understanding of chaplaincy, his love of football and Oxford United entering the Football League in the summer of 1962. Chantry was involved at the club on a weekly basis and especially on match days. Every Christmas he held a carol service in the club bar for players and staff. Mick Brown, manager of Oxford United between 1975 and 1979, recalls Chantry's support when, on 20 March 1977, player Peter Houseman, his wife and two friends were tragically killed in a car accident after a club event. Sadly there are times in the life of a sports club when the unique role of a chaplain is crucial. Chantry's work at Oxford United demonstrated the value of consistent and caring chaplaincy. The same passion for the game also led to Revd Jack Bingham becoming involved in sports chaplaincy but in a different and unique way.

Reverend Jack Bingham

Reverend Jack Bingham, another early pioneer, became chaplain to Stockport County F.C. in the strangest of ways. Bingham, a qualified referee, enjoyed watching football. In his final year of training for Methodist Church ministry at Hartley Victoria College in Manchester, he was assigned a placement at Heaton Mersey Methodist Church, Stockport. On FA Cup third-round day, 13 January 1973, Stockport County played Hull City. Bingham went to watch with a young fan from the church, David Tidswell, now a Methodist minister in North Lancashire. During the game, there was a skirmish between the then Hull City player-manager Terry Neill and Stockport player Ian Lawther. The match referee sent them both off. Jack Bingham felt the Stockport player had been unjustly treated. On hearing in the media that both players were to be suspended, Bingham wrote to the Football Association, explaining what he had seen from the stands. He asked them to reconsider their judgement. This they did and, with Bingham's evidence paramount, Ian Lawther's suspension was withdrawn. The Stockport club was duly informed. In response, they wrote to Bingham, inviting him to become their chaplain. He relished the role, but it was mainly a match-day title. Bingham was not involved much through the week like many current chaplains, but his presence and input were appreciated.

Thus, in the early 1970s, a number of unconnected individuals, for a whole variety of reasons, began to be involved as chaplains of English professional football clubs. Reflecting on these developments, it could be argued that John Jackson, Michael Chantry, Bill Hall, Jack Bingham and Mike Pusey were, to some degree at least, the early pioneers of this ministry. In 1977 another appointment occurred, at Watford Football Club, which was to make an important contribution to the development of sports chaplaincy. It encouraged Christians in Sport to further support sports chaplaincy and, in time, leaders of the Baptist Union of Great Britain (BUGB) to form and support an inter-denominationally focused sports chaplaincy organization which became best known by its acronym SCORE (Sports Chaplaincy Offering Resources and Encouragement).

Watford Football Club

My involvement in chaplaincy at Watford Football Club is recorded in detail elsewhere (see Boyers, 2000; Heskins and Baker, 2006). But I emphasize that it was not something which I actively sought, rather, something which simply came to me. I now see this as divine prompting and guidance. Mike Pusey, chaplain at Aldershot, spoke at my home church in September 1977, saw the nearby Watford FC football ground and urged my involvement with them. Alan

West, Captain of Luton Town FC, provided similar encouragements when also speaking at the same church six weeks later. The following weekend, Graham Taylor, manager of Watford F.C., wrote in the local paper about his desire for the club to become more involved in the community and the community with the club. He invited responses. After discussing and praying about these 'coincidences' with my senior colleague, Revd Richard Harbour, we felt obliged to write to the club, expressing our interest in possible involvement. After two meetings, by December 1977, we were fully incorporated as chaplains in professional football and fully supported by our church.

The club was pleased with the chaplaincy contributions, so we were invited to continue into a second (1978/79) season, at the end of which, the Watford manager Graham Taylor (and my church) confirmed the on-going agreement. Harbour stepped down, but, now ordained and working full time for the church, I continued. It was a pattern for future sports club chaplaincy and a blueprint for later developments. A local church would provide a day or more per week for a minister to serve a local sports club as chaplain offering appropriate confidential, spiritual and pastoral care to all those concerned, whatever their faith background and more often to those with no faith. Relationships and trust with staff and players became the heart of this expression of chaplaincy work.

The first years at Watford were characterized by a steep learning curve. I was familiar with football as an amateur player and as a supporter of Grimsby Town F.C., but came to realize that I knew little, if anything, of the world inside the professional game. These were successful years for Watford – nothing to do with the chaplain, all to do with the management and players. Perhaps God placed chaplaincy there at a strategically successful time? Graham Taylor and his staff were certainly very supportive. The club came to trust its chaplain and value his presence, welcoming me to all parts of the organization. I learned the significance of relationships, trust, confidentiality, consistency and ministry to those facing troubles and crises. I will never forget the accountant who died of cancer at 28; the player's partner who needed a heart transplant; the many private phone calls and conversations; the hospital visits; the home visits to welcome new staff, to follow up a birth or a bereavement. I was pastoring a secular congregation.

Other clubs looked at Watford to consider Taylor's innovations and to evaluate their success; hence, Watford's chaplaincy also attracted interest. I remember visiting several clubs which had enquired about the role and which sought help regarding the possibility of an appointment. I became involved in these processes and as a consequence found myself having to work out how to identify and recruit new chaplains. I sought fellow clergy for whom faith was strong and vital; who were a good fit with the sports world; who were pastorally able, although not necessarily strong as academics, administrators or evangelists and not ardent fans of the clubs concerned. I sought those who genuinely cared about people; whose situations allowed them to give at least one full day per week (and preferably more), to the task; those who appreciated that they had a responsibility to deliver high quality chaplaincy to 'their' club for the sake of future chaplaincies elsewhere.

In the late 1970s and 1980s a steady trickle of football club chaplains were appointed. If I was involved, such appointments invariably came after visits explaining the 'Watford blueprint'. The following observations summarize developments during this period: (1) Watford manager Graham Taylor demonstrated an openness to sports chaplaincy which was of vital importance. He took a risk in this respect, opening the whole club to chaplaincy provision beyond match days and offering continued support. (2) St James Road Baptist Church gave one quarter of my time to the Watford FC chaplaincy, a demonstration of remarkable vision and generosity. The contribution of this particular church to sports chaplaincy in the UK was significant in creating a template for the future. (3) The 1980s tranche of appointments was unlike earlier developments. They did not emerge for unconnected or unique reasons, nor because of denominational allegiances but directly from Watford's chaplaincy which became a pattern for deployment and development which, by and large, was followed by subsequent chaplaincies. (4) The advice to future chaplains was: 'This is how it works at Watford, this is what their chaplain does, and broadly, this is what you should do.' The message was about expectation, regularity, consistency, sensitivity, methodology and ethos. In short, it was about delivering a quality chaplaincy service.

Baptist Union of Great Britain and the formation of SCORE

In the late 1980s CIS was a small-scale organization with limited funds. When the Baptist Union of Great Britain suggested that I should consider leaving normal church ministry to work full time, inter-denominationally, in sports chaplaincy development, CIS strongly encouraged and endorsed this initiative. This decision, to create a self-contained, specialist sports chaplaincy development agency serving all denominations, is one of the major contributions to sports chaplaincy development in the UK. The vision and support of my then Baptist area superintendent Revd Roy Freestone and of Revd David Coffey, the then head of BUGB's Mission Department, and the Union's financial commitment to an organization not just to benefit Baptists but to advance an inter-denominational ministry to help build God's Church and Kingdom are noteworthy. Unequivocally, we can say that without this support, sports chaplaincy in the UK would be much less developed than it is today.

From the outset SCORE sought to be inclusive. All wings of all denominations were welcome to join the network. If sports chaplaincy was to have cohesion and characteristic qualities which all sports could affirm, then all chaplains needed to be included. Some chaplains had emerged as a consequence of their personal initiatives, but they were welcomed. Better to have all (if possible) inside the network, involved, trained, delivering according to the standards of the charity, than by exclusion create a number of unconnected and uncoordinated individuals in similar roles, without any common job description or agreed delivery standards. However, this inclusive approach created problems amongst those who drew boundaries differently. It led to the breakup of the close relationship between CIS and SCORE in the mid-1990s, but that situation was, in time, resolved. By 2003 various sports ministries in the UK had begun to come together on a voluntary basis, to pray, to support each other, and to coordinate common activities. It was a movement with which CIS joined forces from 2005 onwards and the two organizations increasingly found healing and unity. The issue had been doctrinal. In the early days SCORE's prime concern was not about denominationalism, churchmanship or precise credal agreement, but rather, about the delivery of sports chaplaincy to a particular standard. As SCORE grew, it was the principles and practice of chaplaincy which became the vital issue.

A defined code of practice

The code of practice which emerged during the early days of SCORE defined the principles underpinning the organization's work and set out how SCORE chaplains would operate in professional football clubs. On reflection, this was significant for several reasons. Firstly, it demonstrated to clubs that their chaplain was part of a network which aspired to provide excellent chaplaincy in clearly defined ways. It promoted a professionalism about chaplaincy. It took the element of risk out of chaplaincy appointments. Secondly, it defined the dos and don'ts of chaplaincy and provided a clear *modus operandi* for each club and for each chaplain to follow. It became part of the sifting process for identifying potential recruits. The non-acceptance by an appointee of the pattern of chaplaincy to which the club agreed indicated their unsuitability. It meant that all new appointments followed a standard set of practices and ways of working. It was a first real attempt at quality assurance and accountability in UK sports chaplaincy circles. In effect, SCORE was defining what chaplains offered and how they worked.

Of course, establishing a code of practice did not mean that every chaplaincy would be the same. From the outset SCORE understood that each expression of chaplaincy reflected a series of unique factors including the size of the sporting organization concerned, club attitudes towards chaplaincy, the degree of trust placed in the chaplain, and the individual personality traits, sensitivities, and time commitments which chaplains brought with them. Thus, the code of practice was not presented as a mould that every expression of chaplaincy must squeeze itself into, rather it was a template which all new chaplaincies worked around. It spoke to sports of professionalism, to chaplains of responsibilities and to both of foundational and agreed patterns of working. At the same time, it allowed each chaplaincy to be developed in its own way. The code of practice enabled sports to have confidence in chaplaincy appointments. Yet in 1992 an opportunity arose which perhaps did more than any code of practice could do to encourage UK sports to have confidence in the worth and value of chaplaincy.

Manchester United

Although I did not understand it at the time, becoming chaplain to Manchester United F.C. in September 1992 was a major boost to UK sports chaplaincy development. It affirmed the concept at the highest level, which opened doors for chaplaincy elsewhere. Around the UK and in many different sports, interest in chaplaincy multiplied.

In Scotland, where Sir Alex Ferguson is so highly regarded, I found that the Scottish Football Association, the then National Team Manager, Craig Brown, and indeed many football clubs, warmed to chaplaincy because of Ferguson's endorsements. Scottish football club representatives were willing to give me time to explain SCORE's chaplaincy ethos because I worked under Ferguson. In Northern Ireland, my Old Trafford role, the historical 'George Best connection' and links between other Northern Ireland players and Manchester United, appeared to generate interest in SCORE. In Wales too, the Old Trafford links had an impact in conversations about chaplaincy in sport, not least with key personnel at Swansea City F.C. and Swansea 'Whites' RUFC, both of which became bridgeheads for the growth of chaplaincy in that country.

As SCORE became more widely known, an increasing number of sports opened up to the work of the charity with chaplaincy models being established nationally in horse racing, rugby league, rugby union and county cricket. Chaplaincy in horse racing owed much to the Manchester United link. The then CEO of the Racing Welfare charity was willing to meet to discuss chaplaincy purely because of the Old Trafford connection. From those early conversations, SCORE was able to advertise for a post to develop chaplaincy in horse racing which led to the appointment of Revd Graham Locking who pioneered SCORE's work in that sport.

Meeting the growing interest in chaplaincy among sports people throughout the UK was hindered by insufficient funds. However, offers of help in various forms from part-time volunteers to SCORE facilitated further progress. Their roles were vitally important contributions to chaplaincy development, enabling the network to grow, for example, through sports or regional coordinators, when necessary funding was not available.

Over time, my role in SCORE developed to include major sports event chaplaincy. When involved in conversations with the Athens 2004 Olympic Games Organising Committee (by the then Church of England chaplain to Athens, Greece and the Islands, Revd Malcolm Bradshaw), I was immediately given credibility because of my roles as head of chaplaincy at Manchester's 2002 Commonwealth Games and with Manchester United. Later, I found that negotiations for club chaplaincy openings in the UK were helped by my work in Manchester in 2002 and Athens in 2004. Club chaplaincy experience had brought confidence to negotiations for major sports event chaplaincy and indeed vice versa with subsequent club chaplaincy negotiations. Later, in 2010 and 2012, my past chaplaincy experience facilitated further major sports event chaplaincy opportunities.

SCORE and professional sports organizations

The growing support for chaplaincy from organizational bodies within and across professional sports was another contributing factor to its widening appeal. Attitudes changed, from interest to understanding and from approval to affirmation, financial support and public endorsement. Various sports moved along the 'chaplaincy support continuum' at different times and speeds, but the affirmation of the work of SCORE by professional sports bodies was invariably the reason behind the UK sports world coming to view chaplaincy appointments as favourable.

At the 1993 northern sports chaplains' day-conference at Manchester United's Old Trafford stadium, Brendon Batson and David Carr represented the Professional Footballers' Association (PFA) and Alex Ferguson and Dave Bassett the League Managers' Association (LMA). This was early support from professional bodies, soon to be added to by Rick Parry, the first Chief Executive of the English Premier League. Rick Parry understood the value of football club chaplaincy, and a series of meetings led to the Premier League sponsoring SCORE's national football chaplains' training conference at the Lilleshall Sports and Conference Centre, which in 1995 included several speakers from the world of professional football – Rick Parry (CEO of the then Carling Premier League), Dave Richardson (then Football Association youth development coordinator), Gordon Milne (then Chair of the LMA) and Ken Merrett and Ken Ramsden (then secretary and assistant secretary of Manchester United respectively and representing the Football League Executive Staff Association).

Through such conferences, chaplains learned more of the world in which they worked and that world came to know more about chaplaincy and SCORE. After Rick Parry left his role, Premier League support for the SCORE conferences gradually waned but interest has been revived in recent years through significant financial investment for a pastoral support director in English football, Revd Matt Baker. This has given an enhanced profile to chaplaincy and impetus for further appointments. The PFA and its CEO, Gordon Taylor, and the LMA from the days of CEO John Barnwell, have been equally significant in supporting chaplaincy, recognising the benefits it brings to their respective members. Both rugby codes, neither of which as yet has the resources to finance a chaplaincy support officer, also affirm at management and organizational levels, the value of chaplaincy work.

Training, accreditation and qualifications

SCORE, which began in 1990 and became a UK registered charity in 1991, was renamed Sports Chaplaincy UK in 2011 and in 2012 appointed a new CEO, Richard Gamble, a role taken over in 2015 by Warren Evans. Throughout its life under both banners, the organization has sought to increase the professionalism of sports chaplaincy, to move away from anything suggesting that chaplains are simply a collection of sports-consumed clergy living out their broken dreams. The emphasis remains on professionally trained practitioners delivering a quality service that is valued and appreciated by the sporting organizations engaging the chaplains and by all their employees.

The code of practice, the annual training conference, the regional training meetings all helped, but in 2007 SCORE began to discuss a university course to qualify chaplains at postgraduate (certificate, diploma and master's) level. The key academic impetus came from Professors Mike Collins and Andrew Parker at the University of Gloucestershire, with me, John Boyers, contributing from SCORE about practical chaplaincy matters. After a series of meetings, the University validated and approved the new programme, which by September 2010, had recruited its first cohort of students. Since then the course has attracted interest from throughout the UK and beyond and has contributed therefore to the spread of quality chaplaincy and its continued professionalization.

This concern for stronger training and accreditation for sports chaplains has been seen elsewhere. Sports Chaplaincy Australia only accredits chaplains who have successfully completed their Level 1 training course, and also provides a Level 2 course (and other specialist courses) to encourage professional development. Connor's (2003) argument that the quality of sports ministry training inevitably has a direct impact on the quality of ministry itself, is surely universally true. Thus, in the US there is an emerging body of literature which seeks to examine issues of accreditation and professionalism in the field of sports chaplaincy (see Dzikus, Waller and Hardin, 2011; Waller, Dzikus and Hardin 2010). Appropriate training and accreditation must be part of the professionalization of sports chaplaincy in any country where the ministry is emerging. Such work, it seems, is too important to be left to untrained enthusiasts doing their energetic best.

Continuity and change

By 2012 my responsibility for leading Sports Chaplaincy UK had been taken over by Richard Gamble at a time when national interest in sports chaplaincy was continuing to grow. Currently, and perhaps most important of all, is the reality that the ideal template, the model of the pastorally proactive, spiritually responsive style of chaplaincy, delivered consistently and sensitively, is strongly present across UK sport. Whatever the precise location – a sports club, a major sports event, a particular sports venue, a whole sport, a team or individuals – chaplaincy support has to be delivered seriously, faithfully and professionally.

In the midst of changes to structures and personnel, the commitment of individual chaplains on the ground in delivering high quality chaplaincy which recipients appreciate and value, is probably the most significant contributor to further chaplaincy development in the UK. So long as recipients endorse this service as being beneficial to their situation, sport will continue to be open to this ministry. Of course, unofficial chaplaincy still takes place by those who seek involvement with sport without any authorization or formal connection to Sports Chaplaincy UK. However, this chapter argues that in order to achieve and maintain excellence in relation to the spiritual and pastoral care that it provides, sports chaplaincy needs to be official and accredited, collaborative and prescriptive with regard to its quality delivery, current oversight and future development.

Conclusion: a final thought

The trajectory of sports chaplaincy in the UK over the past 50 years has been remarkable: two appointments in professional football in the early 1960s, five by the mid-1970s, around 15 by the late 1980s, 40 by the mid-1990s, 230 by 2010, and over 320 by 2015. In this chapter some of the reasons behind this expansion have been evaluated. These include: the good work of the early pioneers, the significance of the work at Watford Football Club, the impetus and contribution of Christians in Sport, the vision of the Baptist Union of Great Britain, the work of SCORE and Sports Chaplaincy UK, the importance of training and a generic code of practice, the influence of Manchester United, the support of professional sports bodies and the quality delivery of excellent on-the-ground chaplains.

However, further to my brief presentation of the conceptual and historical aspects of the evolution of sports chaplaincy, I believe that there is one overriding influence: God. In the long and complex story of sports chaplaincy's rise in the UK, beyond all the various and significant human factors is one ultimate factor: that it was God's purpose to bring a strong chaplaincy presence to the sports world. Sociologists and historians may have alternative theories that inform this story but I offer this single underlying theological explanation: God willed it.

Note

1 I wish to thank the following for their invaluable contributions to this chapter: Mick Brown (former manager, Oxford United FC), Revd Richard Bryant (former chaplain, Newcastle United FC), Revd Canon Bill Hall (former chaplain, Middlesbrough FC), Revd Mike Pusey (chaplain, Aldershot FC), Revd David Tidswell (Methodist minister, North Lancashire), Revd David Tully (former chaplain, Newcastle United FC), and J. Stuart Weir CEO, Verite Sports.

References

Boyers, J. (2000). *Beyond The Final Whistle*, London: Hodder & Stoughton.

Connor, S. (2003). *Sports Outreach: Principles and Practice for Successful Sports Ministry*, Tain, Ross-shire: Christian Focus.

Dzikus, L., S. Waller and R. Hardin (2011). 'Collegiate Sport Chaplaincy: Exploration of an Emerging Profession', *Journal of Contemporary Athletics*, 5/1: 21–42.

Gamble, R., D. Hill and A. Parker (2013). '"Revs and Psychos": Impact and Interaction amongst Sport Chaplains and Sport Psychologists in English Premiership Football', *Journal of Applied Sport Psychology*, 25: 249–64.

Heskins, J. and M. Baker (2006). *Footballing Lives: As Seen by Chaplains in the Beautiful Game*, Norwich: Canterbury Press.

Jackson, J. (1984). 'A View of Chaplaincy', *Methodist Home Mission Report*, 128: 31–4.

Linville, G. (2014). *Christmanship: A Theology of Competition and Sport*, Canton, OH: Oliver House Press.

Waller, S., L. Dzikus and R. Hardin (2010). 'The Collegiate Sports Chaplain: Kindred or Alien?', *Chaplaincy Today*, 26/1: 16–26.

3 Sports chaplaincy and North American society

Strategies for winning in the club house

Greg Linville

Introduction

North American sports chaplaincy is presently facing various obstacles and criticisms. Hoffman (2010) poignantly argues that American sports chaplains and sports ministries have lost their prophetic voice in the sports world. Elsewhere, sports chaplaincy ministries have been condemned by critic and author Tom Krattenmaker (2010). Amidst such difficulties and dilemmas, US sports chaplains are in need of solid theological truths and biblically based philosophical foundations to re-envision their methodological models.

Whilst I agree wholeheartedly with Hoffman's claims and, indeed, share some of Krattenmaker's concerns, I believe that there is a more critical issue at stake here; that is, that North American sports chaplaincies presently operate in line with what might be described as an ineffective and inefficient sports outreach model. With this in mind, the purpose of this chapter is to explore how US sports chaplaincy might become a more effective and efficient venture through a re-envisioning of its foundational principles. Hence, the questions addressed in the following discussion are: What keeps North American sports chaplaincy from realizing its potential and what changes are needed in order that the current operating model becomes more effective and efficient? The chapter is based upon insights from my own personal journey from disillusionment with US sports chaplaincy to re-envisioning its potential through the lens of theological truths. I articulate some of the criticisms surrounding the North American model and, more importantly, offer suggestions for redeeming both the people of sport and the culture of sport through a transformed approach to sports chaplaincy. I argue that the answer to future effectiveness and efficiency lies in learning from the past, hence, it is to this subject that I initially turn.

The past

Questions concerning the present and the future of North American sports chaplaincy are best served by surveying what has gone before, including an overview of the historical distinction between traditional US sports chaplaincy methodologies and those germane to the UK. There would appear to be a number of differences between the two, four of which are set out below:

Speaking versus serving

A key function of many US sports chaplaincies is the holding of weekly (religiously based) meetings in which the gospel is verbally proclaimed to players, coaches and others involved with athletic teams. Conversely, the role of sports chaplains in the UK has a tendency to be altogether more pastoral where emphasis lies on the 'ministry of presence' (see Chawner, 2009; Heskins and Baker, 2006; Holm, 2009).

Professionalism

American sports chaplains are often 'professional' in the sense that chaplaincy is the main, or major, part of their job description. Many are employed by sport-related para-ministries. UK sports chaplains are more likely to serve as volunteers and are often employed in other fields or by a local church. This raises questions over terminology. Throughout this chapter I use the term 'sport-related para-ministry' to refer to sports ministries not operating within the context of a local church as compared to those which do operate within this context. This stems from a belief that all ministries are 'within' the Church. Some are organized and implemented under the auspices of the local church, others, such as 'para' ministries, are organized on a wider scale, but, in my view, all are within the Church and not outside of or beside it. In terms of my own theological positioning, the term 'para-ministry' is preferred (over 'para-church') based upon a fully developed theology of the Church.

Vision

Whereas sports chaplains in the UK primarily seek to relationally serve the pastoral needs of athletes and coaches, the primary goal of North American sports chaplains has traditionally been to 'seek and save the lost'. This is not to say that UK sports chaplains do not evangelize or that US sports chaplains do not serve pastorally. Rather, this particular distinction has more to do with the emphasis and philosophy of evangelism.

Proclamational or incarnational

The predominant model in the UK in terms of evangelism is one in which chaplains are more discreet and (as already noted) more relationally oriented, whereas North American chaplaincy has a tendency to be seen as more verbally proclamational. Again, this has to do with emphasis and philosophy – but also perception.

From my very first day in the role, I knew that being chaplain to a professional sports team would not be easy. Things became glaringly apparent as I walked into a dark clubhouse where 'chapel' was to be held. I found there the baseball team's newly acquired and homeless centerfielder sleeping on the floor. He was the only player to attend chapel that week. Twenty-plus years and literally thousands of players, managers, coaches, officials and team administrators later, I have experienced the highs and lows of sports chaplaincy. I have learned that the US model has great potential but that it has a number of flaws as currently conceptualized, organized and practised. These flaws stem from a myriad of reasons: (1) formal theological/ministerial training and preparation for sports chaplains is not commonly available; (2) the purpose and goals of sports chaplaincies are sometimes confusing, including what spiritual success is and is not; and (3) quality time and contact with players is often limited, seasonal and sporadic.

A further problem surrounds the way in which US sports chaplaincy is sometimes seen to hamper the spiritual development of the very people who it is designed to help by unintentionally stifling the long-term spiritual growth of athletes. Sports chaplaincy in the US has much potential but has often lacked critical analysis in terms of what is necessary for true effectiveness.

The present

It could be argued that the US sports outreach movement consists of three primary expressions: (1) local church sports ministry, (2) sport-related para-ministry and (3) camp-based sport and recreation ministry. The local church part of the movement is by far the largest, with tens of thousands of churches owning and programming sports facilities. Though significantly smaller, sport-related para-ministries carry an influence belying their number. This chapter focuses on these two groups.

The US sports outreach movement began in the years following the world-wide economic depression of the 1930s, expanding in the decade following the end of the Second World War and possibly peaking at the turn of the millennium (Ladd and Mathisen, 1999). I say possibly because it may grow and become more influential in the near or distant future, but I predict that it will appear in history as a bell shaped curve, peaking between 1980 and 2000 and slowly declining over the next few decades. The relevance of historical overview is that the evaluation of aging and (some would argue) failing models, can lead to change and re-envisioning. I believe that in the case of the US sports outreach movement, these models have been traditionally based on underdeveloped theological truths and somewhat misguided philosophical principles. I say this because it appears that US sports chaplaincy is falling short of expectations. Anecdotal stories circulate about how particular chapel meetings affect individual players and coaches, but there is also evidence that North American sports chaplaincy is ineffective and inefficient in its methods and this requires critical analysis.

Ineffectiveness of sports chaplaincy

The issues upon which the ineffectiveness of US sports chaplaincy is based lie amidst notions of culture and motivation and include: (1) the impact of secular multi-culturalism on professional and elite sport, (2) the culture of elite sports chaplaincy, (3) the motivation of individual sports chaplains, and (4) the motivation of professional athletes and coaches.

Impact of secular multi-culturalism

There is a danger that sports chaplaincies in the US are becoming ineffective spiritually because of the multi-cultural expectations of their hosts: the professional, collegiate, club or school team. North American sports chaplains face an increasingly secular and, at times, hostile environment. Freedom to 'preach the gospel' is sometimes curtailed especially where this is at odds with the athletic goals and expectations of the host institution (Babb, 2014). Restrictions on inviting athletes, coaches and managers into a personal relationship with Christ are ever more prevalent. Chapels are required to be inclusive and not simply multi-denominational but also multi-faith. Chaplains may face the threat of dismissal should they advocate too strongly a 'Christmanship' ethic of not working on Sunday or if they fail to comply with the host team's (and its sponsors) policies or activities when such are not compatible with a biblical ethic.

In addition, chaplains are increasingly faced with choosing between authentic Christianity or capitulating to the demands of 'sportianity' (see Deford, 1976; Hoffman, 2010; Linville, 2014). Sportianity is a popular cultural term used to describe those who make sport their God and their participation in sport their religious activity. Chaplains must often choose between being faithful to Christ or capitulating to the demands of the pluralistically minded world of sport which is increasingly sold out to a 'sportianity ethic' – the way in which athletes, who have made sport their God, participate in sport and allow such involvement to impact upon their moral judgements. There is the possibility that chaplains will have short tenures if their biblical teachings contradict to any significant degree the goals and objectives of sportianity. Such practices run the risk of promoting and perpetuating a weak and anaemic faith in Christian athletes. One outcome of this is that some chaplains may become more concerned about being admitted into the inner sanctums of sport than they are about speaking out and confronting its evils (see Hoffman, 2010).

Culture of elite sports chaplaincy

The authentic spiritual formation of athletes and coaches has the potential to be compromised by the culture of elite sports chaplaincy in four distinct ways. The first is restricted time. Sports chapels commonly have time limitations placed upon them. I was recently asked to lead a chapel for a collegiate American football team playing in a semi-final National Championship game. I was surrounded by many sincere and eager players who were making an effort and perhaps taking a stand for their faith. It was clearly communicated to me that there was a 15-minute maximum for chapel and that players were not to be late to the ensuing (and more important) pre-game activities. I have been given 5 minutes to lead chapel on many occasions – and never longer than 30.

The second point of compromise has to do with context. Chapels often function as a cross between a motivational talk and a seminar and rarely resemble a formal worship service. Chapel participants are typically seeking inspiration and motivation rather than spiritual development. Some come along to fulfil faith-based obligations: for example, so that they can tell a parent, partner or friend that they have attended church that day. Others come so as not to risk offending the 'gods of the game'. Chapels attended by a manager or coach may attract more players.

The third way that the culture of elite sport can restrict the authentic spiritual formation of its participants has to do with the setting of chapel meetings. Most sports chapels do not occur in places conducive to ministry. On one occasion I was allocated the team owner's executive, field-level loge for chapel. We were closer to home plate than the pitcher would be an hour later. The loge was enclosed but a room-wide window provided excellent views of the infield and beyond. Chapel was scheduled 45 minutes before team (infield) practice but because batting practice had been cancelled, more players came along. These infrequent attenders witnessed a chapel like no other. I stood in front of the glass window. Players, coaches and front office personnel enjoyed the comfortable seats and gazed past me out on to the field. Chapel was usually 15 minutes in length but soon after the opening prayer and reading of scripture I had to curtail proceedings as a consequence of the fact that I was competing with a scantily clad, gyrating female Elvis-impersonator providing pre-game entertainment on the other side of the window behind me.

The fourth point of compromise concerns content. Chapel talks have a tendency to be based on a narrow range of athletic statements from scripture and to be predominantly evangelistic in content. Evangelism is incredibly important but athletes cannot grow spiritually if their biblical diet is limited to athletic metaphors and evangelistic concepts.

In summary, my critique of the culture of elite sports chaplaincy revolves around how North American sports chapels are typically structured and conducted. Time is often short, the context ill-defined, the setting distracting and the content theologically weak and one dimensional.

Motivation of individual sports chaplains

The third reason why the current US model of sports chaplaincy could be considered ineffective has to do with the motivation of sports chaplains themselves. The vast majority of sports chaplains are properly motivated but even the most conscientious might benefit from a self-evaluation regarding the following issues. Each of us who have served as sports chaplains needs to evaluate our motivations for doing so. Is our motivation about being able to associate with elite sports stars honourable? Is sports chaplaincy about accessing game-day tickets, autographs and other sports memorabilia? Unfortunately, some may compromise the gospel to maintain the benefits and prestige of being team chaplain. While it is certainly acceptable to be an appreciative recipient of a team's (or a player's) graciousness, it is something quite different to compromise the key principles of one's faith to remain as a chaplain.

To this end, the following questions need contemplation by all sports chaplains. Are you willing to remain as chaplain if you do not receive any associated benefits? Are you willing to relinquish your status as chaplain if you are not allowed to freely preach the gospel and to carry out discussions and teaching in line with biblical principles? The answers to these (and other) questions determine how effective and efficient US sports chaplaincy will be in the future.

Motivation of professional athletes and coaches

The fourth reason why I consider US sports chaplaincy to be ineffective in its present guise has to do with the motivation of professional athletes and coaches. It is not uncommon for high profile athletes to struggle with the balance between success in sport and faithful discipleship. In over 20 years of serving as a chaplain to professional sportsmen, I have encountered very few athletes and coaches who could be classified as being firmly at the Christianity end of the Christianity–sportianity continuum. Some elite athletes appear to have a faith of convenience more than one of conviction. A number of athletes who fail to reconcile their faith and sporting lives leave sport altogether (Linville, 2014).

In my experience, some of those attending sports chapel think of it as a rabbit's foot or lucky charm and choose sport over faith, especially if choosing faith means losing favour with the team management or their coach. A deeper problem here for sports chaplaincy is the production of dedicated disciples of Christ who regularly participate in a local church and willingly choose an allegiance to faith over an allegiance to sport. In addition, there is the problem of 'platform proclamation'.

Platform proclamation – the winning of high profile athletes and coaches to Christ for the purpose of providing a platform for them to proclaim the gospel – has long been a feature of North American sports chaplaincy ministries. While on the surface this may seem like an honourable goal, it is also flawed by the reality of its consequences. Elite athletes who verbally proclaim Christ but are more committed to success in sport than their faith, and who are not well grounded theologically and spiritually and often fail to live out their faith, may not only find themselves exposed theologically but also personally and spiritually if and when their moral misjudgements become front page news. Rather than aiding evangelism, such events can damage and disrupt gospel endeavours. More importantly, they may damage the faith of the individuals concerned.

Inefficiency of sports chaplaincy

Beyond the reasons that I have put forward for US sports chaplaincy's ineffectiveness, there is a further issue that I wish to raise: it is also an inefficient model.

In terms of a simple cost–benefit analysis, arguments surrounding inefficiencies can be framed around one simple question: could the multi-millions of dollars spent to reach elite athletes through North American sports chaplaincies be paying higher and more efficient dividends? It may be argued that the funds allocated to the work of one sports chaplain could be more efficiently spent if redirected to hire a local church sports-outreach minister. The former may well engage a number of elite athletes, but the latter has the potential to reach many more. Local church sports ministries may also have the potential to be more effective in making dedicated disciples of elite athletes because they reach them in their formative years as children and teenagers. Hence, we must consider whether the results of US sports chaplaincy are commensurate with the investment of resources and effort.

This leads us to a further pragmatic question regarding the current US sports chaplaincy model: Do athletes who participate in sports chapels become active church people? There are various arguments surrounding this issue one of which suggests that sports chaplaincy falls short in the way that it facilitates the transition from chapel to (local) church. My view is that there are three key reasons behind this: (1) players often substitute chapel for church attendance, (2) players' families cannot participate in chapel, and (3) chapels are often administrated and led by sport-related para-ministries.

Players substitute chapel for church attendance

Over the years as a practising sports chaplain, it has occurred to me that most elite athletes and players are not required to report to the team headquarters or ballpark until late Sunday morning or early afternoon and yet habitually avoid church in favour of chapel. This has struck me as strange given that they have plenty of time to attend a worship service and still get to the ballpark venue on time. They choose a 10 to 15-minute motivational talk over an hour of worship, fellowship and biblical teaching. It is pertinent for chapel ministries to hold Bible studies and to minister six days a week, but we must also consider whether providing Sunday chapels runs the risk of aiding spiritual anaemia.

Players, families and chapel

A related consequence of holding Sunday chapels at ballpark venues is the effect this may have on the marriages and families of players. The typical Sunday morning schedule of a professional (male) athlete's family comprises mother/wife/partner and children attending a local church service, while father/husband/athlete relaxes at home and later attends a 15-minute chapel talk at the ballpark. North American chapel ministries would do well to hold players accountable to accompanying their families to church, not simply sending them with a spouse or partner. I realize that the dynamics outlined here are not representative of all athletes nor are they solely the fault of the sports chaplaincies involved. Yet if team chaplains challenged Christian athletes to take responsibility for their family's spiritual well-being, some may respond positively.

Chapels administrated and led by sport-related para-ministries

A third reason why elite sports players may not become active church people is because of the way in which sports chaplaincies are administered. Most of my sports chapel experience has been in professional baseball. Initially, my church commissioned and assigned me to lead the sports outreach to a newly formed minor league baseball team. Many players became involved in church through relationships with church members who provided housing, transportation and met various other needs of players and their families. The outreach of my church appeared to be successful in producing dedicated disciples of Christ until a sport-related para-ministry organization became involved. In the short term, any sense of change was imperceptible, but eventually the methodological model of the para-ministry subtly altered the focus of the work from being one of outreach from a local congregation to that of a rather insular and isolated para-ministry enclave. I was not removed as chaplain to the team nor was I kept from involving my church in the chapel ministry, but after I resigned my position the para-ministry took over the sports chapel and removed it from local church ministry. This resulted in few of the players being connected with a local church.

In summary of the discussion so far, my aim here has been to map the contours of modern-day, elite sports chaplaincy provision in the US. In turn, my intention has been to encourage the sports outreach movement to assess the effectiveness and efficiency of the current methodological model upon which such provision is based. One of the ways that the effectiveness and efficiency of sports chaplaincy might be improved is through a re-envisioning of its practices upon orthodox theological truths and biblically based philosophical principles.

The future

So far I have concentrated my efforts on pondering the nuances of the present problems facing US sports chaplaincy. In the remainder of the chapter, I provide some possible theological and philosophical solutions to the issues which I have raised. A discussion of theological truths leads us to consider three key 'faith–sport continuums': (1) the 'local church–sport-related para-ministry' continuum, (2) the 'disciples–decisions' continuum and (3) the 'Christianity–sportianity' continuum.

The local church–sport-related para-ministry continuum

How many para-ministries did Paul, Barnabas, Silas, Peter or Timothy start? What did the Antiochan church commission Barnabas and Paul to do, create para-ministries or win individuals to Christ and plant churches? In its current form, US sport-related para-ministry may be seen to be based upon a flawed model due to its underdeveloped theological foundations. Theologically speaking, the local church is the vehicle which God ordained for evangelism and discipleship, and its biblically based philosophical principle is to equip church members to reach friends, family and associates through on-going relationships. The apparent end goal of many US sport-related para-ministries is some variation of 'reach, grow and send' athletes for Christ. I believe that there is no more important goal a person or organization could invest their efforts in than to make disciples for Christ. Yet, we must consider whether this goal is being accomplished to the degree once hoped for, or promised, by para-ministries. On the surface, the motivation of some of these ministries appears sound but the methodological models employed seem to be becoming less and less effective.

To be 'para-church' is necessarily to be outside the Church. This is no distinction without a meaningful difference. A theological foundation that does not maintain a focus on planting and enhancing a local congregation is, I would argue, misguided and being called para-church subtly influences those involved to understand their call as perpetuating a para-church organization, rather than to build the Church by planting and equipping local congregations. In order for effective discipleship to take place there is a need for para-ministry staff to take seriously their own commitment to attend and be active in a local congregation and for this commitment to be emphasized in and through their relationships with athletes.

There is a need for local congregations to evangelize and for sport-related para-ministries to produce fully mature disciples who are active members of those congregations. Indeed, both institutions should have the same end goal: to make disciples who 'produce, reproducing, reproducers'. Hence, the relevance of the local church–sport-related para-ministry continuum suggests that if there are shortfalls in the transition from chapel to church then a different model is needed. This means reconfiguring current methodological models of both local congregations and para-ministries based upon philosophical principles which emerge from re-envisioned theological truths.

The disciples–decisions continuum

One day I arrived at my office as the sports minister of a church to find over 200 response cards strewn across my desk. The cards, which had been filled out by young people who had attended a recent local sports outreach rally, were delivered to me by the sport-related para-ministry organization which had sponsored the event. When I called and asked the sports ministry staff member concerned what to do with the cards, he responded by saying that it was his job to win people to Christ and the church's job to disciple them.

Theologically, there is a significant difference between someone making a 'decision for Christ' and them committing to becoming a 'disciple of Christ'. Sports chaplaincies which focus solely on facilitating 'decisions for Christ' may be seen to be ineffective because such an operational model is based on an underdeveloped theology. Correctly understood, a decision for Christ is a most important step in the overall spiritual journey, but it is only one step. The ultimate theological goal is to develop dedicated disciples of Christ who consistently and continually participate in a local congregation.

At one level, one might argue that so long as everyone is focused on evangelism and discipleship then there is no need to question how such things are achieved. Yet, if para-ministries are so successful, we might legitimately ask, why has this success not manifested itself in the growth of the local church? If the philosophy of sport-related para-ministry organizations is so significant and if the methodologies of sports chaplaincies, mega-sports outreach events, platform proclamation and mass-media communication of the gospel are so fruitful, then why has US church attendance continued to dwindle? Of course, it could be argued that church attendance would have fallen even lower had it not been for para-ministry endeavours. There is logical truth to this but little hard evidence to back up the claims. Thus, the question in relation to the evangelistic efforts of such ventures is not how many decisions for Christ have been recorded but how many disciples of Christ have been added. We might consider assessing the effectiveness of evangelism not only by how many prayed a prayer with a counsellor, filled out a response card at a sports ministry event, raised their hand at a meeting or 'went forward' at a service, but also by how many new disciples of Christ have joined a local congregation and stayed active within it. As an aside, after repeated contacts and communication, none of the young people whose cards appeared on my desk that day ever came to the church.

The Christianity–sportianity continuum

I have argued that effective gospel ministry through sports chaplaincy depends upon a clear commitment to choosing Christ as Lord rather than serving the god of sport (Josh. 24:15). This continuum has already been articulated but a reprise of it is necessary to complete the theological picture.

As I have explained elsewhere, the Christianity–sportianity conundrum is not always an either/or proposition (Linville, 2014). One certainly can worship and honour God through sport, but sport should not become an athlete's god in terms of time, effort, allegiance or priority. In addition, wherever sport requires an accommodation or capitulation of one's faith, the Christian sportsperson should choose God and follow his commandments (ibid.). This is uniquely encountered by athletes with regard to Sunday participation in sport and Christian athletes often struggle with this theological principle. It could be argued that when sports chaplains ignore this truth they miss an opportunity to provide a relevant biblically based philosophical principle for athletes and coaches who participate in chapel. If Christian sportspeople forgo church attendance and participation in order to take part in athletic training, games and meetings, then they run the risk of communicating that their faith is, at best, a secondary commitment and that sport is their god. US sports chaplains and sport chapel ministries seldom proclaim a gospel encouraging total commitment to a Christian ethic as articulated by God's commands and principles, and thereby articulate an implicit sponsorship of sportianity over Christianity.

Conclusions: a way forward

My aim in this chapter has been to assess the current model of sports chaplaincy within the US and to mount a critical appraisal of its generic methodology. At the same time, I have put forward a series of propositions as to how we might re-envision the work of sports chaplains in line with specific theological truths and philosophical principles. If the ultimate aim of sports chaplaincy is to grow the Church by making disciples of Christ (who are committed, participating members of a local congregation), it is important to consider what kind of strategy might best facilitate this goal.

In one sense, the way forward seems clear: to use sport-related para-ministries to equip and enable local congregations to undertake effective, relevant and successful evangelism and discipleship. I would argue that developing dedicated disciples who follow Christ above all else (even if this means sacrificing their athletic careers), including being active in a local congregation on a Sunday, should be the ultimate goal of both sport-related para-ministries and local congregations. Imagine what might happen if such para-ministries collectively chose to work through a local congregation by equipping and empowering church members? What might be accomplished if local congregations were empowered to reach out to their local minor league baseball teams? Such mobilization and training of church lay people has the potential to result in significant gains for the Kingdom.

To this end, I believe that the methodological model of North American sports chaplaincy can, and should, be re-envisioned in the following three ways: First, empower and equip the local church. Rather than doing the work of making disciples, sport-related para-ministries could focus on mobilizing the church to do this work by equipping and empowering the parishioners of local congregations. Every chapel leader should be a member and active participant of a local congregation, commissioned by a local congregation and jointly supervised, trained and equipped by a local congregation and a para-ministry organization.

Second, abstain from holding chapel services on Sundays. Sport-related para-ministry organizations would do well to make their commitment to the Church real, by training parishioners of local congregations how to do sports chapel outreach throughout the week and then model how to personally invite athletes and players from sports chapel events to join them in active participation in a local congregation – especially Sunday services.

Third, re-envision success. Sports chaplains and sports chapel ministries would also do well to reorganize and re-evaluate their ministries and how they raise funds. Reorganization could include jointly hiring staff and collaboratively implementing a plan for chaplaincy-based outreach with local congregations. The shared staff member could have three main responsibilities: (1) to train, equip and empower church members to be sports chaplains for all local area scholastic clubs and collegiate and professional athletic teams, (2) to create a culture within local congregations that welcomes those who the chaplains bring to the church and (3) to work to build relevant and strategic programmatic connections that encourage players and their families to flow into the life of the congregation and to enable their growth into mature disciples of Christ.

Re-evaluation entails understanding that success is not simply about holding Sunday chapels at a local ballpark or increasing the number of attendees at team Bible studies but rather how many players, coaches and families become dedicated disciples of Christ and committed members of a local congregation. Raising funds for such work thus becomes somewhat easier because local congregations share in the expense of funding chaplaincy staff salaries. One additional key concept is necessary: to communicate to those who financially invest in sports chaplaincy ministries the changes in how the ministry intends to determine success. I believe investors would welcome the knowledge that their support is being directed towards not only enabling sports outreach at local arenas and sports venues but also that it has the potential to grow elite athletes, coaches and their families into dedicated followers of Christ. This would ensure winning in the clubhouse and in the church.

References

Babb, K. (2014). 'Where College Football is a Religion and Religion Shapes College Football', *Washington Post*, 29 Aug. Available at <https://www.washingtonpost.com/sports/colleges/where-college-football-is-a-religion-and-religion-shapes-college-football/2014/08/29/8d03de32-2dfa-11e4-bb9b-997ae96fad33_story.html>.

Chawner, D. (2009). 'A Reflection on the Practice of Sports Chaplaincy', *Urban Theology*, 3/1: 75–80. Available at <http://www.urbantheology.org/journals/journal-3-1/a-reflection-on-the-practice-of-sports-chaplaincy>.

Deford, F. (1976). 'Religion in Sport', *Sports Illustrated*, 44/16: 88–100.

Heskins, J., and M. Baker (eds) (2006). *Footballing Lives: As Seen by Chaplains in the Beautiful Game*, Norwich: Canterbury Press.

Hoffman, S.J. (2010). *Good Game: Christianity and the Culture of Sports*, Waco, TX: Baylor University Press.

Holm, N. (2009). 'Toward a Theology of the Ministry of Presence in Chaplaincy', *Journal of Christian Education*, 52/1: 7–22. Available at <http://www.academia.edu/1256854/Toward_a_Theology_of_the_Ministry_of_Presence_in_Chaplaincy>.

Krattenmaker, T. (2010). *Onward Christian Athletes: Turning Ballparks into Pulpits and Players into Preachers*, Lanham, MD: Rowman & Littlefield.

Ladd, T., and J.A. Mathisen (1999). *Muscular Christianity: Evangelical Protestants and the Development of American Sports*, Grand Rapids, MI: Baker Books.

Linville, G. (2014). *Christmanship: A Theology of Competition and Sport*, Canton, OH: Oliver House Publishing.

4   Sports Chaplaincy Australia

Cameron Butler and Noel Mitaxa

Introduction

As Australian sports ministry has grown over the past 30 years, it has demonstrated God's sovereignty in the linking of two unlikely partners, a national passion for sport and a cultural ambivalence towards religion and authority. Australia's British heritage has been augmented by post-war mass migration on a similar scale to that witnessed in the US. With a landmass equivalent to North America's mainland states, Australia hosts a population of 23 million, the majority inhabiting towns and cities on its eastern and south-eastern coastlines and remote south-west corner. While North America's first European settlers eagerly sought a land of opportunity, Australia's early European inhabitants were convicts with offences ranging from murder and treason to petty theft. Transported from overcrowded English jails, they experienced a brutal penal regime to which the Church was seen to be intimately connected. Such associations were characterized by early expressions of Christian witness in Australia: for example, the First Fleet's Revd Richard Johnston (Cable, 1967) and, later, Revd Samuel Marsden, described as 'the flogging parson'. Recommended by William Wilberforce, both of these men originally served as chaplains with a genuine enthusiasm for the gospel, thereafter being appointed as magistrates and falling into the enticing trap of grace-giver and judgement-maker (Cronshaw, 2006). Hence, unlike US immigrant dreams surrounding freedom of religion, Australians have traditionally harboured a desire for freedom *from* religion, unless religion can prove its value or credibility.

Meanwhile, Australia's love of sport has traditionally provided a strong social cohesion across ethnic and social class divides. Though this cohesion is tested by good-natured 'tribal' loyalties within and across competitive sports, an affection for sporting activity approaches religious proportion for many Australians (both as participants and spectators). Such trends, Clifford (1989) observes, place an obligation on the church to connect the gospel to sports in relevant ways.

In this chapter we consider the formation and history of sports chaplaincy in Australia. In so doing, we uncover when and where it began and how, in more recent years, it has re-formed and re-branded adopting a movement model in order to facilitate rapid growth and the empowerment of local sport and faith communities. We conclude by discussing the risks and opportunities which lay ahead for sport and chaplaincy in Australia.

Early beginnings

Formal sports chaplaincy in Australia was launched at the elite level in December 1984 with the appointment of Revd Mark Tronson (a Baptist pastor and part-time industrial chaplain) as chaplain to Australia's test cricket team. This appointment proved positive for it opened up the possibility of chaplaincy for other sports clubs and associations. During the 1960s and 1970s retired and current Christian athletes had begun to meet regularly in Sydney, forming the Christian Sports Fellowship to encourage one another in their faith and to support each other in ministry. This group also developed links with high-profile evangelical US sportsmen and women. These links facilitated invitations for Tronson and his ministry colleagues to attend an International Sports Ministry conference in Hong Kong in August 1982, which attracted 186 delegates from 30 nations. Nine Australians attended this event, including Tronson and Revd David Tyndall, an international rugby union referee, who began to share their thoughts and visions for establishing an Australian sports ministry as they travelled home together. They knew that many churches had participated in their own sports competitions or competed in community associations for many years with some larger churches sponsoring visits by international sports outreach groups like Venture for Victory basketball ministry, Sports Ambassadors Service and Christian Surfers. Tronson and Tyndall also recognized that professional sportsmen and women had little or no Christian ministry exposure. This led them through 18 months of networking with the Christian Sports Fellowship, the New South Wales Baptist Union and the Inter-church Trade and Industry Mission (ITIM), the latter of which was entrusted to oversee a fledgling ministry that would provide Christian pastoral care to professional sports figures (Tyndall, 2004).

In February 1984, under the auspices of ITIM, Mark Tronson and Delma Tronson stepped out in faith to launch Sports and Leisure Ministry (SLM), a name that avoided any negative preconceptions from sports agencies about the role or intentions of prospective chaplains. The success of this ministry came through establishing strong links with mainstream churches, rather than adopting a para-church model, so that local churches could support those referred to them. The national board of SLM comprised representatives from the major denominations thereby providing some element of safeguarding around the credentials of prospective chaplains. In 1988, SLM's stated goals were to place chaplains with sports clubs and associations, to provide discipleship for Christian sportspeople, and to assist churches in developing authentic sports ministry. Progress towards these goals gave SLM sufficient credibility to change its name to Sports Chaplaincy Australia (SCA) in August 2005.

Sports Chaplaincy Australia

In 2005 the SLM National Board commissioned its first national director of SCA, Revd Cameron Butler, a long serving SLM chaplain to the Melbourne Football Club in the Australian Football League. Prior to this appointment Butler had trained and served as a local church pastor at Doncaster City Church in Melbourne and had founded and directed an internet-based software development company. Butler consolidated the fledgling ministry and implemented a number of key changes including strategic re-positioning, re-branding and, most critically, clearly articulating the ministry vision and mission to the remaining chaplains, devotees and groups across the existing network. At that stage, SLM had fewer than 45 active chaplains.

In September 2005 Sports Chaplaincy Australia was formally launched with a vision to have chaplains serving in every sports community in Australia. Two significant events led to the reinforcement of this vision. In 2006 Australian universities and sports organizations which were addressing the issue of mental health in sport brought together key representatives from across the nation to the Australian Sport and Mental Health Conference in Melbourne. During an open forum at the conference, a leading national sports administrator declared that Australian sport was in a state of crisis as 'parent coaches' were taking the decision to no longer be involved in sport due to the pressures of having to deal with not only the technical side of activities, but in helping young people with their personal problems (Gannon, 2006).

It was at this stage that the SCA network saw a significant opportunity for local club chaplains. Sports clubs had need for pastoral carers; something that the Christian community could provide and that elite sports would appreciate. This presented the local church with a significant opportunity to serve its community in a highly relevant way. But was this a wish or was it a reality? An impromptu telephone call in 2010 between Glenn Scott, then CEO of Australia's largest sports league, the Victorian Country Football League, and Cameron Butler clarified this. The call led to a meeting at the Melbourne Cricket Ground where Scott invited SCA to assist the League in appointing chaplains to all of their clubs, some 880 in total. Interestingly, most of these clubs were in partnership with netball clubs. The demand for over 1,700 chaplains in only two sports in a small region of Australia again reinforced the need to strategically shift the local church mindset from pastoring a church to shepherding a sports club. The perceived demand for local club chaplains had materialized.

Strategic response

The need to clearly and concretely articulate a strategic response by SCA for both the Australian sports community and the Christian faith community was critical. How would SCA fulfil its vision to place a chaplain in every sports club and which model of growth would the organization adopt? What guiding principles and ideologies were critical for success? What usual dependencies or securities was SCA prepared to let go of for the sake of growing God's Kingdom? Most importantly, the vision which SCA had articulated many years earlier – to see a chaplain serving in every sports club – was considered by those involved as being God's vision more than that of SCA. SCA staff realized that with a chaplain in every club in Australia, or region, or city, the local church would be actively reaching 75 per cent of the country's total population. On average, a sports chaplain in Australia has a pastoral care reach of approximately 500 people in their club and wider community. For every member of a sports club, pastoral care takes place both for the club member and for their extended family, thus providing substantial and strategic reach for God's grace and mercy.

Official government research into sports participation in Australia reveals that over 30 per cent of the population takes part in organized sport each week, with most involved twice weekly (Australian Bureau of Statistics, 2003). Comparatively speaking, the most favourable church attendance figures in Australia (across all Christian denominations) currently sit at 8.8 per cent, which equates to attendance once per month (National Church Life Survey Research, 2001). Indeed, Australians are 40 times more likely to be involved in a sports club community than in a local church. In turn, the above figures indicate that church attendance is declining overall and that sports and recreational involvement is increasing marginally. Strategically, SCA has been challenging the Australian Church to reconsider what it means to shepherd a flock; to rediscover the notion that the flock is not simply made up of traditional church members but also includes the community or crowd which has no shepherd (Mark 6:34).

Point of difference in the sports marketplace

The kinds of questions that face many in the Australian sports industry are: why do we need a chaplain? What does a chaplain do? What can a chaplain do that a sport psychologist or a sports welfare officer or 'caring' coach cannot? Understanding the point of difference of an Australian sports chaplain has become critical in SCA's ability to present chaplaincy to enquiring club presidents, coaches and administrators. The point of difference is simply that sports chaplains provide volunteer pastoral care. When asked what pastoral care is, chaplains relay simple stories about meeting the basic needs of individuals amidst the turbulence of everyday life – divorce, bereavement, injury – issues which counsellors, sport psychologists and coaches do not always have the time, expertise or inclination to deal with (Sports Chaplaincy Australia, 2011). Such an approach is designed to avoid the risk of having to explain pastoral care in an academic, overly religious or philosophical way. Jesus adopted a similarly straightforward model of communication throughout his ministry (see e.g. Luke 10:30). Most sports clubs simply need help with caring for people. As mentioned earlier, many volunteers do not see this as part of their involvement in sport, accepting that it is a worthwhile venture but often not knowing how best to act. A very real risk which accompanies the framing of sports chaplaincy in this way is that it is tempting to professionalize and programmatize it for the sake of conformity or compromise or to generate income. SCA vigorously adheres to the crucial focus of its mission, which is equipping and sending pastoral carers, not 'running programmes'.

Growth: Centre Bounce Teams

Luke 10 has come to be the pre-eminent scripture for sports chaplains in Australia. Here Christ explains to those going into the community that they will see that the harvest is 'plentiful' and instructs them to 'ask the Lord of the harvest, therefore, to send out workers into the harvest field'. With these verses in mind, in 2008 SCA began to focus on a strategic growth response to an ever-increasing appetite for chaplaincy from within the sports sector. Late that year US Fellowship of Christian Athletes sports chaplain Roger Lipe travelled to Australia to discuss with SCA the significance of a movement model based on Brafman and Beckstrom's *The Starfish and the Spider* (2006). After much consultation with key operatives, in 2010 SCA launched its Centre Bounce Team strategy.

Put simply, the Centre Bounce Team strategy seeks to empower the SCA network to further growth. Leaning on the team-sport adage that 'only a few people start the game then the rest of the team join in', SCA sought to reinforce its mission by empowering church and missional networks, to grow the vision. This currently includes groups like Christian Surfers, Youth with a Mission and Youth for Christ. SCA continues to provide free and unfettered resources (and authority) to these pre-existing networks in order to establish a chaplain serving in every sports community. After some six years of implementation, over 100 Centre Bounce Teams operate around Australia in regions, denominations and agencies, actively seeking to identify sports communities who require chaplains, identifying suitable Christians who can serve, and enlisting the help of these groups to appoint them.

Trusted people

Amidst the openness and freedom for growth which SCA engenders in relation to its networks, two fundamental issues are observed: 'trusted people' and the 'guiding principles of Australian sports chaplains'. In turn, SCA provides the Australian sports industry with three significant value propositions: SCA chaplains are very good at providing care, SCA chaplains are free, and SCA chaplains are trusted people. This latter concept is held without compromise. SCA demands that all chaplains are accredited and vetted as trusted people. Notably, the Australian sports industry also requires this. In 2001, after consulting with senior chaplains Peter Nelson – Australia Institute of Sport chaplain in Canberra and Gary Speckman – chaplain to New South Wales Waratah's rugby union, SCA identified a definitive list of guiding principles to ensure the consistency, clarity and effectiveness of sports chaplaincy growth in Australia. These comprise the following: the chaplain's relationship with Christ and others is their ministry; chaplains make time; chaplains build people; chaplains are authentic; chaplains are visible – for visibility is credibility; chaplains maintain confidentiality; chaplains are trustworthy – respecting the office'; chaplains serve without discrimination; chaplains are servant leaders; chaplains are always a guest; chaplains are volunteers; chaplains are discerning; chaplains do ministry 'to' and not 'through'; chaplains keep it pure – no agendas; chaplains are comfortable inviting response; chaplains don't go alone; chaplains are catalysts for growth.

Keeping focus

With an overwhelming desire to respond to the many opportunities for chaplaincy, sports ministry distractions are commonplace. SCA has articulated its vision, mission and day-to-day activities by encouraging its networks to focus on four key activities under the acronym ITAG: Identify, Train, Appoint and Guide chaplains. Behind these activities are some unique ideologies. They include the fact that SCA does not see itself as a para-church organization 'doing' ministry but rather as an organization which empowers the local church to release its people to 'do' ministry. During the 2010 launch of SCA's Centre Bounce Team strategy, Cameron Butler coined the term 'syncra-church' whereby he described SCA's aspiration to be the local church's 'best friend' in mission by 'working in-sync' and not in competition with it. The SCA network assists the local church by providing local church people with the rudimentary skills and understanding necessary to function appropriately in community sectors such as sports. The approach is based on the biblical pattern in Luke 10:1–9. The network runs free, entry-level training for churches and mission agencies to assist with the identification and appointment of local club chaplains.

SCA also appreciates the role of the local church as the primary care-giver and best friend to sports chaplains. It often takes a relatively short period of time before a chaplain reaches his or her level of competency or capacity and needs to draw upon help from their faith community. More importantly, it is the indispensable role of the local church to care for the care-giver during times of tragedy, loss and hardship. The overwhelming difficulty and cost of providing essential peer support for issues like vicarious trauma can be addressed by adopting a healthy New Testament approach to ministry and the care of chaplains as in Luke 10:17–24. Unlike military chaplains or hospital chaplains, sports chaplains in Australia are not recognized professionals who operate under the auspices of government or non-governmental organizations, nor are they employed or paid by their respective clubs. Instead, chaplaincy is provided on a voluntary basis although chaplains can receive support as missionaries if they choose. Their role is significantly more relational than positional whereby the success of their ministry almost entirely hinges on the effectiveness of their ability to build and maintain relationships. They are almost always part-time, usually serving between 4 and 8 hours per week, and all SCA chaplains are governed by a professional code of conduct which includes a statement of faith. In turn, all SCA chaplains are commissioned by their local church and serve their sports community without discrimination. When asked about other faiths, SCA is quick to respond to the notion that its chaplains pastorally care for everyone in their community regardless of religion, belief (or non-belief), ethnicity, gender, age or lifestyle. Any requests by people of other faiths which chaplains are unable or ill-equipped to respond to are referred to the appropriate person, be it an Imam, Rabbi, Priest, psychologist or other faith specialist.

Serving sport

In line with the organizational development and remit of the SCA network, sports chaplaincy provision is expanding in a number of ways. At the time of writing there are over 400 chaplains serving across Australia with many thousands of requests for chaplains continually being received from sporting bodies. What follows is an overview of the key areas where SCA chaplaincy is currently taking place.

Motor sports

As the work of SCA has developed, motor sport officials have been quick to embrace sports chaplaincy because of the inherent dangers of the sport and because many of them have become familiar with chaplaincy at American racetracks and circuits. Over 50 chaplains now serve across the spectrum of Australian motor sports from the annual Australian Grand Prix and the Bathurst 1000 races though drag racing, rallying, speedway and motorcycle racing. One of the central bodies in motorsports in Australia, the Confederation of Australian Motor Sports, has indicated that they would like to have chaplains serving at all events and racetracks around the country, which total more than 500. The opportunity and significance of chaplaincy in motorsport has long been a staple of sports chaplaincy in Australia.

Football

Football in Australia is a smorgasbord of codes: the home-grown Australian Rules, rugby union, rugby league and soccer. At the elite level of each code are many examples of long-serving chaplains, with deep appreciation for their work being shown in numerous formal and personal ways. Australian Rules predominates in the southern states, with ten teams in Victoria. Eight more, in Perth, Adelaide, Sydney and south-east Queensland give the game the widest national exposure of all codes, with some matches attracting crowds in excess of 80,000 during the season and more for finals. Centred around Sydney, the National Rugby League is the predominant rugby code with ten New South Wales teams, three from Queensland and others from Canberra, Melbourne and Auckland, New Zealand.

The National Rugby League's prevalence has undoubtedly come from the fierce rivalry between NSW (Blues) and Queensland (Maroons) in the State of Origin series. The Australian Rugby Union also prevails in New South Wales, Queensland and the Australian Capital Territory with major representative teams in Melbourne and Perth. Though players mainly stem from Sydney's private church schools, chaplaincy emerged largely through a Christian doctor's

(Wallabies' John Best) concern for pastoral care for elite-level players with spinal injuries.

The world game of soccer has more junior participants than any other team sport in Australia, yet its senior-level competition has the lowest media profile of the four football codes. In the past, chaplains have served at the elite level but with the demise of the National Soccer League and recent re-engineering of the National A-League chaplaincy has been more readily adopted by the national youth, women's and local-church based leagues in Victoria, Newcastle and Queensland.

Basketball and Netball

Exported around the world from the US, basketball has deep historic roots in Australian sport. School and community-based basketball and netball centres are as commonplace as any sport nationally. Like soccer, basketball has undergone numerous identity changes and continues to find its place at the national level. Nonetheless, chaplains have, for some time, served in the national competition. Unlike in the US where chaplains serve through college teams, Australian basketball chaplains are increasingly invited to serve in regional sports and basketball centres.

The late John Van Groningen had a significant impact on the Australian basketball fraternity over a 15-year period serving as chaplain to the national basketball team, the 'Boomers', at the Olympic and Commonwealth Games. Van Groningen also recruited many of the current serving national basketball chaplains and invited dozens of national players, like former Boomers captain Jason Smith, to tour outback Australia with him. They participated in 'role model' clinics to encourage and esteem godly and healthy values amongst young, isolated indigenous peoples in the Northern Territory. Such events and experiences proved as life-changing for the athletes as they did for young people involved.

A commonwealth favourite, netball has long been the sleeping giant of Australian sports chaplaincy. Like many other female sports, netball in Australia does not boast a long association with sports chaplaincy though the call for female chaplains in Australia's pre-eminent women's sports is rapidly increasing. The trans-Tasman competition (Australia and New Zealand), known as the ANZ Championship Cup, is leading this call, and local clubs are increasingly seeing the benefit.

Winter sports

With such a short snow season, skiing in Australia is largely recreational. However, a small band of chaplains minister to several snowfields and the New South Wales Institute of Sport high-performance winter sports academy at Jindabyne. Apart from the conventional pastoral care required in the academy, critical incidents are commonplace in the snowfields with major injury trauma and death a prominent part of any winter sports chaplains' ministry. Road trauma and staff relationship issues also feature highly for winter sports ministry. Local snowfield churches continue to be the best conduit for emerging chaplains.

Tennis

Australia has a strong track-record in tennis at the elite level and historically the sport has been well resourced as a recreational pursuit with many churches having their own courts. However, since 1977 only two Australians have won Wimbledon, and Australia has only won the Davis Cup five times. Chaplaincy has had a small but important role to play on the Satellite Tour supporting players who are away from home for long periods of time. In recent years, the Australian Tennis Academy and senior coaches have further explored the idea of chaplaincy and have begun to consider the provision of wider pastoral care for players.

Baseball

Baseball has never had a high profile in Australia, despite being introduced by American prospectors during the 1850s gold rush. After decades of being the chosen winter sport of State and Test cricketers, baseball became a summer sport in 1989 when the Australian Baseball League was formed to attract more national interest. Chaplains were quickly appointed because officials were aware of the role of chaplaincy in US baseball and little groundwork had to be done to establish access and to initiate systems of pastoral provision.

Cricket

Cricket and Christianity have been closely linked in England for over 150 years, with many clergy playing at county level as well as serving as public school headmasters. The NSW Churches Cricket Union (originally known as the Western Suburbs Cricket Union) was formed in 1902, and Canon E.S. Hughes was president of the Victorian Cricket Association from 1932 to 1942.

After the appointment of a Test cricket chaplain in 1984, every state cricket association was prompted to make similar appointments. One important initiative, in conjunction with international umpire Tony Crafter, has been the Life after Cricket programme, which prepares elite cricketers for their exit from the game.

Surfing and Life Saving

In the late 2000s surfing's leading national body the Association of Surfing Professionals approached Brett Davis, chairman and founder of Christian Surfers International, to trial chaplaincy to the men's world tour. With support from SCA, the 12-month trial was successful and led to the Association welcoming chaplains to serve the women's and junior tours. Not long after the appointment of Davis, Abe Andrews served the Pro Tour following the sudden death of three-time Men's World Champion Andy Irons. Many Association of Surfing Professionals chaplains today are being trained by SCA and Christian Surfers International to serve in surfing regions all around the world.

Since 1998 surf lifesaver Terry Legg has served life saving in Australia as senior chaplain and devoted himself to growing credibility in his sport where now over 30 chaplains serve clubs around the nation's dangerous shores. Terry has represented the international sports chaplaincy community at life-saving carnivals around the globe and in 2002 handed his national leadership role to rugby league chaplain Russ Harmon and the newly formed Life Saving Chaplaincy Australia National Committee. Dozens of Surf Life Saving Australia clubs have shown interest in having chaplains and appointments are well underway.

Institutes of sport

Australia's failure to win Olympic gold medals at Montreal in 1976 prompted the establishment of the Australian Institute of Sport (AIS) in Canberra in 1981. In seven subsequent Olympic Games, AIS athletes won 142 Olympic medals, including 33 gold. AIS chaplaincy began in 1989 and was well received by athletes, coaches and staff. Now, many of the State Institutes of Sport have chaplains working closely with Athlete Career and Education coordinators providing pastoral care to high performance athletes and to AIS staff.

Women's sports chaplaincy

For many years sports chaplaincy mirrored elite sport in Australia. Predominately male and typically professional, chaplains were mainly ordained men. There were very few female chaplains, and there was a reluctance in the chaplaincy network to appoint women chaplains simply to accommodate the nuances of political correctness. However in the late 1990s women became more involved, firstly in yachting, netball, cricket, swimming and to the wives of speedway drivers and then among State Institutes of Sport.

National athletics competitor Nett Knox returned to her sport as chaplain after retiring from competition in 1998 and in 2006 became a full-time chaplain serving across a range of women's sports and to several Olympic and Commonwealth Games. In 2006 a unique opportunity arose when Karen Moreton, a local church youth leader and mother with children at a local pony club, was invited by the Dubbo Pony Club Committee to serve as their chaplain. The initiative shown by Moreton led to an endorsement by the NSW Pony Club Association for chaplains to over 250 clubs.

Conclusion: the future of sports chaplaincy in Australia

This chapter has sought to provide an overview of the emergence of sports chaplaincy in Australia during the past 30 years. Similarly, it has sketched a brief overview of the unique style and development of SCA's urban chaplaincy model working closely with the local church and sports community to provide a timely response to community need. However successful the history of SCA has proved, future challenges remain.

Until the mid-2000s sports chaplaincy in Australia was largely focused on high-performance sports. In the coming decades the need to respond to local sports communities will be central to SCA's focus. It is likely that opportunities will emerge in fringe and extreme sports. At this level, similar openings will probably materialize in sports management and amongst indigenous communities.

One concern will be the push by some to license the role of the chaplain. Governments and stakeholder organizations, including some religious denominations, may seek to institutionalize chaplaincy in sport. However, the power of a servant-leadership model (unpaid, non-commercial, volunteer) and the vigorous attention to keeping Jesus Christ and his grace and mercy at the centre of the mission (not the institutional, political, secular or religious agendas of various stakeholders) will lessen the opportunity for these groups to control outcomes.

More exciting will be the complementary opportunities which are likely to emerge from the proliferation of sports chaplains in the areas of training, consultancy and professional services to sports bodies and communities in Australia. To date, many chaplains have served at numerous major sporting events like the Sydney Olympics, the 2001 World Masters Games, the 2003 Rugby World Cup, the Melbourne Commonwealth Games and regional carnivals and regattas are sectors that are also set to grow. However, the greatest potential outcome in the growth of SCA still remains the countless lives and communities who will tangibly come to know the grace and mercy of Jesus Christ through ordinary people serving as chaplains.

References

Australian Bureau of Statistics (2003). *Participation in Sport and Physical Activities Australia*, Canberra: Australian Bureau of Statistics. Available at <http://www.abs.gov.au/ausstats/abs@.nsf/mediareleasesbytitle/4C791011290F82A3CA2577FF0011E7C1?OpenDocument>.

Brafman, R.A., and O. Beckstrom (2006). *The Starfish and the Spider: The Unstoppable Power of Leaderless Organizations*, New York: Penguin.

Cable, K.J. (1967). *Australian Dictionary of Biography*, vol. 2, London: Melbourne University Press.

Clifford, D.R. (1989). *Chairman's Report: SLM Conference*, Adelaide, SA: Specialised Life-Orientated Ministries.

Cronshaw, D. (2006). *Credible Witness*, Springvale, Vic.: Urban Neighbours of Hope.

Gannon, K. (2006). 'Open Forum'. Paper presented to Sport and Mental Health Conference, Hilton on the Park, Melbourne.

National Church Life Survey Research (2001). *National Church Life Survey*. Available at: <http://www.ncls.org.au/default.aspx?sitemapid=2260>.

Sports Chaplaincy Australia (2011). *The Game Plan*, Melbourne, Vic.: Sports Chaplaincy Australia Inc.

Tyndall, D.B. (2004). 'Evangelicalism, Sport and the Australian Olympics', PhD thesis: Maquirie University.

5   Sports chaplaincy at the Olympics and Paralympics

Reflections on London 2012

Duncan Green[1]

Introduction

On 6 July 2005 the awarding of the 2012 Olympic and Paralympic Games to London caught the imagination of the British people. During the following seven years, the UK public watched the progress of the development of the Games, debating such issues as the financial and personal cost and the potential benefits to the residents of East London. Many questions were raised, but in the end, the organizers delivered a Games which were described by the International Olympic Committee (IOC) president, Jacques Rogge (at the closing ceremony of the Paralympics) as 'happy and glorious'. A surge of shared emotion had been released, allowing the nation to 'express parts of themselves which are normally suppressed' (Ellis, 2012: 181).

During the seven years leading up to the opening ceremony of the 2012 Olympics a team was built to undertake the essential detailed planning. This is the story of one small but significant part of that team: the involvement of the faith communities in both the planning and delivery of the Games, which created the infrastructure for a radical and innovative chaplaincy programme. Beginning with my appointment as the Church of England Olympics executive coordinator in November 2007, it follows the development of my role, travelling with the London Organising Committee of the Olympic Games (LOCOG) and being appointed in July 2011 by LOCOG (on secondment from the Church of England) to be its head of multi-faith chaplaincy services. It describes how the chaplaincy service was delivered during the Olympics and Paralympics by members of the five major world faiths to people of every nation and faith: athletes (including coaches, team medical staff and administrators), workforce (all the LOCOG employees and the 70,000 volunteers), media centre (where the 5,800 accredited journalists and broadcasters worked) and even the general public. The unique and novel aspects of the London 2012 chaplaincy are highlighted.

My appointment

My career had seen me serve as priest and vicar in local church ministry, latterly as team rector and area dean at Saffron Walden in Essex and, for the period 1987 to 1994, as youth officer of the diocese of Chelmsford. Involvement in a major sports event was an entirely new experience for which little in my previous roles had prepared me. In the latter part of 2006 the dioceses of Chelmsford (which included what was to become the Olympic Park), London, and Southwark agreed to recruit and fund an Olympic executive coordinator to be a senior appointment in the Church of England. When the job was advertised the bishop of Barking encouraged me to apply. I was appointed, and took up post on 1 November 2007. Whilst the job description gave me a wide-ranging and somewhat grandiose brief, I was sailing in uncharted waters.

It would have been possible for me to fulfil all that the job description demanded from the safe distance of my home office base, but from the beginning I believed that I would better meet the specific requirements of the post if I were located within LOCOG, sharing highs and lows, joys and sorrows with all who were now working under the pressure to deliver the best Games ever. I quickly realized that, if I were to have the influence I desired I would need to seek access not to those at the top of the organization but to those at the bottom. My *modus operandi* was a willingness to serve and to do jobs that no one else wanted to do.

While attending a meeting in late 2007 I came into contact with LOCOG's community relations manager. It was just a chance conversation that developed as we walked from the meeting venue to the underground station and then travelled together on the tube, a journey which was to have significant consequences. It had already become clear to him that, whilst the Olympic movement defined itself as being non-religious, engagement with the faith communities in the East End of London and beyond would be essential to the success of the Games, something he was finding difficult to do. As we talked, he realized that he was making the contact he needed and he asked me if the Church could second someone to LOCOG to take on the role of faith advisor, someone who would be able to advise LOCOG on how it could engage with the faith communities. In such a way is God's Kingdom built: I saw an open door and instantly walked through it. I was delighted and replied that this was the job I had been appointed to do and that I would be only too pleased to assist.

From being an outsider seeking a way in, I now found myself in a pivotal position seconded to LOCOG as multi-faith advisor and a member of the LOCOG Community Relations/Community Engagement Team. Through me the Church and the faith communities could engage with the whole of LOCOG, and LOCOG could engage with the faith communities. Formally, I now had three roles: (1) I had been appointed by the bishop of Barking to co-coordinate the response of the Church of England to the Olympics and liaise with other churches and other faiths, (2) I had been seconded to LOCOG to be their faith advisor and to work with them on how the Olympics would relate to the faith communities and how the faith communities would relate to the Olympics, and (3) I had also been appointed by the bishop of Barking to liaise with More than Gold, the organization established to coordinate the churches' response to the Olympic Games, and I was invited to serve on its executive board. In this sense, I provided a significant link between More than Gold and LOCOG, each seeing me as its representative on the inside of the other.

Although I had a desk in LOCOG's offices on the top floors of the Barclays Bank Building in London's Canary Wharf, my appointment as multi-faith advisor required me to be there only one day per week. However, as well as having a specific job to do, I was also a priest who, 'by his very presence, spoke of a spiritual dimension in life' (Billings, 2010: 49), so it was natural for me to be around the office on most days. This kind of presence required a relationship that was both typical and unique: typical in the sense that it gave me the pastoral, spiritual and prophetic presence within the organization which chaplains to schools and hospitals would recognize; unique in that, because I had not been appointed 'chaplain to LOCOG', there was no expectation that I would conduct services or say prayers in public or wear a dog-collar. I was there to do what needed doing. Through me the church was serving the organization. I was now able to begin to build 'a presence within the structures' of my new found surroundings (Slater, 2012).

One aspect of my job within LOCOG was to advise management on the requirements of the members of the faith communities as they became engaged with the Games. To help achieve this, at the beginning of 2008 I decided to invite the faith leaders to appoint representatives so that a Faith Reference Group (FRG) could be set up. The FRG developed into a key channel of communication. Because it was clear that its importance must be recognized by all the faiths and by LOCOG, the then archbishop of Canterbury, Rowan Williams, hosted its launch at Lambeth Palace with all the faith leaders present. LOCOG made a presentation of the plans for the Games, the archbishop gave his blessing, and the faith leaders gave their support. The archbishop's interfaith officer continued to work closely with me.

The FRG acted as a point of contact and information on the requirements of the faiths on such matters as uniform, food, security and chaplaincy provision, and LOCOG policies on these matters were developed with the advice of the group. As a result catering services ensured the provision of both kosher and halal food in a way that sensitively met the needs and concerns of the Jewish and Muslim communities respectively. As the games would be held during Ramadan, the FRG provided the essential forum for discussing with LOCOG the best way to provide for the needs of practising Muslims. It was planned that spectators and Games workforce would not be allowed to bring food into the official venues, but LOCOG management were aware that special provision would need to be made for Muslims to bring in small amounts of food so that they could end their fasts. As a result of conversations with the FRG, it was agreed that 'break of fast' packs would be provided for athletes and for the workforce.

My relationships with the all the faiths through the FRG, my LOCOG appointment, and my position as a canon of Chelmsford Cathedral gave me the authority to speak on matters of faith. By the middle of 2011 I was deemed to be the natural person for LOCOG to put up to be interviewed by the *London Evening Standard* on how they were planning to respond to the needs of the Muslim community during Ramadan.

The members of the FRG brought with them an in-depth knowledge of the people of the East End of London, so they could not be ignored when they spoke up for those who were or might be marginalized. On their initiative, tickets for the Games were distributed to local children through their faith communities. They were able to channel the outrage of the East End community that the marathon route had been changed so that they would not see the athletes on their streets. Although based with the Community Relations/Community Engagement Team, I was able to relate to other parts of LOCOG. When it was suggested that faith rooms for athletes, staff and volunteers would not be necessary, I was able to work through the Diversity and Inclusiveness Team to make sure that places for prayer and quiet would be provided.

By 2009 I had become recognized in LOCOG as both a trusted friend and confidant and through the FRG the essential source and provider of expertise in relation to all matters of faith and the faith communities in the East End. It was now clear that the FRG's advice and guidance would be invaluable in the planning and delivery of the Games themselves, particularly in relation to the delivery of chaplaincy services. While nowadays a religious centre and chaplaincy is an accepted part of the Olympics, the nature and extent of such provision varies from Games to Games because of the autonomy of the local organizing committee. In 2000, for example, the organizing committee had upset the local faith community by handing over responsibility for chaplaincy to the Sydney police chaplains (Tyndall, 2004). Chaplaincy in Athens 2004 was deemed to have worked well, but in Beijing 2008 the religious centre was staffed entirely by Chinese chaplains. The lack of accredited international chaplains had provoked criticism, particularly from the American Olympic team (Cha, 2008).

In London we were determined to have a chaplaincy which reflected the diversity appropriate to a worldwide event, so adopting the model used in Beijing 2008 was not an option. By the end of 2009 it had become clear to me that (for the first time in the history of the Olympics) there was the potential for there to be chaplains not only to the athletes but also to the Games workforce, media centre, volunteers and out-of-London sites. I could see that LOCOG needed a manager for the faith area alongside the managers for security, catering and the villages. Early in 2010 in consultation with me a job description for the head of multi-faith chaplaincy services was written. Following this a 'concept of operations' was produced, which set out plans for faith services at all the venues where the Games would take place and which will be passed on to the organizers of future Games. This encompassed a bold and wide-ranging vision, proposing a multi-faith chaplaincy service which would be for the overall care – and specifically the spiritual needs – of those of all faiths and none including space for prayer and worship in multi-faith centres for all of the nine faith communities in the UK inter-faith network and for others as required. Such a service would contribute to fulfilling the overall aim of the London 2012 Games in its bid promises of diversity and inclusion. In this sense chaplaincy would not merely provide religious services for religious people, but it would undergird the very heart of LOCOG's bid to stage a Games which would reflect the richness of the UK's multi-cultural and multi-faith society. The intention was that no place where athletes, officials, broadcasters and press, workforce or volunteers would be found should be outside the scope of the chaplains' ministry. In each of the three Athletes Villages there would be a multi-faith centre with space for religious services for the respective faiths, a counselling room, a wash area for Muslims, shoe racks, an office area, reception and the provision of prayer books.

A high level of professionalism would be required of the chaplaincy managers during the Games to ensure that an efficient and reliable service was delivered 24-hours a day. They would keep records and produce reports, liaise with the village management team, work with LOCOG in the training of the chaplains of all faiths, and integrate chaplains into the Athletes Village community. They would also ensure that the multi-faith centre was furnished to the needs of each faith community and that the faith leaders were consulted on any matters of concern. All chaplains were expected to wear a version of the 'Games Maker' uniform which had the word 'Chaplain' inconspicuously located on the epaulettes. Epaulettes opened doors as people respected the chaplaincy badge of office that put chaplains on the same level as doctors and other professionals. An essential part of LOCOG thinking was that chaplains were an integral part of the village services team.

Chaplains reacted very differently to this integral role. Some international chaplains, who had served at other Olympic Games where chaplains had had a unique uniform which instantly identified them, felt that the designated attire presented a series of barriers in terms of relationship building. There was no possibility of chaplains having a separate uniform. LOCOG had decided that they were to be considered Games Makers: that is, part of the volunteer workforce behind the delivery of London 2012, albeit with a specific role. Hence, they had to wear the Games Maker uniform. Others experienced clear benefits from wearing the uniform. A local chaplain said she had found renewed freedom in her ministry by being released from the clerical collar she had worn in the parish all her ministry. She had had to dig deep to find herself and as a result had been in touch with people as human beings and been invited into locations from which other chaplains seemed to have found themselves excluded. Another emphasized the value of wearing the same uniform as everyone else: 'For me, *being part of a community on equal terms was vital*' (original emphasis). This particular individual went on to say that 'the uniform was not a hindrance and actually encouraged one to introduce the meaning of being a man or woman of faith to those who we would engage with'. Another chaplain stated that 'it helped to be recognized as a Games Maker but I felt we should have something [more] distinctive to point us out as chaplains – perhaps "chaplain" written across the back of our jackets'. The manager of the 'roaming team', Jeremy

Fraser, found the dress requirements particularly difficult, feeling that he was often having to explain who he was to people, who had not seen the writing on the epaulette. On the other hand, he readily recognized the benefits of not having attire that marked out faiths separately which, he argued, 'allowed us not to be "our faith" chaplains but "multi-faith" chaplains'. A Muslim chaplain said that her distinctive (Muslim rather than chaplain) dress had led to people contacting her for general help and that this had led to some relating to her as a chaplain. Of course, some cultures relate uniforms to notions of status, hierarchy and authority and this may, at times, have presented itself as a barrier.

Chaplaincy management structure

The 'concept of operations' set out the criteria for the recruitment of chaplains, making clear what was needed to build a successful multi-faith team. Potential chaplains would be expected to have had, for example, previous experience of sports chaplaincy in an official capacity and ideally be able to speak at least one other language as well as English. They would be endorsed by their religious group or denominational leaders and would commit themselves to be available to fulfil the number of shifts required of chaplains before and during the Games. The aim was to build a balanced multi-faith team of chaplains who individually had particular skills to offer. The vision of the first truly comprehensive Olympic Games chaplaincy service had finally come into focus. It made the creation of the post of head of multi-faith chaplaincy services essential. Over the years SCORE (now Sports Chaplaincy UK), had provided chaplaincy to many major sporting events, and might have been thought to be the body to organize chaplaincy at London 2012. However, the FRG had assumed from an early stage that I would take on this role having been involved since the beginning, and it was indeed the case that, while I was clear that it was not in my gift, I was inevitably becoming involved in the recruitment of chaplains through the volunteer scheme.

LOCOG's trust in me, the depth of my knowledge and my vision for a comprehensive chaplaincy service made me the natural candidate for this role. In the spring of 2010 LOCOG agreed that I should be responsible for the delivery of the service, and I was appointed head of multi-faith chaplaincy services. This new role encompassed my previous responsibilities as faith advisor but added to it the task of developing the chaplaincy. I was now responsible to Nigel Garfitt, the director of Games services and villages. At the same time, I continued my original roles as Church of England Olympic coordinator and liaison with More than Gold on behalf of the Church of England. In due course John Boyers, chaplain to Manchester United and founder (and formerly national director) of SCORE was appointed manager of the main Olympic Village multi-faith chaplaincy centre. I had believed that a priestly ministry could be possible in this uniquely secular and officially religion-free setting and I was now in a position to set up the first Games-wide chaplaincy service in Olympic history.

My LOCOG job description listed ten tasks: ten things necessary to deliver 'the best chaplaincy service ever'. It emphasized the primacy of involving all the faith communities in the life of the Games and especially in the creation of multi-faith chaplaincy teams and it built in the detailed work that would be required to achieve this. Through me the Church of England would continue to develop its relationship with the Games, as I travelled the country encouraging dioceses to engage with the Olympics.

Lord Coe, chairman of LOCOG, was very supportive of my role and on 20 May 2012, nearly a year after my appointment as head of multi-faith chaplaincy services and just two months before the opening ceremony, he wrote to me recalling that seven years before, in his presentation to the IOC about why London should host the Olympic and Paralympic Games in 2012, he had spoken about how the diversity and vibrancy of our communities would positively influence the experience of the Games for athletes, spectators and visitors alike. He continued by saying that he knew that stimulating communities to join in would be one of our toughest challenges, and, in order for this to happen, we needed to find respected leaders within our communities. In a generous endorsement of what we had achieved up to this point, he then went on:

> Due to your invaluable stewardship of both the Faith Reference Group and Faith Community Outreach Group we have succeeded at engaging with the main UK faith organisations and a number of localised faith groups to inspire them to join with us on this journey.

His closing paragraph further demonstrated the high regard in which he held my work and the importance of the role that I was now undertaking:

> We were delighted when you joined us in the role of Multi-Faith Coordinator, building into Head of Chaplaincy, thus securing our engagement with faith communities. Thank you so much for the time, expertise and personal effort you have given to this. I am so grateful for everything you have contributed.

Whilst LOCOG had set specific limits on what I could achieve operationally, it had depended on me to define, create and prepare what was needed to deliver a successful chaplaincy service. It was now time to put all of that preparation into practice.

Recruitment, training and requirements

The recruitment of 162 chaplains had been in progress for some time. All came through the volunteer (Games Makers) recruitment programme and were then identified as potential recruits. All of those appointed were ordained and/or affirmed by the governing body of their faith group or denomination as being utterly suited to this task. It was important to appoint chaplains of a variety of faiths to serve all of the official venues: the three Olympic Villages, all of the competition venues as well as logistics and administration centres. Team leaders were appointed for each venue.

The chaplains brought with them a wide range of experience. International chaplains brought many contacts with athletes from their home countries. They would receive induction into the culture and expectations surrounding London 2012. Sports chaplains from the UK brought experience of chaplaincy with athletes in a variety of sports. Local chaplains, either brought previous experiences of chaplaincy or were regarded as having the approach and skills needed. It was essential that each chaplain had both a pastoral heart (simply enjoying 'being' with people to listen and care), and the ability to cope with any eventuality (including an unexpected death), something which is not uncommon at such events. A fundamental requirement for recruits was that they understood that proselytizing, or even overt evangelizing, was not permitted in the Olympic movement and that any such activity could affect the chaplain's accreditation.

We decided to recruit a significant number of international chaplains for the Olympics and the Paralympics. In the end 19 international Olympic chaplains were accredited: five from Europe, four from USA, three from Latin America, two from Asia, and two from Oceania covering all continents of the world and with native speakers in Chinese, French, German, Hindi, Norwegian, Portuguese, Spanish, Swahili in addition to several local or tribal languages. There were seven accredited international chaplains at the Paralympics: three from the USA and one each from Argentina, Australia, Kenya and Switzerland. International chaplains were recruited with the help of J. Stuart Weir and Ashley Null of the Major Events Chaplaincy Committee (MECC) which identified chaplains who had served at previous Olympics or equivalent sports events. The MECC, the network which coordinates the application and recommendation process for Protestant chaplains to major sports events on behalf of the international sports ministry movement, had recommended the 19 chaplains from over 50 applicants on the grounds of experience and contacts with current Olympians in addition to geographical distribution and language skills. The MECC also coordinated accommodation, supplied UK mobile telephones, and provided other practical help for the overseas chaplains.

All chaplains were required to attend a day's training run by John Boyers and me, with the aim of providing all that they would need to perform their role effectively and sensitively. The training, which took place a few days before the Olympics (and Paralympics) started, emphasized the importance of each chaplain working cooperatively and respectfully with other chaplains as a member of a multi-faith (not inter-faith) team whilst also representing and serving their own faith community. They were made aware from the outset that they would be placed on a rota and were expected to fulfil its requirements. It was also made clear that chaplains would be required to act in a responsible manner in their relations with all those with whom they came into contact; they were warned not to use their position for their own benefit, acting always under the direction of the head of multi-faith chaplaincy services and their team leader and within LOCOG guidelines. My position as a member of the Games Services and Villages Team, ultimately responsible to the Head of All Villages Services, firmly located chaplaincy within the LOCOG management structure, giving it both credibility and responsibility. Professionalism, sensitivity, integrity, confidentiality, wisdom in ministry and otherwise appropriate behaviour were expected at all times. The work would be variously spiritual, pastoral and social, always seeking to offer a positive welcome to everyone. Chaplains were challenged to achieve high standards, be welcomed and valued by all and beneficial to everyone's Games experience: 'the best chaplaincy service ever'. That these aims and standards were achieved was essential to chaplaincy being accepted at this and all future Olympic and Paralympic Games and indeed at all major sporting events.

Olympic chaplaincy in practice

The model of chaplaincy followed at London 2012 was based on the style of 'being present' which I had developed in the years that I had worked with LOCOG: caring and being alongside people rather than seeking to convert them. Indeed, such a 'ministry of presence' is one which is common to both sports-related and wider chaplaincy roles (see Boyers, 2000; Chawner, 2009; Heskins and Baker, 2006; Holm, 2009; Paget and McCormack, 2006; Threlfall-Holmes and Newitt, 2011; Wood, 2011). Hence, those who had served as chaplains in such environments were familiar with the model, including many chaplains of other faiths who joined the team, as they had already served in multi-faith chaplaincy teams in, for example, hospitals or prisons. For others, this kind of role did not come so naturally; some felt more at home in the chaplaincy centre rather than wandering around making contact with people as opportunities arose. We also established a roaming team, which covered all of the London venues where staff and volunteers worked outside of the Olympic Park itself. At any major sporting event decisions have to be made about how much freedom chaplains will be allowed in order to operate effectively within the Games environment. After discussion with village management, I was able to establish that a roving brief was essential if chaplains were to be available whenever and wherever they might be needed, whilst at the same time recognizing that athletes' and officials' living space could be entered only by invitation of the athletes or other team members. The fact that many reports written by village managers after the Games mentioned the value of having chaplains around demonstrates the success of this policy.

Compared perhaps with some other major sporting events, the Olympic movement places significant emphasis on security and the protection of people's personal space, emphasizing that the village is the athletes' home whilst at the Games. I was made aware of some reports that, at previous Games, chaplains had intruded into athletes' quarters without permission and LOCOG was very concerned that there should be no such incidents in 2012. Initially some LOCOG managers wanted to restrict chaplains to the religious centre, where they would wait for athletes to come to them, but I was able to negotiate their right to move freely around the village but not into 'athletes-only' areas except by athlete invitation, a restriction that some chaplains found frustrating. After the Games it emerged that there had been some confusion about access to athlete-only areas with a number of chaplains thinking they were not allowed into athletes' dining or residential areas at all. International chaplains, who had experienced having easy access to athletes at events elsewhere in the world found this particularly difficult, but these frustrations were worked through as the Games progressed and many found that, once they had made contact with an athlete, they were able to develop a relationship. Being known as an athlete before becoming a chaplain was a definite advantage. One chaplain, who had been an elite wrestler and who had attended many international wrestling events over the years, was given permission by the venue manager, to be with the athletes and was seen by the organizers as adding value because of his expertise and contacts.

Chaplaincy and the Multi-Faith Centre

LOCOG went out of their way to provide the best accommodation there had ever been at the Games for the multi-faith centre, so that it was possible to provide an ideal place for official and formal religious services to take place for the five mainstream religions: Buddhism, Christianity, Hinduism, Islam, Judaism and for other faiths as needed. The multi-faith centre, which was located on the second floor of a building next to the fitness centre and close to the athletes dining room, was also a quiet place for private prayer, contemplation and meditation. It provided a base in and from which chaplains could work and where they could be contacted easily and immediately. It proved to be an area of both religion and friendship, where any who came could find experienced religious leaders, pastors and counsellors. During the Paralympics ground floor rooms were also made available for both worship and counselling. It was important in the short time available to make the chaplaincy services and centre known as widely as possible: a presentation was made to each national team as they arrived and the centre was in a well-signposted, central location in the village. Beyond the Olympic Park, the roaming team encouraged managers to highlight chaplains' availability with notices at check-in or in the canteen, perhaps a note in the daily briefing. We left a book in each quiet space for visitors to write comments and left our mobile telephone numbers so that we could be contacted. Chaplains at the other sites also found ways of making their facility and contact information known.

There were some reports of athletes and officials finding it difficult to locate the multi-faith centre. This is perhaps inevitable in such a large complex where people were only staying for a short time. But, as one chaplain reported, when they found it they experienced 'a place of quiet, calm, counsel, spiritual support and inspiration for athletes, their staff, work force and volunteers'. It proved to be a place of special importance to Muslims who needed a readily accessible venue for prayer, it being Ramadan. Chaplains spoke of the importance of having facilities for any who came asking for Mass or prayers to be said with them. Through the generosity of the Bible Society and the Muslim Council of Great Britain, the chaplaincy was able to supply copies of the Sports Bible, New Testament or Koran respectively to the significant numbers of athletes who asked for them. Irish boxer, Katie Taylor, wrote of her experience of the multi-faith centre:

> I'm a creature of habit and I usually feel out of sorts if I don't get to go to church for a few weeks, so I was delighted when a letter was dropped into my room from one of the pastors in the Olympic Village to say there were a few services going on during the Games. He had heard that I was a Christian. There was an area in the village called the Faith Centre. They had a room for Buddhists if they wanted to meet, another room for Hindus and one for Christians, different rooms for different religions. The first time I went was midweek. There were only a handful of people there. One of the Jamaican sprinters was there, Sam Henry-Robinson was her name. She went on to win a silver medal with the 4×100 relay team. I really enjoyed the service so I went back on the Sunday morning, and this time the place was jammed with athletes. The service was run by the athletes themselves, many of them got up and shared a story of something amazing God had done for them. Brigetta Barrett from the USA was there, she won a silver medal in the high jump. Another girl from New Zealand stood up and told how she was the first from her country to ever qualify in her swimming event, and she thanked God for that. The 400m runner LaShawn Merritt, who had won gold at the Beijing Olympics, was there too. The common denominator was God working for them. There was something powerful about that. I found it to be emotional just listening to people speaking about how God helped them. Apart from winning the gold medal, this was probably my stand-out experience of the Games.
>
> (Taylor, 2012: 167)

It was precisely to meet the spiritual needs of athletes like Katie Taylor that we had worked so hard over several years.

Conclusion

The award of the 2012 Olympic and Paralympic Games to London in 2005 gave the country seven years to prepare for the events themselves. Because of the vision of the bishop of Barking, who established a post of Church of England Olympics coordinator later that year, the church and faith community had also almost seven years to develop its own strategy around how it would respond to and maximize this opportunity. Having such a substantial lead-time made it possible to achieve chaplaincy provision more extensive in scope and remit than at any previous Games. Being appointed to that post at such an early stage enabled me to travel with the London Organising Committee of the Olympic Games and to gain the confidence of key people that led to my appointment first as LOCOG's multi-faith advisor and then as head of multi-faith chaplaincy services. As an Anglican priest, seconded to the organizing committee, I was able to model to LOCOG staff the type of chaplaincy that I wanted to introduce to the Games. The formation of the Faith Reference Group was another important step in ensuring that organizing committee members grasped the importance of the role that the faith community could play in the delivery of the Games.

In Beijing 2008 the Olympic religious centre had been staffed by a small number of Chinese chaplains. In London we were determined to have a chaplaincy which reflected the diversity appropriate to a worldwide event and which, for the first time, would encompass not just athletes and team members in the Olympic Village but also media and Games workforce. Our team of 162 chaplains covered all continents, the world's major religions and languages serving not only in the main Olympic Village and Olympic Park but at the other villages and competition venues. A similar chaplaincy programme, albeit on a smaller scale, operated for the Paralympics. In addition to the training provided by LOCOG for all volunteers (Games Makers) we held our own chaplaincy specific training to ensure that members of the chaplaincy team understood the professionalism, sensitivity, integrity and wisdom that the role would require.

In my view, two key things contributed to what we were able to achieve at London 2012; one was my early appointment almost five years before the games took place, the second was gaining the respect of LOCOG through a willingness to serve, often by taking on jobs that no one else wanted to. It was a privilege to be part of the planning, development and implementation of ground-breaking chaplaincy. It is my hope that future Olympic organizing committees might learn from our experience and build on it.

Note

1 I am grateful to J. Stuart Weir (Verite Sport) for his assistance in editing my London 2012 report to produce this chapter and for the tremendous work and support offered by the Revd David Read who was my theological consultant during my years serving the Games and was key to producing the final Games report.

References

Billings, A. (2010). *Making God Possible: The Task of Ordained Ministry Present and Future*, London: SPCK.

Boyers, J. (2000). *Beyond the Final Whistle*, London: Hodder & Stoughton.

Cha, A.E. (2008). 'Some Olympians Dissatisfied with Religious Center', *Washington Post*, 14 Aug. Available at <http://www.washingtonpost.com/wp-dyn/content/article/2008/08/13/AR2008081303772.html>.

Chawner, D. (2009). 'A Reflection on the Practice of Sports Chaplaincy', *Urban Theology*, 3/1: 75–80. Available at <http://www.urbantheology.org/journals/journal-3-1/a-reflection-on-the-practice-of-sports-chaplaincy>.

Ellis, R. (2012). 'The Meanings of Sport', *Practical Theology*, 5/2: 169–88.

Heskins, J. and M. Baker (eds) (2006). *Footballing Lives: As Seen by Chaplains in the Beautiful Game*, Norwich: Canterbury Press.

Holm, N. (2009), 'Toward a Theology of the Ministry of Presence in Chaplaincy', *Journal of Christian Education*, 52/1: 7–22. Available at <http://www.academia.edu/1256854/Toward_a_Theology_of_the_Ministry_of_Presence_in_Chaplaincy>.

Paget, N.K., and J.R. McCormack (2006). *The Work of the Chaplain*, Valley Forge, PA: Judson Press.

Slater, V. (2012). 'From Practice to Policy: Theological Reflection on being a Chaplain', practitioners' workshop for people involved in chaplaincy, Ripon College, Cuddesdon, 21 April.

Taylor, K. (2012). *My Olympic Dream*, London: Simon & Schuster.

Threlfall-Holmes, M., and M. Newitt (eds) (2011). *Being a Chaplain*, London: SPCK.

Tyndall, D. (2004). 'Evangelicalism, Sport and the Australian Olympics', PhD thesis. Macquarie University.

Wood, S. (2011). *Keeping Faith in the Team: The Chaplain's Story*, London: Longman, Dartman & Todd.

Part II

Conceptualizing sports chaplaincy

6   Doing sports chaplaincy in a fatherless age

Nick J. Watson

Sport chaplains . . . should simply maintain a strong, steady, and resolute presence.

Maranise, 2014: 5

Introduction

Sport chaplaincy in the Western world is practised in a socio-cultural context that is often characterized by widespread family breakdown and dysfunction. Social scientists and Christian commentators have described the era following the Second World War as a 'fatherless generation', in which moral and social ills have exponentially increased due to the absence of good father-figures (Blank-enhorn, 1995; Sowers, 2010). Of course, fatherlessness is not the only determinant that leads to social and moral problems. Empirical research has shown that unemployment, poverty, lack of education, drug and alcohol abuse amongst many other variables, all play their part (Centre for Social Justice, 2011; The White House, 2012). Nonetheless, the human and financial impact of father-lessness on societies in the West (and globally) is aptly demonstrated by the fact that both UK and US governments have instigated aggressive and costly strategies to combat the deleterious effects of this problem (sometimes through sport). The pervasive message of Blankenhorn's (1995) seminal text, *Fatherless America* has eventually caught the attention of policy-makers in Washington. As part of a Father's Day address to an African American community in Chicago, US President, Barack Obama – himself familiar with paternal absence as a boy – reflected on the terrible price of fatherlessness in American society:

> If we are honest with ourselves, we'll admit that what too many fathers are is missing – missing from too many lives and too many homes. They have abandoned their responsibilities, acting like boys instead of men. And the foundations of our families are weaker because of it . . . . We know the statistics – that children who grow up without a father are five times more likely to live in poverty and commit crime; nine times more likely to drop

out of school and twenty times more likely to end up in prison. They are more likely to have behavioural problems, or run away from home, or become teenage parents themselves. And the foundations of our community are weaker because of it.

(Obama, 2004, cited in Stibbe, 2010: 19)

Millions of those people participating in sport (from grass roots to professional level), have experienced fatherlessness in some way; that is, they have a 'deficit of love and affirmation' due to a 'physically' or 'emotionally' absent father. Therefore, whether they are conscious of the fact or not (such emotional and spiritual wounds are often buried in the unconscious), arguably they would benefit from the 'soul care' or 'fathering' of a significant other. Chaplains who work in sport offer this service and herein lies the rationale for providing an analysis of the wider socio-cultural and spiritual context in which sports chaplaincy occurs.

Since its birth in the 1970s, and particularly over the last decade, there has been a significant increase in the development of national organizations, media attention (Rudd, 2013), practitioner books (Heskins and Baker, 2006; Lipe, 2006) and academic practitioners calling for the professionalization and accreditation of sports chaplaincy (Dzikus, Waller and Hardin, 2010; Null, 2008; Watson and Parker, 2014). I contend that these developments are, at least in part, a response to the increased need for soul care in sporting locales. This is especially pertinent for professional sportspersons due to the many pressures, expectations and demands of twenty-first-century elite sport. An extensive body of interdisciplinary research has shown that suicide/suicidal ideation, varying levels of depression and maladaptive anxiety and the subsequent relational and professional difficulties that follow, are frequently reported by professional athletes (Watson, 2011). Following the institutional professionalization and commodification of sport in the 1960s, more and more athletes it seems are in need of, and are drawing on, the services of sports chaplains, sport psychologists and 'emotionally intelligent' coaches and managers (Gamble, Hill and Parker, 2013).

This exploratory chapter examines the socio-cultural and spiritual context in which sports chaplaincy (in professional sport) is practised, in light of the pandemic of fatherlessness in modern western culture. The chapter is structured around four thematic sections which were identified in a recent review of literature on sports and Christianity: (1) a biblical overview of fatherlessness and fatherhood; (2) fatherlessness in the modern era; (3) social, political and Christian initiatives to combat fatherlessness (in and through sport); and (4) the role of sports chaplains in the soul care of the fatherless (Watson and Parker, 2014). In conclusion, I reflect upon the 'central calling' of sports chaplains with regard to how they might deal with fatherlessness, as and when it arises, as an underlying issue in the course of their everyday work. My first task is to provide a biblical foundation to examine fatherlessness in the modern era and its relationship with sports chaplaincy.

Fatherhood and the fatherless in the Bible: a brief reflection

The fatherhood of God is a central doctrine and narrative throughout the biblical canon. While the explicit use of the term 'Father' is limited in the Old Testament, in the New Testament it appears 65 times in the Synoptic Gospels and over 100 times in the Gospel of John (Stein, 1996). Through the life, death and resurrection of Jesus, a monumental shift occurs in creator–creature relations, as all humans are now afforded the opportunity to come into an intimate relationship with a Father God. Yet it is worth examining the notion of God as Father (and the fatherless and orphan) in the Old Testament, not least because the God to whom Jesus prayed and related to (as recorded in John's Gospel), was principally a God shaped by Jewish scriptures and traditions.

Undoubtedly, Jesus would have recited the Shema (Deut. 6:4) on a daily basis within the Jewish community, a prayer in which God was known as Yahweh (although Jesus would have said 'Adonai', 'My Lord'), and it is worth quoting Wright (2007: 17) at length, to elaborate this point:

> When Jesus thought of God, spoke of God, reflected on the words and will of God, set out to obey God – it was this God, Yahweh God, that was in his mind. 'God' for Jesus was the named, biographied, character-rich, self-revealed God Yahweh, the Holy One of Israel .... But of course, Jesus also knew this God of his scriptures in the depth of his self-consciousness as Abba, as his own intimate personal father. Luke tells us that his awareness was developing even in his childhood, and it was sealed in baptism, when he heard the voice of his Father, accompanied by the Holy Spirit, confirming his identity as God's beloved son. So in the consciousness of Jesus the scriptural identity of God as Yahweh and his personal intimacy with God as his Father must be blended together.

That Jesus called God his Father was deeply offensive to the Jewish leaders of the day, something that was embedded in Judaic history, theology and tradition. Only 15 times in the whole of the Old Testament is God specifically called by the name Father – for example, as the father of the nation of Israel (Deut. 32:6; Isa. 63:16; Jer. 3:4, 19) and the father of specific individual Bible characters (2 Sam. 7:14; 1 Chron. 17:13; Ps. 68:5). On other occasions – for example when the nation of Israel is described as God's son (Exod. 4:22–3; Hos. 11:1–4) and the theme of adoption is evident in narratives pertaining to the fatherless, orphans and widows (Ps. 27:9–10; 68:4–6) – father imagery is clearly deployed. In short, the fatherless, the orphans and widows, experience the father's heart in compassion, care, protection, authority, discipline, love, provision, strength and gentleness in the Old Testament (Deut. 10:18, 14:28–30; Ps. 68:5–6; Prov. 23:10–11; Isa. 1:17; Zech. 8:10). Indeed, there is a strong 'covenantal' dimension to the father–son metaphor in the Old Testament, which is something that reflects the relational and familial nature of the way God chose to relate to his people.

The scarcity of explicit or indirect references to God the Father in the Old Testament, Stein (1996) suggests, is predominantly due to its frequent usage in ancient Near-Eastern culture, where it was used in Canaanite fertility religions that involved inappropriate sexual content. Given that there is no evidence in pre-Christian Jewish scholarship of the Jewish community referring to God as 'Abba' (Wright, 2007) – an Aramaic term that conveys intimacy and which was used by children addressing their earthly fathers ('Daddy') – Jesus' teaching and testimony on the fatherhood of God, was indeed, radical and revolutionary.

An exegetical or systematic analysis of the Father–Son relationship (within a Trinitarian framework) is well beyond the scope of this chapter. That said, from John 1:18 onwards, where the importance of the Father is introduced into the storyline, the theology of John's Gospel cannot solely 'be swallowed up in Christology' (Stibbe, 2006: 1), as has been the case historically in Johannine studies. Perhaps one of the most illustrative passages of John's Gospel with regard to the centrality of the fatherhood of God, is in chapter 20 where, after the resurrection event, Jesus says to Mary Magdalene: 'Do not hold on to me, for I have not yet returned to the Father. Go instead to my brothers and tell them, I am returning to my Father and your Father, to my God and your God' (John 20:17). Commenting on this passage, Stibbe (2006) makes clear that Jesus' use of the personal pronoun when speaking with Mary, denoting that God was now her Father (following the redemptive work of the crucifixion and resurrection), points to the coming of the Holy Spirit and the adoption of humans from a position of orphan-hood (John 14:18) into intimate relationship with Abba. This concept is most clearly expressed in Paul's theological narrative that describes our 'adoption as sons' (Rom. 8:1–17), which is something that confers a remarkable dignity and status on believers in Christ.

These attributes of the Father's heart and character – compassion, love, gentleness, care, protection and guidance – are among those required of the chaplain working in modern-day sports settings. Many theologians, spiritual writers and social scientists have argued that the modern world (in particular the West) is suffering from a pandemic of fatherlessness. In light of the prophetic words of Malachi, 'I will send you the prophet Elijah before the great and dreadful day of the Lord comes. He will turn the hearts of the fathers to their children, and the hearts of the children to their fathers; or else I will come and strike the land with a curse' (Mal. 4:5–6), some have even tentatively suggested that this 'fatherless generation' may have eschatological significance (Kendall, 2004; Sowers, 2010; Stibbe, 2010). This is rooted in the premise that the prophet's oracles have double prophetic meaning, both foretelling the ministry of John the Baptist in first-century Palestine (Luke 1:17) and the 'day of the Lord' that will be heralded by modern-day prophet(s) that will result in the consummation of God's Kingdom. While it is important to carefully weigh such ideas (Matt. 24:36–44; see also Canfield, 2014) and to be aware that fatherlessness has characterized other imperial societies through history (Hübner and Ratzan, 2011), it is worthy of note, as I now turn to analyse fatherlessness in the modern era.

To what extent, we may ask, are many Western nations living under the self-imposed 'curse' of fatherlessness that the prophet Malachi spoke of?

Fatherlessness in the modern era

Social scientist, David Blankenhorn (1995: 1), communicates the frightening scale and impact of fatherlessness in the US (which has the third highest divorce rate in the world):

> Fatherlessness is the most harmful demographic trend of this generation. It is the leading cause of declining child well-being in our society. It is also the engine driving our most urgent social problems, from crime to adolescent pregnancy to child sexual abuse to domestic violence against women.

Fatherlessness and its many deleterious effects are, of course, not confined to the US, with many academic researchers, social commentators and Christian leaders identifying it as a 'global pandemic' (Stibbe, 1999, 2010). The alarming rise in fatherlessness, in particular in modern industrialized societies, is also mirrored in the world Church with a significant drop in male church attendance across the denominations during the last two decades. Taylor (2014: 2) has recently argued that 'the crisis in religious practice in the western world is intimately related to the crisis in fatherhood, since it is from God, as St. Paul tells us, that all paternity on this earth is named (Ephesians 3:15)'. Taylor goes on to call for a more adequate theology of maleness and of fatherhood to help counter fatherlessness in the modern era. This is something that has more recently been addressed by theologians, psychologists and sport scholars (e.g. Aune, 2010; Vitz, 1999; Watson, 2013) and through the birth of numerous Christian ministries with a focus on the fatherhood of God. In turn, a flood of popular books have appeared on this topic, from both Protestant (Dalbey, 2003; Eldredge, 2001, 2009; Piper and Grudem, 2012) and Catholic commentators (Rohr, 2012).

The reasons for a family becoming fatherless or experiencing fatherlessness (even where a father is physically present) are numerous and complex. Examples include the death of a father, the physically absent father (from divorce or parental relationship breakdown), the achievement-driven father, the abusive father, and the abdicating or apathetic father. The emotional and spiritual wounds that result from fatherlessness are deep, enduring and affect males and females very differently, but are no less devastating (Sowers, 2010). Longitudinal research conducted over the last two decades illustrates the worrying statistics and the social impact of fatherlessness in the modern-world (ibid.; The White House, 2012). According to Stibbe (2010: 20), children who are fatherless in the US are:

8 times more likely to go to prison
5 times more likely to commit suicide
20 times more likely to have behavioural problems

20 times more likely to commit rape
32 times more likely to run away from home
10 times more likely to abuse chemical substances
9 times more likely to drop out of high school
33 times more likely to be seriously abused
73 times more likely to be fatally abused
One-tenth as likely to get As in school
Have a 44% higher mortality rate
Have a 72% lower standard of living

These US-based statistics in many ways reflect the situation across the globe, for example, in Britain and Western Europe, Australia, Africa and South America (e.g. Fatherhood Institute, 2013). A number of scholars have, however, raised concerns about the flawed methodological design of some of these studies and the validity of their statistical findings (especially when cited by particular political or religious groups that may wish to promote a specific agenda). For example, in a commissioned report that examined fatherhood and fatherlessness in Australia, Flood (2003) raises a host of questions with regard to research design, the apparent confusion between correlation and causation and the selective use of resulting evidence which, he suggests, often manifests itself in simplistic claims with regard to the relationship between fatherlessness and social problems. More broadly speaking, commentators from the media, academia and politics all consistently acknowledge that fatherlessness is a weighty social issue that leads to multiple social, financial, emotional and political problems (Cabrera and Tamis-LeMonda, 2012). This has led to an exponential increase in the number of studies on men and family issues, principally emanating from social science and social policy disciplines including those concerning the subculture of sports (see e.g. Messner and Sabo's [1990] *Sport, Men and the Gender Order*), which is itself grounded in the rise in the late 1980s and early 1990s of the academic field of men's studies (see also Kimmel, Hern and Connell, 2004). Nonetheless, it was not until recently that the first major study of fathering in the context of sport and leisure was published.

Picking up on this wave of critical enquiry into the relationship between maleness and sport, Kay (2009: 1), editor of *Fathering through Sport and Leisure*, states that 'sport and leisure researchers ... appear to be riding on a tide of interest in fathers and fatherhood. With so much mounting evidence that fathers place leisure at the heart of their parenting'. But the circumstances surrounding postmodern models of fatherhood are 'complex and contradictory' and thus 'it is increasingly unclear what the role of a father is, and perhaps even less clear, what it "should" be' (ibid. 7). While Kay's social-scientific text is a welcome and timely addition to the literature, its limitation from a Christian stance is its lack of a foundational theology of fatherhood: a relatively clear and objective model of what a father should be. As Stibbe (2010: 25), a New Testament scholar and church minister, states, when writing on the issue of fatherlessness, 'nothing is going to change [significantly] until we understand that this is a spiritual issue'.

I agree, and after identifying the scale and significance of the problem of father-lessness in Western industrialized society I now turn my attention to recent political and Christian initiatives which seek to combat fatherlessness.

Social, political and Christian initiatives to combat fatherlessness

In response to the scourge of fatherlessness in modern societies, over the last two decades a wide range of political, charitable and church-based initiatives have emerged with the aim of combating the problem of absent fathers, through research, political lobbying, intervention programmes and legislative amend-ment. In the UK, the Fatherhood Institute (1999), the Centre for Social Jus-tice (2004), the Marriage Foundation (2013) and those with a Judea-Christian foundation, the Relationships Foundation (1994) and XLP Mentoring (1996) are examples of these. There is also a rapidly developing Church-based move-ment emerging in the UK and US that seeks to combat fatherlessness through the intentional adopting and fostering of children (Bergeron, 2011; Kandiah and Kandiah, 2013). Collectively, these organizations address family break-down and dysfunction (and thus, fatherlessness) in a variety of ways, not least because of the £44 billion cost to the British taxpayer (Benson, 2014), which is reflected in the UK government's strategic launch of the Childhood and Fam-ily Task Force (2011).

In the US, there is a similar National Fatherhood Initiative (1994) and the Mentoring Project (2006), whose president, Dr John Sowers, has written an important book on the theology of fatherlessness based on his doctoral thesis (Sowers, 2010) and which includes a number of examples of mentoring in and through sport. Sowers, is also a 'Champion of Change' in President Obama's Responsible Fatherhood Working Group (The White House, 2012), which led to the launch of the President's Fatherhood Pledge. Within the microcosm of sport there are also, encouragingly, a number of practical initiatives with a Christian underpinning that have a specific vision to address paternal absence and to bring life, hope and God's love to children. Of course, the use of mentor-ing in sport through coaching and teaching (regardless of affiliation, or not, to a religious group), is a well-documented method by which to inculcate desir-able character attributes and to promote healthy civil engagement, in particular, with vulnerable and disadvantaged groups (Crabbe, 2009; Graveling, Collins and Parker, 2014; Meek, 2013; McCloskey and Bailes, 2005). But my focus here is on the response of the Christian community (individuals and organizations alike) to the problem of fatherlessness and how sport can act as vehicle for mentoring and fathering.

Perhaps the best-known and largest sports organization to actively seek to rejuvenate 'godly manhood' and to encourage fathering from a Christian world-view, which is based in the US but has global reach, is the Promise Keep-ers (1990). The former NFL player and college-football coach Bill McCartney founded this organization which (perhaps somewhat predictably on account of its conservative evangelical position on biblical notions of manhood) has attracted critiques from secular and feminist sociologists (e.g. Claussen, 2000) and Catholic commentators (Rohr, 2012). Another organization that is arguably much less evangelical in its approach, yet which was also founded by an ex-NFL player and Christian minister, Joe Ehrmann, is Coach for America (a division of Building Men and Women for Others Inc.). This ministry organization gained national recognition in the US following the publication of *Season of Life* (Marx, 2003; see also Ehrmann, Ehrmann and Jordan, 2011). While more 'pastoral' than overtly 'evangelical', the pedagogical philosophy of John Wooden, the renowned US basketball coach and devout Christian, was also imbued with a strong 'fathering element' (see Williams and Denney, 2011). Tony Dungy, a former Super-Bowl-winning coach, who has worked extensively with the Fellowship for Christian Athletes (1952–), a US-based sports ministry organization, and who is a national advocate for many US-based fatherhood initiatives, has written a number of books addressing fatherlessness and the importance of mentoring and relational skills through sports coaching (Dungy, 2010).

While there are significantly fewer Christian-based initiatives in the UK that have used sport to combat fatherlessness, encouragingly the sports ministry organization Ambassadors Football (1993–), recently organized a 'father's football project' in the inner-city London borough of Tower Hamlets with a view to encouraging fathers to engage more with their children. In South Africa, Cassie Carstens, chaplain to the South African Rugby World Cup winning team of 1995, has recently started a movement called the World Needs a Father (2011–) that uses sports amongst a host of other social and cultural drivers to educate and convey the love of God.

The practical sport and faith initiatives noted above all provide a sign of light and hope that the problem of fatherlessness can, in part, be met through the vehicle of sport (and fundamentally the Christian gospel expressed through fathering in this context). But what role can individual sports chaplains play in addressing such a widespread and endemic societal problem as fatherlessness?

The role of sports chaplains in the soul care of the fatherless

It may seem unrealistic to suggest that chaplains working in sport could have much of a redemptive and corrective impact on this fatherless generation. Based on the premise that Christians are called to be a 'faithful presence' in our culture (Hunter, 2010) and to 'love' those individuals that God brings across their paths, I argue that sports chaplains play a somewhat understated and yet increasingly vital role in addressing the wounds of the fatherless in sporting environments. Chaplaincy in sport is a ministry calling in which the incarnational testimony of a Christ-like life carries much weight: 'preach the gospel, and if necessary use words', as St Francis is reputed to have said. Along these lines, US-based sports chaplain, Roger Lipe, has recently provided a mandate for the critical reassessment of the role of the chaplain in sport which calls for the resurrection of the concept of 'shepherding or fathering' and, in turn, a Christo-centric starting-point for reflections on this topic:

> The present world of sport and much of sports ministry is characterized by three primary weaknesses. 1) The prevalence of compartmentalized lives; that is a lack of integrity. This is easily seen in situations like the fall of coaches, players, and even prominent Christian athletes. 2) The horrible lie of performance based identity. A player's sense of personal worth may rise or fall based upon his most recent performance on the field of competition. A coach's sense of God's pleasure with her may ride on her team's win/loss record. Even worse, a sport chaplain's sense of his or her being in God's will can be shaped by the relative success or failure of the teams being served. Each and all of these scenarios are emblematic of the terrible lie that assaults the hearts of sports people. 3) The collapse of the American family structure. Most of the young men and women whom we serve are now from single parent families. They start their lives relationally and spiritually handcuffed. Worse still, if they are so blessed as to be athletically gifted, they may find that their coaches, teammates, agents, peers, lovers, even their parents and sport chaplains use the player for their own personal gain.
>
> (Lipe, 2013)

If many of the sports people that chaplains relate to 'start their lives relationally and spiritually handcuffed' due to family breakdown and dysfunction, then clearly the fathering role is immediately brought to the fore in sports chaplaincy practice. While I am sure that chaplains from across the globe have often 'stood in the gap' and taken on the role of father (or mother) in their ministry in sport, this has never been made explicit. However, Waller and Cottom's appeal (this volume) for the revival of the shepherding dimension in pastoral theology, sports chaplaincy training and, thus, the hearts and minds of individual practitioners is implicitly tied to the notion of fathering and the central message of this chapter.

In the high-pressure world of modern-day professional sport in which a significant moral vacuum exists (McNamee, 2010), men and women in sports need the love of God the Father mediated to them through those who love and know him. Writing during the 1970s, the era in which the sports chaplaincy movement began to take shape, Henri Nouwen, in his classic pastoral reflection, *The Wounded Healer* (1979), spoke of the need for the alienated, the fatherless, those who have failed, to receive the Father's presence through others, to be listened to, to be gently guided and to be loved. And herein lies the mystery and beauty of servant-hearted chaplaincy to those in sport. A paradoxical role in which, at times, little seems to be achieved, yet where the Kingdom of God is manifest and the heart of the Father is revealed to players (and support staff) who are in a state of crisis or transition, experiencing failure, grief or stress – or who simply need a non-judgemental friend or mentor whom they can trust.

Conclusion

Sports chaplains need to be affirmed and encouraged of the importance and timeliness of their vocation in an age of fatherlessness and in a highly competitive sports world in which they are often marginalized, overlooked, undervalued and undercompensated. Their presence is the Father's presence; they are God's whisper in a setting often characterized by deep insecurity and the ever-present threat of rejection.

While some are called to be evangelists, prophets or teachers in the local church or on a national stage, sports chaplains are essentially called to love the one – the athlete, coach, manager, administrator, official, board member. The call for more chaplains who have a pastoral heart has recently been documented by Galli (2011), who bemoans church leadership models which overemphasize the need for 'prophetic and charismatic' leaders (of course, leaders with these characteristics are also needed). He argues that such emphasis 'inadvertently denigrates every clergyperson who is a . . . chaplain – in hospitals, in the military [and sport] . . . as if these ministers are second-class clergy' (Galli, 2011: 1). On the contrary, I agree with the great spiritual writer, Oswald Chambers, who suggested that loving the one is the way that the Father will 'sweep the earth with His saints' (Chambers, 1935). Little Christs revealing the heart of the Father to the broken, lost and hurting in all of our societal institutions (the market place) including the competitive and transient world of professional sport. The recent growth in sports chaplaincy training and accreditation, as documented in this book, is a vital encouragement for the profession. Nevertheless, as Jesus knew Yahweh intimately as his Abba, I would argue that the most important thing for sports chaplains in the busy modern era is to take time to fellowship with the Father, for, 'you can't give, what you yourself have not received'.

References

Aune, K. (2010). 'Fatherhood in British Evangelical Christianity: Negotiating Mainstream Culture', *Men and Masculinities*, 13/2: 168–89.

Benson, H. (2014). *£46bn Bill won't get a Mention in the Budget: Four Zero-Cost Measures to Reduce It*, Marriage Foundation (UK). Available at <http://www.marriagefoundation. uk/Shared/Uploads/Products/77955_MF%20pre-budget%20special.pdf>.

Bergeron, L.E. (2011). *Journey to the Fatherless: Preparing for the Journey of Adoption, Orphan Care, Foster Care and Humanitarian Relief for Vulnerable Children*. Bloomington, IN: Westbow.

Blankenhorn, D. (1995). *Fatherless America: Confronting our Most Urgent Social Problem*, New York: Harper Perennial.

Cabrera, N.J. and C.S. Tamis-LeMonda (eds) (2012). *Handbook of Father Involvement: Multidisciplinary Perspectives*, 2nd edn, London: Routledge.

Canfield, K. (2014). 'The Modern Fatherhood Movement and Ministry to Fathers in the Faith Community', *Family Ministry Today* (18 Oct.). Available at <http://www.sbts.edu/family/2011/10/18/the-modern-fatherhood-movement-and-ministry-to-fathers-in-the-faith-community/>.

Centre for Social Justice (2011). *Strengthening the Family and Tackling Family Breakdown: Fatherlessness, Dysfunction and Parental Separation/Divorce*, policy paper. Available at <http://www.centreforsocialjustice.org.uk/UserStorage/pdf/Pdf%20reports/StrengtheningtheFamily.pdf>.

Chambers, O. (1935). *My Utmost for His Highest*, Uhrichsville, OH: Barbour Books.

Claussen, D.S. (2000). *The Promise Keepers: Essays on Masculinity and Christianity*, Jefferson, NC: McFarland.

Crabbe, T. (2009). 'Getting to Know You: Using Sport to Engage and Build Relationships with Socially Marginalized Young People', in R. Levermore and A. Beacom (eds), *Sport and International Development*, London: Palgrave, 176–97.

Dalbey, G. (2003). *Healing the Masculine Soul: How God Restores Men to Real Manhood*, Nashville, TN: Thomas Nelson.

Dungy, T. (2010). *The Mentor Leader: Secrets to Building People and Teams that Win Consistently*, Carol Stream, IL: Tyndale House.

Dzikus, L., S. Waller and R. Hardin (2010). 'Collegiate Sport Chaplaincy: Exploration of an Emerging Profession', *Journal of Contemporary Athletics*, 5/1: 21–42.

Ehrmann, J., P. Ehrmann and G. Jordan (2011). *Inside Out Coaching: How Sports can Transform Lives*, New York: Simon & Schuster.

Eldredge, J. (2001). *Wild at Heart: Discovering the Secret of a Man's Soul*, Nashville, TN: Thomas Nelson.

—— (2009). *Fathered by God: Learning what your Dad could Never Teach You*, Nashville, TN: Thomas Nelson.

Fatherhood Institute (2013). *Pushing Fatherhood up the Agenda: Annual Report 2012–2013*. Available at <http://www.fatherhoodinstitute.org/wp-content/uploads/2013/11/FI-Annual-Report-12-13-Final-Web.pdf>.

Flood, M. (2003). *Fatherhood and Fatherlessness*, Australian Institute Discussion Paper no. 59. Retrieved from <http://www.bouverie.org.au/webfm_send/205>.

Galli. M. (2011). 'Why We Need More "Chaplains" and Fewer Leaders: What's a Pastor For?', *Christianity Today*, 1 Dec. Available at <http://www.christianitytoday.com/ct/2011/decemberweb-only/morechaplains.html>.

Gamble, R., D. Hill and A. Parker (2013). '"Revs and Psychos": Impact and Interaction amongst Sport Chaplains and Sport Psychologists in English Premiership Football', *Journal of Applied Sport Psychology*, 25: 249–64.

Graveling, R., Collins, M. and Parker, A. (2014). 'Faith, Sport and Disengaged Youth', *Journal of Religion and Society*, 16: 1–17.

Heskins, J., and M. Baker (eds) (2006). *Footballing Lives: As Seen by Chaplains in the Beautiful Game*, Norwich: Canterbury Press.

Hübner, S.R. and D.M. Ratzan (eds) (2011). *Growing up Fatherless in Antiquity*, Cambridge: Cambridge University Press.

Hunter, J.D. (2010). *To Change the World: Tragedy, and Possibility of Christianity in the Late Modern World*, Oxford: Oxford University Press.

Kandiah, K., and M. Kandiah (2013). *Home 'for' Good: Making a Difference for Vulnerable Children*, London: Hodder & Stoughton.

Kay, T. (ed.) (2009). *Fathering through Sport and Leisure*, London: Routledge.

Kendall, R.T. (2004). *Between the Times: Malachi God's Prophet of the Old Testament*, Tain, Ross-shire: Christian Focus Publications.

Kimmel, M., J. Hern and R.W. Connell (2004). *Handbook of Studies on Men and Masculinities*, London: Sage.

Lipe, R. (2006). *Transforming Lives in Sport: A Guide for Sport Chaplains and Sport Mentors*, Kearney, NE: Cross Training Publishing.

—— (2013). 'Re: The Significance of Sport Chaplains, Sport Mentors, and Character Coaches in the 21st Century', blog entry, 15 Nov. Available at <http://sportchaplains portmentor.blogspot.com/2013/11/the-significance-of-sport-chaplains.html>.

McCloskey, J., and J. Bailes (2005). 'Follow the Leader: Kids need Better Mentors, Heroes', in *When Winning Costs too Much: Steroids, Supplements, and Scandal in Today's Sport*, New York: Taylor Trade Publishing, 21–35.

McNamee, M. (ed.) (2010). *The Ethics of Sports: A Reader*, London: Routledge.

Maranise, A.M.J. (2014). 'The Sport Chaplain: Adding a "Game" Face to the Many Faces of Chaplaincy', *Inside Homeland Security*. Available at <http://www.abchs.com/ihs/WINTER 2013/ihs_articles_cover.php>.

Marx, J. (2003). *Season of Life: A Football Star, a Boy, a Journey to Manhood*, London: Simon & Schuster.

Meek, R. (2013). *Sport in Prison: Exploring the Role of Physical Activity in Penal Practices*, London: Routledge.

Messner, M.A. and D.F. Sabo (eds) (1990). *Sport, Men and the Gender Order*, Champaign, IL: Human Kinetics.

Nouwen, H.J.M. (1979). *The Wounded Healer: Ministry in Contemporary Society*, New York: Doubleday.

Null, J.A. (2008). 'Some Preliminary Thoughts on Philosophies of Ministry and their Literature', in D. Deardorff II and J. White (eds), *The Image of God in the Human Body: Essays on Christianity and Sports*, Lewiston, NY: Edward Mellen Press, 241–74.

Obama, B. (2004). *Dreams from my Father*, New York: Three Rivers Press.

Piper, J., and W. Grudem (eds) (2012). *Recovering Biblical Manhood and Womanhood: A Response to Evangelical Feminism*, 2nd edn, Wheaton, IL: Crossway.

Rohr, R. (2012). 'Men and Spirituality', in R. Woods and P. Tyler (eds), *The Bloomsbury Guide to Christian Spirituality*, London: Bloomsbury, 338–46.

Rudd, A. (2013). 'Clubs Turn to Chaplains for Guidance as Pressures on Players Grow', *The Times*, 29 Mar.: 80–1.

Sowers, J. (2010). *Fatherless Generation: Redeeming the Story*, Grand Rapids, MI: Zondervan.

Stein, R.H. (1996). 'Fatherhood of God', in W.A. Elwell (ed.), *Baker's Evangelical Dictionary of Biblical Theology*. Available at <http://www.biblestudytools.com/dictionaries/bakers-evangelical-dictionary/fatherhood-of-god.html>.

Stibbe, M. (1999). *From Orphans to Heirs: Celebrating our Spiritual Adoption*, Abingdon: Bible Reading Fellowship.

—— (2006). 'Telling the Father's Story: The Gospel of John as Narrative Theology', in J. Lierman (ed.), *Challenging Perspectives on the Gospel of John*, Tübingen: JCB Mohr, 170–93.

—— (2010). *I am Your Father: What Every Heart Needs to Know*, London: Monarch Books.

Taylor, A. (2014). 'Fatherless Churches', *First Things*. Available at <http://www.firstthings.com/web-exclusives/2014/01/fatherless-churches>.

Vitz, P.C. (1999). *Faith of the Fatherless: The Psychology of Atheism*, Dallas: Spence Publishing.

Watson, N.J. (2011). 'Identity in Sport: A Psychological and Theological Analysis', in J. Parry, M.N. Nesti and N.J. Watson (eds), *Theology, Ethics and Transcendence in Sports*, London: Routledge, 107–48.

—— (2013). 'Fatherlessness and Fathering in the World of Sport: Muscular Christianity and Beyond', paper presented at the Christian Society for Kinesiology and Leisure Studies Annual Conference, Baylor University, Waco, TX, June 12–14.

—— and A. Parker (2014). *Sport and the Christian Religion: A Systematic Review of Literature*, Newcastle upon Tyne: Cambridge Scholars Publishing.

The White House (2012). *Promoting Responsible Fatherhood: Every Father Taking Responsibility for his Child's Intellectual, Emotional and Financial Well-Being.* Available at <http://www.whitehouse.gov/sites/default/files/docs/fatherhood_report_6.13.12_final.pdf>.

Williams, P., and J. Denney (2011). *Coach Wooden: The 7 Principles that Shaped his Life and Will Change Yours,* Grand Rapids, MI: Revell.

Wright, C.J.H. (2007). *Knowing God the Father: Through the Old Testament,* Downers Grove, IL: IVP Academic.

7 Sports chaplaincy in a post-traditional religious context

Ed Uszynski

Introduction

Individuals seeking to minister in the role of sports team chaplain in modern-day North America must navigate the realities of contemporary spirituality and the differing forms religious life takes among its constituents. They find themselves wading through the maturation of transformative upheavals still radiating from the 1960s, producing a reality that reflects the tumultuous cultural turns that took place during that period of US history. The modern chaplain negotiates not only the constantly unfolding social history surrounding the concept of religion itself but also its implications for individual spiritual seekers in this moment. Where members of a society once understood their collective and largely shared religious sensibilities as a sacred canopy shrouding their entire lives, they now think of their own individualized spirituality, considering religion not as a worldview binding a people, but rather a consumerist slice of their individual existence, the notion of the sacred itself a matter of human construction. This chapter considers the move toward this individualized notion of spirituality and its implications for those seeking to minister within its parameters.

The challenge of the 'religious turn'

While ascribing a cultural shift to any one set of circumstances in history always oversimplifies, much of what constitutes modern North American spirituality should be understood against the backdrop of a particularly tumultuous decade in the last century. In the mid-1960s Harvey Cox (1966) popularized the now axiomatic contention that a constantly decreasing number of people – with emphasis on those living in the US – would derive their personal and cosmic values and explanations from traditional forms of religion. His words popularized and effectively brought to a tipping point an intellectual movement that had been gaining momentum since the Enlightenment swept through Europe two centuries before: God is dead (or is quickly dying) along with the hierarchies and powers that perpetuate his existence – with science killing them all.

While the historical narrative of almost any recorded epoch of human history is decorated with the sacred in both practical and institutional forms, the

belief that theological superstitions, symbolic liturgical rituals and sacred practices were products of an antiquated past that would be outgrown in the modern era took hold in unprecedented ways. Forces of modernization loosened
the dominance of clerical understandings of what constituted the sacred and
intensified – at least theoretically – the disenchantment of the world, while the
materialistic notion that humanity sat in the centre of the universe empowered
people with their own sense of subjective agency.

Of course, the assertion that the rise of scientific progress would cause religion itself to fade ever-more from the public square and diminish people's
appetite for religious fare was only half right. Indeed, while formal religious
institutions waned, the people of North America were as religious as ever (ironically, perhaps more so) but in decidedly different ways than before. Though
denominational life would statistically decrease, personal pursuit of spirituality
in all its various and available guises would actually accelerate in the closing
decades of the twentieth century. Religious life in the US – its customary
hierarchical approaches significantly disrupted and thrust into a major period
of redefinition – would increasingly move away from being characterized by
a communal experience founded on communicated doctrine in the pursuit
of a God, toward an individual experience based on identity-seeking and self-
realization in the pursuit of autonomy. One sociologist in particular prognos-
ticated the future effects of this shift and saw not only the demands it would
make on those seeking to cultivate a spiritual life, but also what implications
would arise for those seeking to minister to them.

Thomas Luckmann and the prediction of a self-centred spirituality

Though hardly alone in writing about the spread of secularization and the
concurrent waning of traditional, hierarchical modes of religious life in the last
decades of the twentieth century, sociologist Thomas Luckmann wrote with a
particularly prescient understanding of certain predictable consequences resulting from this shift as it was taking place.

In 1967 Luckmann wrote *The Invisible Religion*, a book incisively describing
both the immediate and anticipated realities in view of the religious life being
absorbed into the social landscape of his time. Luckmann predicted that people,
while being free from the weight of religious institutions and the demands of
dutiful religion, would now face the burden of constructing their own forms
of religiosity to fill the gap left by organized religion's retreat – they would
be free essentially to create their own personalized canon of religiosity. Individuals would need to determine what counted as sacred, what gave meaning and purpose to life, what list of values a life could be moulded around.
These processes of personal construction also entailed the shaping and formation of individual consciousness and personality, work influenced historically
by the church or other predominant public institutions but now left almost
entirely to the private sphere. According to Luckmann (1967: 97), the move

away from hierarchical institutions like the local church 'left wide areas in the life of the individual unstructured and the overarching biographical context of significance undetermined' – creating a shapeless mass of choices waiting to be sculpted by each individual subjective artist.

Luckmann considered this the chief defining and most revolutionary characteristic of modern society – that personal identity formation would essentially become a private phenomenon, that the unstructured and undetermined aspects of one's person would be arranged almost entirely through subjective choice. People are left – for better or worse – to figure out who they are, why they are and where they fit into the cosmic order essentially on their own. Beyond offering doctrinaire teaching on matters of life and death, traditional religious institutions had historically taken the primary role in prompting individuals to view themselves through comprehensive identity prisms – with a significant percentage of people deriving identity from the community of the Church and the teaching of the Bible – yet now their loss of effective control over the population, left such work to an ever increasing percentage of individuals themselves. For Luckmann, individual identity, meaning and significance became substantially privatized, and the primary 'spiritual' pursuit of modernity became subjective or biographical identity formation and the quest for self-realization. Thus, ministers of the gospel (whether among athletes or not) would from then on operate primarily in the waters of 'moralistic therapeutic deism', a pervasive philosophy featuring a hands-off god who leaves humans to discern for themselves not only how to be good according to their own shifting standards but how to be constantly, maximally happy and self-satisfied (Smith and Denton, 2005).

Cut loose from the strictures of overbearing outside influences on their individual consciousness, North Americans, Luckmann (1967: 117) asserted, would now pursue 'a radically subjective form of "religiosity" characterized by a weakly coherent and nonobligatory sacred cosmos and by a low degree of "transcendence" in comparison to traditional modes of religion'. With no single obligatory sacred system or hierarchy holding sway over public consciousness, in its place the autonomous consumer would select certain religious themes from the assortment available and build them into a somewhat precarious private system of ultimate significance, producing a constantly changing variety of ultimate meanings, which would leave in its wake a fragile and constantly changing sense of personal identity.

The quest for identity and self-understanding in our current cultural moment

Almost fifty years later, we live and experience the maturation of Luckmann's insights. In describing the cultural moment just after the turn of the twenty-first century, sociologist Sean McCloud (2007: 300) contends that it is a period of extreme modernity, characterized by 'fewer set identities, fixed roles, and uncontested grand explanatory schemes'. The product of late-modern technical

newness and fullness of being with, where life and world wondrously conjoin' and argues that the spiritual life is essentially the awakening and manifestation of the soul. Thus, both sport participation and sport fandom 'enable us to realize that we can recognize, create and participate in the "unguarded moment" (ibid.) where we gain a new reading of existence, that moment when 'the sense of rapturous enjoyment, at-one-ment, and the epiphany of "spiritual aesthetics" occurs'. At their best, sports offer both participants and spectators 'experiences of the ineffable outside the constraints and parameters of religious institutions' (ibid. 96).

Yet, by Grimshaw's own reckoning, defining these undeniable experiences as 'transcendent' is to rely on a postmodern understanding of the word itself and implicitly assumes that 'spiritual' must be defined within a materialistic understanding of the universe. That is, if we deny the spiritual world or the possibility that a non-material someone or something may exist not merely outside but also throughout the space–time continuum, then we have no other option but to redefine the notion of transcendent by limiting it to the highest experience available to our human senses within the world as we know it. Thus, while athletes are predisposed to understand transcendent as something outside the ordinary experience of everyday humans, an experience potentially available to them and their fellow athletes at the height of their athletic performance, they nevertheless set parameters around the word that fall short of what the gospel promises.

An orthodox Christian position acknowledges the interpenetration of the spirit world with the physical world. While each can be separately abstracted for discussion, God as the source of both an invisible spiritual world and visible material creation affirms the physicality of his created beings (and the subsequent joy they may experience as a result of that embodiment), while desiring their perception of a world breaking into their own from outside, a spiritual world that literally interpenetrates every pore of material existence for those who acquire eyes to see.

The reigning modern philosophy does not seek to be infused by anything from outside this world but rather to find an autonomous yet satisfying personal ground-zero within it. In a disenchanted world we might find great solace in anything that gives us whiffs of something 'other' along the way – even if that transcendent other remains ironically and entirely this worldly – and sport competition may provide that for elite athletes who reach their athletic and physical summit. The possibility that a sports team or individual player may embody this postmodern sense of transcendence through performance, enabling him, as Grimshaw (2000: 97) suggests, to 'burst totally and completely, yet fleetingly, into the *now*', is certainly a goal worth pursuing. There is nothing wrong with experiencing the fullness of a total release performance and the natural high that comes with it; however, the Christian chaplain should help an athlete discern the difference between worshipping the experience itself versus worshipping the giver of the experience. Properly understood, the postmodern notion of transcendence can actually function sacramentally in the life of the athlete, making visible the invisible mysteries of God while pointing to Him as the giver and sustainer of such experiences.

This involves, among other things, stretching the theological imagination of the athlete by introducing and developing categories of thought that include mental plausibility structures geared toward exploring Jesus as God come in the flesh, that introduce the wonders of a future age as depicted in the book of Revelation, that renew the mind by meditating on the truths of the Triune God's gospel as related in the Bible. It is perhaps indicative of our cultural moment that far too many preachers and ministers shy away from teaching the Bible with an aim toward engaging the audience's imagination. In many cases their own imaginations have been dulled by too much concern with bursting totally and completely, yet fleetingly, into the now. Christian ministers must do the work of confronting their athletes with glimpses of another world, however dimly lit it may be.

Proposition 3: Athletes are positioned to be more pluralistic in their beliefs than the average person. An effective sports chaplain will help athletes understand how the Gospel compares to and intersects with other belief systems and social imaginaries.

Humans, even those still characterized by fundamentalist leanings, seem to carry a measure of impulsive pluralism within them – despite doctrinal demands to the contrary – and are constantly negotiating competing belief systems. That is, while our desire to answer questions of ultimate concern may be finally answered within one system, that same system, even if predominant in the life of the believer, may also find competition from another belief network that touches the immediate concerns of everyday life.

Consequently, a person may not practically settle on just one system to capture their religious imagination. Even those who profess ultimate allegiance to one form or another may indeed find under close surveillance that their lived experience is divided out among several competing belief systems, a bricolage that produces religion à la carte. Wade Clark Roof (1999) calls the current social environment a 'spiritual marketplace' where North Americans actively seek out and incorporate various worldview elements to fit their individual needs and aspirations. Sean McCloud (2007: 298) notes 'the increased visibility of combinative religious practices among Americans', where 'combinative means the improvisory picking, mixing, and combining of beliefs and practices from a variety of religious traditions', a practice that has become 'a more visible and accepted part of public discourse in the contemporary era'.

While this is true of the North American population in general, athletes may be more prone to pluralism than the average non-athlete simply because of their exposure to and interaction with teammates, opposing teams' players and different coaches over the course of a playing career. They learn to work with others whose thinking and beliefs about core issues of life may be entirely contrary to their own. The team dynamic practically forces different views of the world into the consciousness of each player, and long times spent together practising, travelling, eating and playing open opportunities for these differing beliefs to be shared.

Within this cacophony of worldviews, the God revealed in the Bible positions himself with all or nothing propositions. The narrative thread coursing throughout the biblical text pits Jehovah against all other gods, and, while people mingled their beliefs just as fluently then as now, such practice gets swiftly condemned in just one commandment: 'I am the Lord thy God . . . . You shall have no other gods before me' (Exod. 20: 1–2; Deut. 5: 6–7). Indeed, the story of both testaments could be summarized in people's unwillingness to resist their urge toward idolatry of various sorts, constantly allowing other pursuits to take first place in their own heart.

An effective chaplain will help players negotiate the many belief systems and their associated idols that compete for primary allegiance in the athlete's heart and mind. To this end, the chaplain must be competent in understanding the core beliefs of different worldviews and able to give a response for how the claims of Christianity interact with the various dimensions of relevant social imaginaries. John B. Thompson (1984: 6) defines the 'social imaginary' as 'the creative and symbolic dimension of the social world, the dimension through which human beings create their ways of living together and their ways of representing their collective life'. As a social imaginary apologist, the chaplain is constantly asking and answering the question 'How do various approaches to organizing life compare and relate to one another, and how does the gospel interact with each of these beliefs?' Hence, she is competent at taking the raw material of popular culture, the language of communication media and the symbolism of college life and deconstructing it, exploring its inherent meanings, symbolic reach and psychological power to shape the individual life.

The chaplain also acts as a guide through the practical realities of choosing one way of thinking and living over another, while at the same time revealing the idols of the heart that so easily pollute the true worship of God. Rarely in popular media are social imaginaries (other than perhaps the Christian worldview) held accountable for their actual effects in the lives of real human beings. A good chaplain does this not in a condemnatory manner, but with a sobriety that takes seriously the adage that ideas have consequences and choices to organize one's life around a particular philosophy (even if done unconsciously) will manifest themselves on the surface of one's life eventually.

Besides being exposed to different beliefs, athletes standing out from the rest of the team by believing anything too stringently or becoming a lone voice championing any particular belief system (whether traditionally secular or religious) get frowned upon by gatekeepers of most teams. It is an unspoken though generally understood maxim: 'Don't let your beliefs – in anything – get in the way of what we are trying to accomplish as a team.' Therefore, regardless of upbringing or predisposition about their own beliefs, most athletes have been conditioned to operate as pluralists by praxis if not conviction. They are encouraged to live as practical relativists, living fluidly among a mixed bag of worldviews, subtly encouraged to steer away from dogmatism of any kind – outside of total commitment to the sport they play. Indeed, for the athlete there is a self-preserving safety in worldview pluralism.

A Christian chaplain, however, brings a 'narrow gate' (Matt. 7:13–14) approach to her message, helping an athlete understand the uniqueness of the gospel in relationship to all other belief systems alongside the call to single-minded discipleship inherent in following Christ. The role cannot be diluted to simply being an interesting and knowledgeable worldview sage, but must include the prophetic call to identify and turn away from all other idols, a lifelong work that begins with a resolved mind to genuinely follow Christ, repenting of a pluralism that denies God his proper place on the throne of life.

Conclusion

This chapter has attempted to situate sports chaplaincy in the current cultural moment, taking into consideration how modern religiosity plays itself out among people, before considering the specific manifestations of those inclinations among athletes. As sociologists like Thomas Luckmann argued in the last half of the twentieth century, the decade of the 1960s saw a substantial decrease in people's reliance on institutional religion to establish personal identity, to portray and demarcate the idea of transcendence and to offset the relativization of truth claims. Perhaps more than at any time in recent history, people would be left to their own inclinations to cultivate their religious appetites and to search for answers relative to identity, transcendence and truth. Indeed, we now live in the society Luckmann and others envisioned almost half a century ago.

Sports parallel institutional religions quite nicely in what they provide, including a strong sense of significance and identity developed among a group of teammates who function practically as a sectarian congregation, moments within competition that 'transcend' daily life and opportunities to be exposed to various worldviews. But they do nothing to fully satisfy or counter the emptiness of an identity forged in performance; they do not offer a glimpse of something beyond their material existence; they add to but cannot help a person sort through the claims of various social imaginaries and their merits. To have someone – in this case, a chaplain – who can point beyond these socially constructed boundaries may play a critical role in the spiritual formation of an athlete seeking something outside the norm.

The role of sports chaplain includes coming alongside the athlete to help him or her wade through the realities of their quest for stable identity, to help him entertain the possibility of a dimension beyond the visible and to help her adjudicate truth claims. The effective chaplain helps a seeker move away from endless seeking toward a place of habitation, recapturing a sense of dwelling in the midst of a culture that has almost completely conceded that this possibility remains entirely beyond our grasp.

The Christian chaplain must understand the incredibly powerful (though ultimately superficial) religiosity derived by athletes from their participation in sport, while unapologetically inviting the athlete to trade in his identity garnered from sport for an identity conferred by Christ. They can cultivate and open the eyes of the athlete to see another reality, helping them consider a space–time continuum that extends beyond what can be seen in this world. They can hold up the supremacy of the gospel in the relativistic race toward nihilism, helping them remove all other gods competing with Christ for dominion in their life. That is the challenge of sports chaplaincy (and really any kind of ministry) in our age: to help athletes see that while sports do indeed provide Grimshaw's 'postmodern salvific moments' which are undeniably powerful and identity shaping and at times even worldview altering, they can never satisfy the soul like 'Christ in you, the hope of glory' (Col. 1:27).

References

Cox, H. (1966). *The Secular City: Secularization and Urbanization in Theological Perspective*, New York: MacMillan.

Giddens, A. (1991). *Modernity and Self-Identity: Self and Society in the Late Modern Age*, Stanford: Stanford University Press.

Grimshaw, M. (2000). 'I Can't Believe my Eyes: The Religious Aesthetics of Sport as Postmodern Salvific Moments', *Implicit Religion*, 3/2: 87–99.

Lipe, R.D. (2013). *Free to Compete: Reflections on Sport from a Christian Perspective*, Kearney, NE: Cross Training Publishing.

Luckmann, T. (1967). *The Invisible Religion: The Problem of Religion in Modern Society* [Problem der Religion in der modernen Gesellschaft], New York: Macmillan.

McCloud, S. (2007). 'Liminal Subjectivities and Religious Change: Circumscribing Giddens for the Study of Contemporary American Religion', *Journal of Contemporary Religion*, 22/3: 295–309.

Null, J.A. (2004). *Real Joy: Freedom to be your Best*, Ulm: Ebner and Spiegel.

Roof, W.C. (1999). *Spiritual Marketplace: Baby Boomers and the Remaking of American Religion*. Princeton, NJ: Princeton University Press.

Smith, C., and M.L. Denton (2005). *Soul Searching: The Religious and Spiritual Lives of American Teenagers*, Oxford: Oxford University Press.

Thompson, J.B. (1984). *Studies in the Theory of Ideology*, Berkley: University of California Press.

Wuthnow, R. (2009). *After Heaven: Spirituality in America Since the 1950s*, Oxford: Oxford University Press.

8 Reviving the shepherd in us

Pastoral theology and its relevance to sports chaplaincy in the twenty-first century

Steven N. Waller and Harold Cottom

> In entering the footy world (or any world!) the chaplain must also empty himself of the privileges and indeed the reputation that he may be accorded in the religious world from where he has come. He enters the world with empty hands – he has not the skill of a trainer or the inspirational techniques of a coach, nor the administrative methodology of a manager or CEO. He comes bearing the humble mantle of one who comes to serve, who comes with the promise of care and compassion, who will listen without reproach or report to the coach!
>
> B.G. Stewart, n.d.: 17–18

Introduction

In his essay 'The Pastoral Ministry of Sports', Carlo Mazza makes a stirring observation that many serving in sports ministry perhaps overlook. He speculatively poses the question of where the pastoral ministry in sports fits into the scheme of professional pastoral ministry. The essay begins with the following statement:

> It is curious to notice that within the specializations in theology today, there is not a specific sector dedicated to the so-called 'pastoral ministry of sport'. Actual trends in theology don't seem to be fascinated by an aspect of life that involves millions of people, sportsmen, fans, spectators.
>
> (Mazza, 2008: 31)

Interestingly enough, other chaplains and educators unfamiliar with pastoral ministry in sporting contexts have made similar observations. This is especially true in the US among the community of chaplains, namely those that are affiliated with organizations such as the Association of Professional Chaplains and the American Association of Pastoral Counsellors.

In this chapter we seek to: (1) examine the biblical and theological aspects of pastoral or 'shepherding' ministry; (2) elaborate upon the integration of pastoral theology and sports ministry; (3) elucidate upon some of the challenges facing shepherding ministry in sporting contexts; and (4) use pastoral theologian

Andrew Purves' theological framework – which undergirds the concepts of the crucifixion and resurrection of ministry – in order to rejuvenate sport-based pastoral ministry. Our discussion is anchored in sports chaplaincy in the US, but many of the points that we raise are applicable to sports chaplains on a global scale. The need for a coherent pastoral theology which guides the work of sports chaplains is essential to their contribution across the world.

Pastoral theology as the foundation of shepherding

Pastoral theology is the strand of theology concerned with the practical application of scripture to the 'care of souls' (Kurian, 2005). The term is often considered synonymous with pastoral counselling or pastoral care (Kinast, n.d.). Likewise, pastoral theology encompasses many of the requisite skills used by those in pastoral ministry which includes preaching, evangelizing, administration and caring for the troubled, the sick, the penitent and the bereaved (Lartey, 2003).

The literary works of classical pastoral theologians such as the Cappadocians – Basil of Caesarea, Gregory of Nyssa and Gregory of Nazianzus – John Chrysostom, Martin Bucer and Richard Baxter help to ground both the theology and practice of those who provide spiritual care for others. The body of scholarly work produced by pastoral theologians such as Seward Hiltner, Thomas Oden, John Patton, Richard Olsen, Emmanuel Lartey and Andrew Purves provides unique insights into the integration of pastoral theology and contextualized ministry. Hiltner, often referred to as the 'father of modern pastoral care' and a pioneer in the development of pastoral theology used the term 'shepherding' to operationalize the integration of practical theology and the work associated with pastoral care (see Hiltner, 1958). The shepherding aspect of pastoral theology grounds the work and ministry of sports ministers and sports chaplains. It is sound pastoral theology that informs and guides the work of sports ministry generally and sports chaplaincy specifically.

The shepherd in the Bible and theology

The term 'shepherd' is used in a variety of biblical, theological and practical contexts. In *Reconstructing Pastoral Theology*, Purves (2004) suggested that shepherding is much more than a mere metaphor. He stated that, 'shepherding appropriately connects the identity and work of God and the caring work of the church' (p.xxvii). Biblical shepherds may be literal or metaphorical: those literally in charge of sheep and those practically in charge of the spiritual oversight and guidance of people. Pastoral counsellor and renowned professor of pastoral care and counselling Jay Adams defines a shepherd in contemporary terms in the following manner: 'One who provides full and complete care for all of his sheep. The shepherd knows that sheep are helpless (Isa. 53:7), are followers (John 10:3–5), are likely to wander and stray (Isa. 53:6), but under the watchful care of the shepherd they do not lack' (Adams, 1975: 5). Furthermore, Oglesby describes the shepherd as 'one who knows the flock and is known by the flock. The shepherd genuinely loves the flock and is willing to sacrifice for their welfare' (Oglesby, 1990: 1164).

In his earlier book *Pastoral Theology in the Classical Tradition* (2001), Purves similarly used the pastoral theology of Gregory of Nazianzus to anchor both sound pastoral theology and the shepherding and pastoral role that some are called to. Purves notes that in his *Second Oration*, 'In the Defence of his Flight', Gregory refers to pastoral care or shepherding as 'the art of arts' (Gregory of Nazianzus, *Orations*, 2.16) and that the shepherd directed by Christ, 'a Shepherd to shepherds and a Guide to guides' is to guide the flock that Christ himself presents, spotless and worthy of heaven (ibid. 117). Moreover, in the *Second Oration*, Gregory draws a distinction between the 'physician of souls' and those who treat the ailments of the body as emblematic of pastoral work. Through the lens of Gregory, the pastor/shepherd is greater than the physician because the pastor diagnoses and treats the maladies of the soul (Purves, 2001: 17). To wit, the pastor/shepherd has the innately more difficult task of 'the diagnosis and cure of our habits, passions, lives, wills, and whatever else is within us by banishing from our compound nature (body and soul) everything brutal and fierce, and introducing and establishing in their stead what is gentle and dear to God' (Gregory of Nazianzus, *Orations*, 2.18).

Shepherd imagery in the Bible

In more than 200 biblical passages, the customs of shepherds are used to illustrate spiritual principles; for example, shepherds are compared to spiritual overseers (Num. 27:16–17; Eccles. 12:11; John 21:15–17), and 'sheep without a shepherd' symbolize vulnerable people in need of leadership and protection (Matt. 9:36; Mark 6:34). Ideally, the shepherd should have the traits of the shepherds alluded to in the Bible: strong, devoted and selfless.

The New Testament uses the term 'shepherd' 16 times. Some New Testament references use a shepherd and sheep to illustrate Christ's relationship to his followers who, in turn, describe him as 'our Lord Jesus – the great Shepherd of the sheep' (Heb. 13:20). Jesus spoke of himself as 'the good Shepherd' who knew his sheep and would sacrifice his life for them (John 10:7–18). In John 21, Jesus exhorted and commissioned Peter to feed his sheep. Jesus is also referred to as 'the Shepherd and Guardian of your souls' (1 Pet. 2:25) and 'the chief Shepherd' (1 Pet. 5:4). Additionally, the Pauline writings apply the word 'shepherd' to church leaders. While issuing a warning about 'fierce wolves' (false teachers), Paul admonishes the Ephesian elders to oversee and care for the flock (Acts 20:28–30).

Implications for those serving in shepherding roles in sport

Notwithstanding the rich biblical tradition of the shepherd and the task of shepherding, it is incumbent upon all who are called to this facet of ministry in sport to have an understanding of the biblical mandate that is assigned to caring for God's people in sporting contexts. Keeping the role and function of the shepherd in mind – valuing the sheep, leading, guiding, protecting, carrying the weak, locating the lost and, most important, being accountable to the great Shepherd – is of paramount importance to the work of the ministry leader as shepherd (Lartey, 2003).

For as much as creating and managing sports ministries and serving the people of sport is tantamount, perhaps the greatest challenge to us all is not to lose sight of Christ, our sense of purpose or the people we serve. This is not to devalue the other vital functions of contemporary sports ministry, it simply suggests that we must keep 'first things first'. Similarly, Patton (1993) urges the recognition that an important element of shepherding is creating a 'community of care' where 'remembering' is a part of the human condition and because God remembers. Moreover, Jacobs (2012: 3) ardently suggests that all pastoral care-givers/shepherds must create a 'personal theology' in order to effectively serve those placed in their charge. This theology must be anchored in one's experience with God, thoughts about caring for others in different places in the human experience, as well as one's understanding of the vocation of pastoral care. This personal theology should undergird all pastoral actions. In summary, in sports ministries across the globe, our first priority must be the sheep and executing the God-given task of shepherding.

Challenges to the shepherd in the twenty-first century

Some critics argue that the biblical and theological concepts of shepherding are outdated and irrelevant in postmodern times. In *Pastoral Theology*, Thomas C. Oden (1983: 51) argued to the contrary stating: 'rather than prematurely rule out pastoral images as meaningless to modern consciousness, we do better to listen carefully to them so as to ask how they resonate vitally with contemporary human aspirations'. There are several challenges that sports chaplains face regardless of the geographic location of their ministry, including finding time to shepherd effectively and the need for self-care toward the end of sustaining the ministry.

Finding the time to shepherd

We live in an age where sports chaplains are often forced into a mode of multi-tasking and prioritization of ministry efforts. In some cases, how we allocate time to the various facets of ministry can be a challenge. In this age of busyness, losing sight of key tasks may yield collateral physical and spiritual damage. One of the most significant challenges to those shepherding people of sport is gaining the time to watch over the many sheep that constitute the flock. A good friend and consummate college sports chaplain at the University of Tennessee, Knoxville, Roger Woods once elaborated on the difficulties of shepherding a large flock of National Collegiate Athletic Association Division 1-A athletes while lecturing on our sport and religion course. He stated,

> Pastoring athletes in a large athletic program like ours has its challenges. One of the greatest challenges is watching over the more than 550 men and women that play at a highly competitive institution like ours and in an ultra-competitive conference like the SEC [Southeastern Conference]. The pressures of academics, athletics, their faith and life in general can get to be a bit overwhelming at times. This is why one of the biggest parts of my job is making sure I have contact with the people I serve. Being present matters.
>
> (Woods, 2013)

Shepherding, exercising the caring and watching over functions, as Woods notes, is a crucial responsibility not to be minimized. For example, Paget and McCormack (2006: 90) provide a meaningful account of the necessity of staying close to high performing athletes as their shepherd in the following vignette:

> It was the day after the game, and he was angry at the world. When you are responsible for the play that cost your team the championship, what's left for a fired, 28-year-old athlete? Where are the fans now? When the chaplain came over; he just sat in silence until the athlete began to talk about the embarrassment and fears for his future. There was no resolution that day, but a suicide was averted and young man knew he wouldn't have to be alone in his pain.

Shepherding requires a large investment of time and personal attention to be in tune with the needs of the athletes, coaches and families that are part of the flock of the sports chaplain. In order for sports chaplains to be able to meet the challenges that come with their ministries, they must strongly embrace the need for self-care.

The shepherd and self-care

An important facet of pastoral theology is self-care, an area that sports chaplains often neglect. Chaplains and other professional clergy are expected to be spiritually, emotionally and physically available to serve others when called upon (Doehring, 2013). The same expectations are true of sports chaplains. Withstanding the rigour of shepherding the people of sport in the twenty-first century, the shepherd's health may begin to dissipate. Long hours, stress, travel with teams and attending to the needs of one's own family can take its toll especially if the need to care for oneself is not addressed. Moreover, the sheer compassion required to care for the souls of players, coaches and families can also be spiritually taxing. Ultimately, rest, proper nutrition and spiritual care of self are required to sustain the pace needed to effectively serve. Even Jesus, the Chief Shepherd, took time away from a burgeoning fast-paced ministry to care of himself (Mark 6:30–31, 45–6). One of the greatest threats to sports chaplains amidst the busyness of their working lives is compassion fatigue.

Compassion fatigue

Compassion is a complex emotion that allows care-givers to hold and sustain themselves in emotional balance while also holding an individual's despair in one hand and their hopefulness in the other. It requires an inner conviction and resilience – a passion of personal ethics, and personal beliefs. In an attempt to operationalize the term 'compassion fatigue', D.W. Stewart (2012: 2) suggests that 'the helper does not personally suffer the event but, because of the helper's empathetic interaction with the sufferer, the helper becomes overcome by the trauma(s) as if it were his or her own'.

Compassion fatigue is progressive and escalates over time. Some of the common symptoms include intrusive thoughts, sleep disturbance, anxiety and loss of hope (Stewart, 2012). Contributing factors are age, lack of on-the-job experience, history of previous trauma, lack of support, repetitive exposure to trauma victims, co-dependency relative to those being ministered to, frequent exposure to negative events in a short time and a lack of balance between work, rest and play (Adams, Boscarino and Figley, 2006; Ferguson, 2007; Stewart 2012). Compassion fatigue has been widely examined in the literature among military, hospice, healthcare and corporate chaplains (Auld, 2010; Kruger, 2010; Stewart, 2012). To date, there has been no research conducted on compassion fatigue among sports chaplains.

When left unattended compassion fatigue can lead to burnout. The intensity that accompanies care-giving for people of sport can trigger compassion fatigue, especially when the relationships with players, coaches and families are close and personal. A similar scenario is that of the athlete or coach who fails to perform up to par on a high visibility stage and where the sports chaplain, in an act of compassion, begins to internalize the sense of failure and loss of the individual concerned. For as much as the two are tied together by their faith and sporting experience, failure to create a healthy distance from such circumstances can lead to compassion fatigue in the sports chaplain.

As sports chaplains, we may find that many demands are placed upon us – demands which are often difficult to understand and which may lead to the accumulation of pressure. These pressures often produce a physical, emotional and spiritually strain on our lives which may lead us closer to burnout (Thompson, Amatea and Thompson, 2014). Ultimately, it is important for us to acknowledge that we need to take time out on a regular basis in order to replenish our physical and emotional energies.

Strategies for self-care

How do we as shepherds sustain ourselves in the face of the many challenges of sports chaplaincy? First, we must regularly make the effort to maintain our spiritual resources through daily meditation, prayer, Bible reading and worship. Without question, God wishes to minister to our needs and to be involved in our experiences through these spiritual practices. Understanding His shepherding presence in our life can provide an incredible resource as we deal with stressful situations. Constantly reminding ourselves that God is in the midst of our struggles and that He encourages us to let him bear the weight of our burdens (1 Pet. 5:7) is a great source of comfort and strength. Second, we need to care for our physical body. The stronger we are, the easier it is for us to cope with tension created by the rigours of ministry. Small but often overlooked things such as diet and proper nutrition, exercise, rest and engaging in healthy leisure pursuits as time permits all help us to effectively manage the stresses and strains of chaplaincy in the twenty-first century. Doehring suggests that the beginning of the resolution to the problem of self-care among those in ministry involves a heightened level of spiritual and theological integration, which has self-care as a primary outcome (Doehring, 2013). In essence, shepherds must intentionally care for themselves while caring for others.

Reclaiming the role of the shepherd

As we understand the biblical, theological and practical aspects of shepherding the people of sport, we are acutely aware of the diverse range of challenges that confront those involved in sports chaplaincy. Surrounding all of these issues is the moral and professional imperative to uphold the key tenets of caring for the souls of others including the traditional pastoral functions of healing, guiding and sustaining. When this delicate balance of caring and managing ministry becomes imbalanced, how do we find our way back to the primacy of ministry? North American sports chaplain and author Roger Lipe captures the need to revisit and re-think the role of the sports chaplain through the lens of the shepherd in the following excerpt:

> The present world of sport and much of sport ministry is characterized by three primary weaknesses. 1) The prevalence of compartmentalized lives; that is a lack of integrity. This is easily seen in situations like the fall of coaches, players, and even prominent Christian athletes. 2) The horrible lie of performance based identity. A player's sense of personal worth may rise or fall based upon his most recent performance on the field of competition. A coach's sense of God's pleasure with her may ride on her team's win/loss record. Even worse, a sport chaplain's sense of his or her being in God's will can be shaped by the relative success or failure of the teams being served. Each and all of these scenarios are emblematic of the terrible lie that assaults the hearts of sports people.
>
> (Lipe, 2013)

The genesis of reclaiming and reviving the shepherd for sports chaplains is to revisit the personal call to this facet of ministry. Prayerfully seeking the will of God about one's calling into sports chaplaincy can be rejuvenating. It helps to locate or re-locate where we are in ministry and understand why we remain involved. Withstanding all of the entanglements and distractions of sport ministry it becomes relatively easy to lose focus and not hear the directive voice of God clearly. Additionally, making sure that the call, ministry activity and journey are anchored in Christ is equally important. As the apostle Paul wrote, 'in him we live and move and have our being' (Acts 17:28). Christ must be at the very nexus of everything done in sport chaplaincy.

Second, a re-examination of the pastoral theology we bring into ministry is essential. As we operationalize our pastoral theology as shepherds there must be an on-going integration of our experiential location and theological reflection. The continued transformation of the individual as a shepherd should be a by-product of this integration. New insights and revelation about the shepherding aspect of sports chaplaincy should also emanate from this process. Neither theology nor the shepherding (pastoral ministry) may function in isolation if pastoral theology is understood correctly.

Third, a loving but critical examination of our personal practice of shepherding by respected and qualified peers and colleagues can be exceptionally useful in helping us to re-engage and refocus properly. Proverbs 27:17 provides useful insight into the value of others in this sub-field of ministry: 'As iron sharpens iron, and one person sharpens the wits of another'. Periodically, we miss some of the intricacies related to sports chaplaincy that can be can detrimental to the people we serve and the overarching ministry. Seeking wise counsel (Prov. 1:23; 20:18) and truth from trusted colleagues about everyday working practices can help to reinvigorate the individual and the specific ministry to which they are called.

Finally, having the ability to get fresh ideas from other shepherds can help revive the spirit of the sports chaplain. Conferences, training seminars, professional development institutes, as well as a growing body of contextualized literature that integrates Bible, theology and reflective practice, continue to prove useful in the professional and personal lives of sports chaplains. Moreover, taking advantage of opportunities to enhance one's professional identity (Dzikus, Waller and Hardin, 2012; Waller, Dzikus and Hardin, 2008, 2010; Waller et al., this volume) and elevate the field of practice through available professional certification programmes will help the practice of shepherding.

But what if all of the aforementioned are not enough to re-calibrate the ministry given to us? If the sports chaplain can no longer embrace the primacy of the pastoral or shepherding role then should his or her ministry be permitted to continue by the entity responsible for oversight? This raises further serious questions about why the ministry exists at all and where it is heading. Perhaps the crucifixion and subsequent resurrection of the ministry born after the name of Jesus Christ is necessary to recreate it anew.

Crucifying and resurrecting the ministry of sports chaplaincy

What happens when the sports chaplain loses focus and begins to drift from his or her charge? What guiding, yet corrective action can be taken to re-orient a ministry that becomes leader-focused as opposed to Christocentric and people-focused? For as much emphasis we place on building ministries and shepherding people, the stark reality is that our ministries are not redemptive in their own right.

In *The Crucifixion of Ministry*, Purves (2007) discusses two specific areas on which we as shepherds need to concentrate. The first is conceiving ministry as our own ministry and the second that ministry must be understood as a sharing in the continuing ministry of Jesus Christ (Purves, 2007: 12). Periodically, shepherds become so attached to their ministry and the pay-off (positive or negative) they cannot see that their focus is displaced. In a pathological sense when there is more 'me' than 'thee' in ministry, a level of caustic toxicity exists. Subsequently, as Purves (2007: 13) elucidates, 'all that we think we should do and can do and are doing in ministry must be put to death .... Even when we conduct them from the best spiritual, therapeutic and moral motives, they are not redemptive. Only the ministry of Jesus is redemptive'.

Moreover, every now and then some have the propensity to develop a 'messiah complex'. Essentially, we begin to feel that we must carry the burden and solve all of the problems of those who we have been called to engage and shepherd in ministry. We fail to realize that our ministry is a privilege and that we are partakers of the ministry of Jesus Christ. The sometimes necessary crucifixion of ministry is the prelude to our audacious confidence in the power of the resurrection. We crucify it on two levels: (1) to self, letting Christ's ministry rule and abide, and (2) to the distractions that draw us away from our primary call – caring for the souls of those we serve. God, with full intentionality, will slay our ministries when we move away from the centre, Jesus Christ. The joyful aspects of crucifying ministry are in finding an incarnate Christ and anticipating the power and presence of a resurrected Christ at the very centre of a resurrected sport ministry. In this process, the chief Shepherd rejuvenates and restores the ministry shepherd. The simple truth is that we cannot enjoy a resurrected ministry unless we are willing to suffer the painful death of the ministry.

In the follow up to *The Crucifixion of Ministry*, *The Resurrection of Ministry*, Purves (2010) endeavours to show how living in the hope of Jesus' resurrection can help those involved in pastoral ministry (regardless of the context), subdue the mourning, discouragement and sense of regret that comes from a slain ministry. In essence, Purves argues that God establishes our ministries on their proper ground in the ministry of the resurrected and ascended Jesus, and subsequently we minster in the joy and hope of life in Him. Through the power of the Spirit we become inextricably joined together with Jesus, and we share in both his resurrected life and his resurrected ministry. Invariably, the end can be a new, relevant and exciting pastoral ministry anchored in sport that is re-aligned with Christ at the very core. The renewed ministry becomes alive and is permeated with Jesus' ministry. The shepherd sees his responsibility clearly through the eyes of the chief Shepherd and views the people and the ministry he or she is steward over in a new light. The re-birth of ministry in the power of Christ re-focuses and re-energizes those that are associated with the ministry. From the vantage point of the shepherd, he or she can now stand steadfast in the fulfilment of their duties, knowing that their sense of empowerment to care for sheep has been renewed. Sports chaplains that are fuelled by resurrection power can go about the work of shepherding with a new confidence in the healing power of Christ working in and through them.

Conclusion

Sports chaplains in the twenty-first century are uniquely qualified to address many of the issues with which people of sport are confronted. If we will lovingly lead and go about the work of being 'shepherds after God's own heart' that are led by him (Jer. 3:15) and led by the caring, resurrected ministry of Jesus, we can make a meaningful impact on the lives of the people of sport. If we rely upon the work and office of the Holy Spirit (John 14:25–6) to remind us of the significant shepherding duties associated with such a role – sustaining, guiding, healing and reconciling – we can make a tremendous difference.

Lipe (2013) eloquently and poignantly reminds us that the challenge to those currently working in sports ministries globally is threefold: (1) to conduct ministry, regardless of the level or venue, with a Christ-centred heart, and to fully integrate the presence and power of Christ in all of life: sport, ministry, family, all of it; (2) to guard against a performance-based identity on multiple levels; and (3) to make a meaningful difference in the lives of the people of sport through the gospel in order to positively influence, teams, communities and global society. For athletes and teams performances and results matter; for sports chaplains pastoral and spiritual effectiveness is the goal, but neither is the ultimate end. Medal counts, records and personal bests are great moments in time; self-sustaining ministries that flourish represent the work of Christ in the arena of sports, but salvation, growth in Christ that yields 'good fruit' (Matt. 7:17; Luke 13:6–8), and guarding the very souls of those in our charge is everything.

Sports chaplains can protect their resurrected ministry by focusing on God in their ministry, understanding and doing pastoral theology in a sporting context and re-establishing a roadmap for their work. The great hope for sports chaplains, as shepherds and stewards of the sporting world, should not be rooted in the success or experience of their ministries *per se*, but in the gospel message of Jesus Christ.

References

Adams, J.E. (1975). *Shepherding God's Flock: A Handbook on Pastoral Ministry, Counseling, and Leadership*, Grand Rapids, MI: Zondervan.

Adams, R., J. Boscarino and C. Figley (2006). 'Compassion Fatigue and Psychological Distress among Social Workers: A Validation Study', *American Journal of Orthopsychiatry*, 76/1: 103–8.

Auld, A. (2010). 'Canadian Military Chaplains Suffering Burnout, Compassion Fatigue at High Rates', *Canadian Press*, 16 May. Retrieved from <www.winnipegfreepress.com/life/health/cdn-military-chaplains-suffering-burnout-compassion>.

Doehring, C. (2013). 'New Directions for Clergy Experiencing Stress: Connecting Spirit and Body', *Pastoral Psychology*, 62: 623–38.

Dzikus, L., S. Waller and R. Hardin (2012). 'Case Studies of Collegiate Sport Chaplains', *Journal of Sport and Social Issues*, 36: 268–94.

Ferguson, S. (2007). 'Clergy Compassion Fatigue', *Family Therapy Magazine*, 2 (Mar.–Apr.): 16–19.

Hiltner, S. (1958). *Preface to Pastoral Theology*. Nashville, TN: Abingdon Press.

Jacobs, M.R. (2012). 'Creating a Personal Theology to do Spiritual/Pastoral Care', in S.B. Roberts (ed.), *Professional Spiritual Care and Pastoral Care: A Practical Clergy and Chaplain's Handbook*, Woodstock, VT: Skylight Press, 3–11.

Kinast, R.L. (n.d.). *How Pastoral Theology Functions*. Retrieved from <http://theologytoday. ptsem.edu/jan1981/v37–4-article2.htm>.

Kruger, T.L. (2010). 'Keys to Resilient Practice in Contemporary Chaplaincy', PhD thesis: Lancaster Theological Seminary.

Kurian, G.T. (2005). *Nelson's Dictionary of Christianity*. Nashville, TN: Thomas Nelson.

Lartey, E.Y. (2003). *In Living Color: An Intercultural Approach to Pastoral Care and Counseling*, 2nd edn, Philadelphia, PA: Jessica Kingsley.

Lipe, R. (2013). 'Re: The Significance of Sport Chaplains, Sport Mentors, and Character Coaches in the 21st Century', blog entry, 15 Nov. Available at <http://sportchaplainsport mentor.blogspot.com/2013/11/the-significance-of-sport-chaplains.html>.

Mazza, C. (2008). 'The Pastoral Ministry of Sport: Taking Stock and Looking Ahead', in *Sport: An Educational and Pastoral Challenge*, Vatican City: Libertia Editrice Vaticana, 31–59.

Oden, T.C. (1983). *Pastoral Theology: Essentials of Ministry*. New York: HarperOne.

Oglesby, W.B., Jr. (1990). 'Shepherd/Shepherding', in R.J. Hunter (ed.), *Dictionary of Pastoral Care and Counseling*, Nashville, TN: Abingdon Press.

Paget, N.K., and J.R. McCormack (2006). *The Work of the Chaplain*, Valley Forge, PA: Judson Press.

Patton, J. (1993). *Pastoral Care in Context: An Introduction to Pastoral Care*, Louisville, KY: Westminster John Knox Press.

Purves, A. (2001). *Pastoral Theology in the Classical Tradition*, Louisville, KY: Westminster John Knox Press.

—— (2004). *Reconstructing Pastoral Theology: A Christological Foundation*, Louisville, KY: Westminster John Knox Press.

—— (2007). *The Crucifixion of Ministry: Surrendering our Ambitions to the Service of Christ*, Downers Grove, IL: InterVarsity Press.

—— (2010). *The Resurrection of Ministry: Serving in the Hope of the Risen Lord*, Downers Grove, IL: InterVarsity Press.

Stewart, B.G. (n.d.). *Sports Chaplaincy: A Pastoral and Theological Exploration*. Available at <https://slmaustralia.securehost3.com/download/articles/A%20Summary%20of%20 a%20Theological%20and%20Pastoral%20Exploration%20of%20the%20Role%20of%20 Sports%20Chaplains%20in%20Australia%20-%20Grant%20Stewart.pdf>.

Stewart, D.W. (2012). 'Compassion Fatigue: What is the Level among Army Chaplains?', *Journal of Behavioral Health*, 27/1: 1–11.

Thompson, I.A., E.S. Amatea and E.S. Thompson (2014). 'Personal and Contextual Predictors of Mental Health Counselors' Compassion Fatigue and Burnout', *Journal of Mental Health Counseling*, 36/1: 58–77.

Waller, S., L. Dzikus and R. Hardin (2008). 'Collegiate Sport Chaplaincy: Problems and Promise', *Journal of Issues in Intercollegiate Athletics*, 1: 107–23.

Waller, S., L. Dzikus and R. Hardin (2010). 'The Collegiate Sports Chaplain: Kindred or Alien?', *Chaplaincy Today*, 26/1: 16–26.

Woods, R. (2013). 'Holistic Care for Athletes', lecture, RSM 580: Religion and Sport in Global Society, University of Tennessee, Knoxville, 29 Jan.

9 Gospel-shaped sports chaplaincy

A theologically driven sport ministry

John B. White

Introduction

Christian sports chaplains undertake pastoral care as specialists in public contexts outside traditional places of congregational life and worship, not unlike chaplains in other secular settings. Sports chaplains experience ministry on the margins of congregational life proper (Threlfall-Holmes and Newitt, 2011). Holst (2006) describes this for hospital chaplains as walking between two worlds – religion and medicine, which, for the purposes of this book, means a walk between religion and sport, or the church and the institutions of sport. Consequently, this walk between different contexts raises a number of concerns, if not conflicts and tensions, which Christian chaplains need to address if they are to negotiate the ideological differences and power struggles. For example, because many sports chaplains are embedded in Olympic, professional and collegiate sporting contexts, they are serving privileged individuals in positions of power.

The economic and social advantages possessed by these individuals can conflict with and even distort gospel virtues such as those taught in the Sermon on the Mount (Kotva, 2012). Conflict is exacerbated by the fact that the nature and values of sport can be juxtaposed with concerns such as those posed by the environment, poverty, hunger, disease, unemployment and illiteracy. These everyday moral matters are also ecclesial dilemmas when considering how to justify the time and resources spent on sport (let alone sports chaplaincy), when the world is in pain and suffering (Twietmeyer, 2007). Additionally, there are plenty of instances in the world of sport of sexism, racism, exploitation of athletes, violence and religious discrimination, which bump up against gospel patterns of speech and action. In this chapter, I consider two main questions: how are the convictions of the gospel fundamental to Christian sports chaplaincy, and how should the good news inform and transform the way in which these sports chaplains serve? My claim is that the culture of sport requires sports chaplains to be apprehended and shaped by the whole gospel: this is a theological task and responsibility.

To explore these questions, requires an understanding of what the gospel is so that sports chaplains minister in a manner worthy of the gospel (Phil. 1:27–30).

What this means in principle and practice has everything to do with how well chaplains embody the good news in the liminal spaces of ministry in sport. Biblical interpretation is complex but what I am interested in here are general biblical themes.

Gospel truths: what is the Gospel?

The gospel is the good news about God's saving work in Jesus Christ. The God of the gospel confronts our human existence, for as Paul asserts it is God's power that brings salvation (Rom. 1:16–17), accomplishing redemption in the salvific acts of Jesus Christ (Rom. 3:21–6). Newbigin (2003) writes about this confrontation as God in Christ breaking into and becoming present in our human history, calling for healing and liberation from the idolatrous powers that oppress. The good news is about Jesus, who liberates or saves us from sin, to which this world is in bondage, estranging humans from God and one another.

The apostle Paul accents the gospel he was entrusted with as the 'ministry of reconciliation', for he writes that 'in Christ God was reconciling the world to himself' (2 Cor. 5:18–19). This claim witnesses to the reality of reconciliation for the work of Christ 'had as its effect the bringing of the "the world" back to God' (Green and Baker, 2011: 84). Paul makes it clear in this passage (2 Cor. 5:11–21) that God in Christ is both the source and substance of the good news. Reconciliation is 'in' and 'through' Christ: the events of his death and resurrection alone are the means. That implies, if God is the gracious subject who initiates reconciliation, then humans are the objects, since the problem of sin and estrangement lie with humans who inhabit a world that needs a comprehensive restoration. God's action in Christ reconciles sinners and the world to himself and inaugurates a cosmic renewal of all of life (Collins, 2013).

Paul concludes his exposition of reconciliation as an event in which Christ's death is the punishment for sin; He took away our sin in that He takes our place by suffering and dying the death of a sinner on the cross. Paul further claims that the result of Christ's death is that 'in [Christ] we might become the righteousness of God' (2 Cor. 5:21). Here Paul connects being reconciled to God (2 Cor. 5:18–20) and Christ's death with the biblical concept of being made right with God. God's forgiving activity of reconciliation means we become the righteousness of God. Although there are a plurality of images and other pertinent passages for elucidating the atonement (Green and Baker, 2011) and even more explicit references to justification (Romans 3–5), Paul's point is that the sacrificial death of Jesus is the basis for sinners being declared righteous. Reconciliation means human beings stand in a right relationship with God, because our justification is accomplished in the event of the cross; Christ as the means of our justification exchanges our state of sin for the righteousness of God (Collins, 2013). This truth of the gospel is that God justifies the ungodly or sinners (Rom. 4:5). In the Christian tradition, the consequence of humankind's transition from one condition into another is because Jesus Christ became what we are as sinners in order to make us what He is. This final point is important in the proceeding discussion on justification and sport.

The trajectory of 2 Corinthians 5:11–21 reminds us that ministry is the direct consequence of the good news concerning Jesus Christ. Just as God called Paul to the ministry of reconciliation, God graciously invites sports chaplains to implement reconciliation as a witness to God's new way of life in Christ for the world of sport. What follows is a discussion of two specific inferences for sports chaplaincy that come from an affirmation of the good news as articulated in terms of the cross event. The first explores a pastoral care implication concerning personal identity, whilst the second mines a prophetic implication of doing sports chaplaincy.

Gospel conclusions for sports chaplaincy

Justification and sport: pastoral considerations of personal identity

If justification is accomplished in the event of the cross, then the glory of the cross says, 'No!' to sportspersons' absurd and hopeless efforts to justify themselves in and through their performances (White, 2012). This is not to say that sportspersons cannot gain a relative appreciation for who they are as they play sports: namely, healthy pride and confidence which fits a proper love of self. However, the 'gospel according to sport' is self-justification, for it attempts to travel the penultimate road of sports as an ultimate authority for determining personal worth. This gospel proclaims and performs a plausibility structure, which legitimizes self-justification, counter to faith in Christ alone. Coakley (2009) explains sociologically that this quest is real because the normative culture's sport ethic is an over-conformity to particular interpretations of values, norms, and goals of sport. What often follows is that the identities of sportspersons become habituated to this logic and thus cemented in sport itself. According to Hughes and Coakley (1991: 312), athletes who most commonly adopt this sport ethic are those 'whose identity or future chances for material success are exclusively tied to sport', because 'self-identification becomes lodged within sport'. Indeed, Hughes and Coakley go on to argue that 'the role of the athlete (player, climber, skier, runner, etc.) becomes extremely salient to a person's identity' (ibid. 318).

How self-justification works: relationships and recognition

German theologian Eberhard Jüngel helps to explain further what this concept of justification means existentially within contemporary society. He describes how our lived experiences connect to and mediate a pre-understanding of the meaning of justification. He claims that 'to justify something, to justify oneself, to be justified – these are primary life-processes that occur daily' (Jüngel, 1999: 28). Humans normally justify their actions when they fail or when something is misunderstood by vindicating or defending themselves. On a more basic level, when people justify themselves, they assert that their lives fundamentally have a meaning. Jüngel further states that this worldly life process, the act of justification, always occurs before some authority or other. He holds that these different authorities function as courts of law in that the event of justification summons us before others, whether that tribunal is a human institution, myself or even before God (although God relativizes all others because He is the true source and means of justification). The nature of life is such that we exist before these kinds of forums which question and evaluate us: that is, athletes before their teammates, opponents and spectators; coaches before media and management; children before their parents; and so on. In these events, a person existentially experiences her or himself ordered to appear before someone to justify her or himself. We even do this before ourselves, which Jüngel concludes is our own conscience serving as a tribunal. With this whole account, the challenge of justification is how everyday life inculcates evaluative interpretations about a person's identity, which form her or his self-understanding as something she or he must vindicate, regardless of the relationship or sphere of life.

Jüngel (1999) argues that there are two essential aspects of our humanity, which explain why we justify ourselves. The first is that because we exist and live as social creatures in relation to others (even to ourselves), our existence implies a responsibility before others, ready to be summoned to accountability and hence, to defend and to justify, if necessary. The second aspect is the human longing for approval: we were made in such a way that we depend on recognition. As Jüngel (1999: 29) states, 'the will to justify ourselves springs from this fundamental anthropological need for approval'. The problem with this drive for approval or self-justification, when understood in relation to sport, is that even though sport performances may witness to a person's identity and even temporarily satisfy the demands of this tribunal, they do not merit God's justification and so leave this desire for justification unsatisfied. With regard to the human condition Jüngel goes on to argue that theological reality rebukes all human attempts at justification, since the 'one who is in the wrong before God is incapable of any such things. Before God, no wrong can be made right. Before God, all "making right" is excluded' (ibid.).

Kelsey (2009) verifies that what is so dangerous about human attempts at self-justification is that they skew reality. Humans falsely believe that they author the worth and meaning of their lives and identities. This can make us too dependent on the acknowledgement and affirmation of others. If our identities and self-worth are fully contingent on the affirmation of others, then we are in a treadmill that is in 'bondage to the assessment of others' (Kelsey, 2009: 873). For Kelsey, inherent in self-justification are beliefs and habits that something is wrong enough with humanity to question the worth of human life and thus, seek justification in reference to some penultimate strategy. Kelsey sees any existential 'hows' (strategies) that try to bring worth to personal identities apart from reconciliation in Christ as deeply insecure and this 'insecurity generates a living death of endless and vicious cycles' (ibid.). The only solution to this problem is found in the gospel in which God's reconciliation blesses and establishes the unrighteous as righteous; God justifies and so people are given definitive approval and forgiveness through the word of God's grace (Jüngel, 1999).

The 'Gospel according to sport' in Friday Night Lights

In *Friday Night Lights*, Buzz Bissinger describes this pre-understanding of justification through his ethnographic narrative about how one high-school (American) football team seemed to animate Odessa, a town in West Texas, holding it together in some sense. Bissinger and his family relocated from Philadelphia to spend a year interviewing and learning the ethos of this town, where almost 20,000 fans would show up on a Friday night because 'football went to the core of life' (Bissinger, 2000: xii). Bissinger chronicles how unresolved and complex tensions related to 'race', sport, education, religion and politics fuelled a community to seek justification vicariously in and through the works of their high-school coaches and athletes. In turn, he interrogates how coaches and athletes experienced this tribunal or others' expectations and its effect on the identities of the main characters. One main character, in particular, is Boobie Miles, who until his tragic knee injury in a scrimmage game was perceived as the anointed one. He relentlessly sought recognition from others with his apparent invincibility and requisite attitude in football boosting his team and town's aspirations for proving themselves. Boobie exemplifies what Coakley (2009) argues happens when athletes equate their identities with their sporting prowess and performance: they overconform to the normative values of sport. Bissinger reports, for example, how Boobie stood existentially before different tribunals (members of his family, uncle L.V., fans, media, teammates, coaches, opponents and rivals, the team physician, Caucasians and African-Americans, teachers and college recruiters) which summoned him to meet their expectations. These generalized others socialized Boobie to earn their recognition, justifying whether his life project to make it to 'the pros' and be somebody would prove meaningful.

Although Boobie's story extends the problem of justification beyond the New Testament, his example illustrates the issue of justification as it relates to identity amongst athletes. Moreover, Boobie's context for justifying himself is a competitive zero-sum game which means, according to Kelsey, that he is driven to compare himself with others (Kelsey, 2009): a logic which necessarily means that there must be a winner who justifies his or her identity and a loser who does not. Before Boobie's injury he commanded respect, securing and winning his identity, but after his injury his winning status became vulnerable, begetting deep insecurity and tentativeness in how he played, for he was no longer a winner and the balance of affirmation shifted to the success of other teammates.

Kelsey (2009) argues that this way of defining personal identities binds humans to a vicious cycle of death, which in Boobie's case was driven by the vice of envy. Bissinger accounts for Boobie's envy (along with other emotions) in how he reacted toward Chris Comer, a teammate who had replaced Boobie in the backfield after his injury as the new distinguished running back. Prior to Boobie's injury, he had succeeded in defining his identity as successful, since he was the honoured athlete who had earned the praise of others. During this time, Boobie even cheered Comer's accomplishment as a running back second to Boobie, presumably, because when he compared himself to Comer, Boobie had kept his status as the winner and thus, Comer was not a real threat to his identity. This comparison only increased Boobie's own sense of righteousness. Bissinger (2000: 15–16) notes the dramatic shift after Boobie's injury:

> As the season progressed and Comer became a star while Boobie languished, the cheers [from Boobie] stopped. He made no acknowledgement of Comer's score. He sat on the bench, his eyes staring straight ahead, burning with a mixture of misery and anger as it became clear to him that the coaches had no intention of playing him tonight . . . . He sat on the bench and felt coldness swirl through him, as if something sacred inside him was dying, as if every dream in his life was fleeing from him and all he could do was sit there and watch it disappear amid all those roars that had once been for him.

Bissinger gives voice to how Boobie's emotions illustrate the inner workings of this cycle of death with Boobie feeling alienated and estranged not only from himself but also from others, for in comparison, his own worth and value are diminished and denigrated. In sum, Boobie's identity is condemned to this false quest for success through social approval.

When applying Kelsey's analysis, Boobie's case draws attention to how personal identity can get distorted by the 'gospel according to sport'. The logic of self-justification in sport occurs when sportspersons answer the existential question 'Who am I?' with 'My sport performance justifies my personal identity.' It is theologically problematic to reduce one's worth to one's athletic abilities, since self-justification only further estranges sportspersons from God, others and themselves, keeping them in their condition of sin which leads to death in many complex and nuanced ways (personally, socially and spiritually).

The Christian Gospel speaks to the 'Gospel according to sport'

The 'gospel according to sport' affords sports chaplains opportunities to embody and speak the Christian gospel as it confronts the liminality between God's justification and self-justification. The gospel erupts in such elemental crises in which life and death confront personal identity (Jüngel, 1999). Here is a cultural discourse and practice in which the true gospel meets vulnerability and neediness. This helplessness as illustrated for many is a chain of tragic self-justifications which paradoxically can set the stage for sportspersons who are downtrodden and heavy-laden with this burden to prove themselves, to receive the good news 'like cold water to a thirsty soul' (Prov. 25:25). The word of reconciliation about Jesus Christ addresses all of humanity at the core of their personhood, for what it means to be truly human is grounded in Christ; it is a new union as derived from God's undeserved gift of righteousness, a consequence of Christ's death and resurrection. 'The word of the cross' (1 Cor. 1:18), when contextualized for sport, constrains sports chaplains to address sportspersons where they are and as they are, to be reconciled to God (2 Cor. 5:20) and, thus, to experience the benefit of God's grace as forgiveness of sin.

The good news is a radical paradigm shift through which a sportsperson's whole existence is reinterpreted, emancipating them from their living lies and death (Jüngel, 1999). The quest for self-justification is over, and they are now justified by faith in Christ. It is the unconditional nature of this event of justification and its application that has always frustrated and offended the world, especially in zero-sum contexts and for those who believe that their works or winning should determine their standing or identity. What lurks primarily in this way of human self-understanding is an identity that is actualized by what athletes do, namely, their performative works of righteousness. Works righteousness is incompatible with and condemned by the doctrine of justification. God's final word of justification puts an end to this achievement-oriented quest for finding one's true identity (White, 2011).

Prophetic imagination for sports chaplaincy

If justification as revealed in the message of the cross radically breaks into, conflicts with and judges this present (evil) age and the old way of life under sin (2 Cor. 5:14–21), then the good news prophetically calls into question the status quo. Paul employs apocalyptic imagery when he uses such language as 'new creation' (2 Cor. 5:17) to describe how Jesus' death made effective the miracle of a new 'world-order change' (Green and Baker, 2011: 88–9). The cross not only declares a new state of affairs for sinners but for the entire cosmos, in that the power of the gospel speaks to all spheres of life.

> The cross is a sign of what happens when one takes God's account of reality more seriously than Caesar's. The cross stands as God's (and our) eternal no to the powers of death, as well as God's eternal yes to humanity, God's remarkable determination not to leave us to our own devices.
>
> (Hauerwas and Willimon, 1989: 47)

Jesus Christ crucified means God judges what is evil. Ironically, God chose the folly of the cross to accomplish this. How Jesus died was offensive and scandalous to the Greco-Roman world (1 Cor. 1:18–30). The cross was a horrible, gruesome form of punishment in an honour-and-shame based culture that the Romans used to intimidate observers and to humiliate the subversives, criminals, outcasts and rebellious slaves who were put to death. The reality of Christ crucified is at odds with many aspects of the world in its present fallen form.

Moreover, Jesus embodied the Kingdom's good news in his life and ministry by advocating justice for the marginalized and defying the use of violence (Sider, 1993).

Taking a prophetic stance on problems in sport

An immediate implication is that just because the people and institutions of sport act in a particular way, it does not necessarily follow that this is the way it should be:

> [Christ's] death publicly exposes and condemns all of the sporting world's abuses of God's intention for the human body [and personal identity], all of sports' spiritual, moral and relational lies like pride, envy, idolatry, violence, disrespect, greed, cheating, taunting, preening, and the vitriol and anger of coaches and parents [and athletes].
>
> (White, 2012)

Sports chaplaincy which does not take a prophetic stance on these abuses is not grounded in the gospel, since good news reveals how the bad news oppresses and harms human beings. Furthermore, because justification stands at the centre of how chaplains should relate to a world that cries for justice, ethics is core to the doctrine of justification. How sports chaplains must think and act has ethical significance for who they are as new creations and what should be done to put things right.

Newbigin (1986) understands the power of the gospel to transform the entire human situation. The reach of the gospel, in his view, is cosmic, since Christ as Creator and Redeemer reclaims and restores all. Not only are individuals and creation affected, but the social order is also to be transformed: human institutions, such as sport, are affected by human sin and are in need of the gospel's leavening influence and renewal. The gospel story applies to the entire human race and all creation. Who we are and what creation and culture should be finds its meaning in relation to the story of Jesus. For sports chaplains, their witness in word and deed is not then merely to individual souls getting saved, but to a gospel directed to the whole person and the whole culture of sport. Ellis (2014) notes that the tendency of sports chaplains and ministries is to keep their public engagement to that of evangelism and individual pastoral care, but because of the reality of the whole gospel this witness remains incomplete. The gospel demands that sports chaplains widen their concerns to include systemic and social issues ('race', family, economics, gender, media practices and so on). The gospel poses an inclusive ministry focus.

This gospel conclusion further problematizes the narrow construal of the gospel to the spiritual dimension, to organized religion, to the individual, to the after-life or to the soul. Frank Deford originally reported a similar observation almost 40 years ago having interviewed individuals from prominent sport ministries in North America. He lamented the fact that these chaplains neglected to consider social and moral matters: cheating, the evils of recruiting, dirty play, racism (Deford, 1976). Why does this happen?

A diagnosis of the problem of neglect: a malfunction of sports chaplaincy

Volf (2011) explains that one reason for this neglect is because of idleness of faith. Chaplaincy idles when chaplains fail to obey the prophetic demands of the gospel, not doing what they should, getting stuck, because of what Volf sees as a result of the power of systems. All institutions operate from some kind of ideology for ensuring order and positing what is acceptable and not acceptable. Chaplains do not serve and work in a vacuum but in a context dependent on processes such as economic and political relations and values. The dominant culture of sport, for example, overpoweringly narrates how each contributing part fits into the whole, including coaches, athletes, management, families, chaplains and media. Each part needs to play a role in order for the whole to operate efficiently. The power of such systems with their own convictions and interests, according to Volf, can tempt and trap chaplains, just as it can sportspersons, to act and to assume roles in accordance with the normative values of sport instead of the gospel. Budde and Brimlow (2002) recognize how easy it is for chaplains then to get co-opted by different worldviews and purposes, especially since their positions require them to conform materially, affectively and spiritually to the formative processes within the power structures and practices of an institution. Here is where the practice of the gospel in sports chaplaincy is especially susceptible to compromise.

In their research on the roles and responsibilities of collegiate sports chaplains, Dzikus, Hardin and Waller (2012) show how two chaplains at different (US) public universities were used by athletic departments to promote a positive image for their sport programmes. The University of Tennessee, Knoxville, football team featured their chaplain in the *2007 University of Tennessee Football Guide* with testimonials about the chaplain's role being to mould athletes into well-rounded players, making them into good men and inspiring the entire university, which the guide used as a public relations and recruitment strategy. Because the chaplain is accountable in some sense to this football programme, then his own loyalty to and the programme's acceptance and endorsement of him relates to their institutional interests. Their assessment and use of him in this programme was based on whether he upheld the university's ideals. So long as this chaplain conforms to this programme, he receives institutional blessing. Although the cause of the gospel takes up human flourishing and even contributes to the common good in sport (Christian chaplains care about the well-being of coaches and players), our witness to the gospel can be altered by the normative purposes and values of sport. That is, the prophetic direction of the gospel must resist equating the scandalous nature of the gospel with the exclusive message and distorted values of an institution like football. The gospel entails that chaplains interpret their work, and what it means to be human, which in the case of the University of Tennessee's guide is what it means to be a man, in a manner worthy of the gospel. However, this prophetic conclusion of the gospel does not mean a chaplain is out to confront for confrontation's sake, nor does it imply that the gospel and sport are incommensurable. On the whole, what is at stake in the University of Tennessee's guide and use of their chaplain are their normative judgements about what makes a well-rounded, good man. Gospel-driven chaplaincy envisages what it means to be fully human in terms of God's revelation in Jesus Christ. The good news concerning Jesus Christ is the true goal of our humanity, and it is in his image that we are conformed (Col. 3:10). This brings into relief how the agenda of the University of Tennessee's guide might get confused, if not conflated with that of the gospel. Implicit in this confusion is a tacit accommodation. While the chaplain may facilitate chapels, religious meetings, lead weekly devotionals and Bible studies and meet for personal counselling and discipleship, the ideology of American football (or of any institution for that matter) and how this material, embodied performance forms a male, can compete with and be antithetical to a gospel understanding of what it means to be a man.

This is troubling, for as Messner (2007) argues, because sports are sites for constructing gender, then this conception of masculinity embedded in the University of Tennessee's guide reproduces traditions and conventions concerning masculinity and shapes reality. Although many other social institutions and experiences contribute to gender identity, organized sport in general and American football in particular produces scripts about masculinity which are not neutral or value-free. Fogel (2011) refers to 'sporting masculinity' as one particular script to which male athletes subscribe in order to meet the expectations of their peers. So, for instance, when being a good man as promoted by the University of Tennessee's guide is associated with physical toughness and power, aggression, heroic conquests or slogans such as 'no pain, no gain', then 'sporting masculinity' is not consistent with the model given by Jesus Christ. Practically this means that, even though the chaplain encouraged the individual piety of the coaches and athletes, unless he analysed and exposed how such hegemonic myths of manhood and personal identity located in the power of this social system can oppress and exploit sportspersons, then he condoned institutional evil. Again, just because certain notions of masculinity and the attendant behaviour are part of the given order of sports, it does not follow, according to the gospel, that this is the way it is supposed to be.

Furthermore, might this chaplain's failure to confront the sin of systems be perceived as divine validation of the goals and objectives of the University of Tennessee's guide (Kotva, 2012)? Consider, also, how the presence of the gospel in this example is not so much a distinct way of life, but is morphed by and into this institution's rhetoric and practices (Volf, 2011). Not only does religion use sport in this form of sports chaplaincy, but sport uses religion (Coakley, 2009). This trivializes the gospel and domesticates its transformative power. When religion is used for public relations and as a tool for recruitment, it sacralizes an institution's power structures.

Additionally, in sport where such malfunctions exist, the gospel should awaken sports chaplains to question the power of the system when athletes are instructed to do something – deliberately take out an opponent, feign injury, employ tactics which purposefully intimidate both physically and psychologically or hate the other side – which outside sport many would not affirm (Volf, 2011). Obedience to the institution of sport may contradict Christian moral convictions.

A Gospel-shaped solution: prophetic inquiry and criticism

In order to counter and resist such strategies, chaplains need to incorporate what Brueggemann (2001: 13) calls the prophetic imagination, which is 'to nurture, nourish, and evoke a consciousness and perception alternative to the consciousness and perception of the dominant culture around us'. Since this critical stance is intrinsic to the gospel, the prophetic role is part of the calling and responsibility of the sports chaplain. In this sense, sports chaplains are moral leaders, not only spiritual advisors giving pastoral care to support players and coaches.

The gospel emboldens the prophetic vision, since in Jesus Christ incarnated, crucified and resurrected the old has passed and the new has come (2 Cor. 5:16–17), giving sports chaplains in their union with Christ the prophetic imagination to discern the difference between the way things are and the way they should be in Christ. This prophetic imperative invokes a myriad of questions, which chaplains can and should raise. What are the morally wrong actions and systemic injustices in how sports are currently organized and practised? How is the human body abused and misused in sport? How should chaplains advocate justice for women, gay, lesbian and disabled athletes and other minorities in sport? What are the economic injustices and disparities in sport? How have the economic interests of the National Collegiate Athletic Association and other sporting organizations exploited sportspersons and misshaped sport? What kind of reform should we advocate in relation to players' rights? Admittedly, because the prophetic voice has often been absent in sports chaplaincy, and because chaplains are normally in post by way of privilege, the challenge to existing policies and practices is significant (Ellis, 2014), but such voice is necessary for the sake of the whole gospel, for the whole sportsperson and for the whole culture of sport.

Furthermore, when chaplains fail to critique the moral and social matters that Deford wrote about in *Sports Illustrated* in 1976 including racism and sexism, they risk supplanting the direction of the gospel and, instead, tolerate norms internal to the social order of sport. Instead of responsibly witnessing to the new order as inaugurated by Christ's death and resurrection, their evangelistic witness underwrites what this cultural discourse considers best, for this gives chaplains relevance while preserving the status quo (building character, winning, team unity, making good men, excellence and so on). There is a tragic trade-off when the gospel is confused with sport, and, moreover, the more the chaplain conforms then the less likely the gospel's call for repentance and correction will be heard, for it loses its distinct voice and identity (Volf, 2011). Volf (2011: 95) aptly states that the gospel 'means the good news – something good, something *new*, and therefore something different'. Again, this does not mean that the prophetic stance of the gospel is merely dissent in that it only condemns what is wrong within a particular context (Biggar, 2011), for Jesus Christ as the source and substance of the good news affirms the created order as revealed in the incarnation and resurrection (O'Donovan, 1994).

Conclusion

In this chapter I have argued that the gospel justifies sinners which can not only liberate sportspersons but can transform how chaplains imagine and relate to such cultural realities as sport. The good news concerning Jesus Christ is both the basis of the identity of all sportspersons and the reason for sports chaplains to confront prophetically the concrete theological predicaments of the people of sport. The gospel calls chaplains back to the work of Christ as definitive for how they care for the people of sport. When sportspersons reflect and practise a distorted identity, chaplains must graciously speak in word and deed God's perspective on sport and life, no longer from an worldly vantage point but 'in Christ' as a 'new creation' (2 Cor. 5:16–17).

References

Biggar, N. (2011). *Behaving in Public: How to Do Christian Ethics*, Grand Rapids, MI: Eerdmans.
Bissinger, H.G. (2000). *Friday Night Lights: A Town, a Team, a Dream*, Cambridge, MA: Da Capo.
Brueggemann, W. (2001). *The Prophetic Imagination*, 2nd edn, MN: Fortress Press.
Budde, M.L., and R.W. Brimlow (2002). *Christianity Incorporated: How Big Business is Buying the Church*, Grand Rapids, MI: Brazos.
Coakley, J. (2009). *Sports in Society: Issues and Controversies*, 10th edn, Boston, MA: McGraw-Hill.
Collins, R. (2013). *Second Corinthians*, Grand Rapids, MI: Baker Academic.
Deford, F. (1976). 'Religion in Sport', *Sports Illustrated*, 44/16: 88–100.
Dzikus, L., R. Hardin and S. Waller (2012). 'Case Studies of Collegiate Sport Chaplains', *Journal of Sport and Social Issues*, 36/3: 268–94.
Ellis, R. (2014). *The Games People Play: Theology, Religion, and Sport*, Eugene, OR: Wipf & Stock.
Fogel, C. (2011). 'Sporting Masculinity on the Gridiron', *Canadian Social Science*, 7/2: 1–14.

Green, J.B., and M.D. Baker (2011). *Recovering the Scandal of the Cross: Atonement in New Testament and Contemporary Contexts*, 2nd edn, Downers Grove, IL: InterVarsity Press.

Hauerwas, S., and W. Willimon (1989). *Resident Aliens: Life in the Christian Colony*, Nashville, TN: Abingdon Press.

Holst, L. (2006). 'The Hospital Chaplain: Between Worlds', in L. Holst (ed.), *Hospital Ministry: The Role of the Chaplain Today*, Eugene, OR: Wipf & Stock, pp. 12–27.

Hughes, R. and J. Coakley (1991). 'Positive Deviance among Athletes: The Implications of Overconformity to the Sport Ethic', *Sociology of Sport Journal*, 8/4: 307–25.

Jüngel, E. (1999). 'On the Doctrine of Justification', trans. J. Webster, *International Journal of Systematic Theology*, 1/1: 24–52.

Kelsey, D. (2009). *Eccentric Existence: A Theological Anthropology*, vol. 2, Louisville, KY: Westminster John Knox Press.

Kotva, J.J., Jr. (2012). 'Hospital Chaplaincy as Agapeic Intervention', in M.T. Lysaught et al. (eds), *On Moral Medicine: Theological Perspectives in Medical Ethics, 3rd Ed.*, Grand Rapids, MI: Eerdmans, pp. 260–8.

Messner, M.A. (2007). *Out of Play: Critical Essays on Gender and Sport*, Albany, NY: SUNY Press.

Newbigin. L. (1986). *Foolishness to the Greeks: The Gospel and Western Culture*, Grand Rapids, MI: Eerdmans.

—— (2003). *Signs Amid the Rubble: The Purposes of God in Human History*, ed. Geoffrey Wainwright, Grand Rapids, MI: Eerdmans.

O'Donovan, O. (1994). *Resurrection and Moral Order*, 2nd edn, Leicester, UK: Apollos.

Sider, R. (1993). *Good News and Good Works: A Theology for the Whole Gospel*, Grand Rapids, MI: Baker.

Threlfall-Holmes, M., and M. Newitt (eds) (2011). *Being a Chaplain*, London, UK: SPCK.

Twietmeyer, G. (2007). 'Suffering Play: Can the Time Spent on Play and Games be Justified in a Suffering World', *Quest*, 59(2): 201–11.

Volf, M. (2011). *A Public Faith: How Followers of Christ Should Serve the Common Good,* Grand Rapids, MI: Brazos Press.

White, J. (2011). 'Sport and Christian Ethics: Towards a Theological Ethics for Sport', PhD thesis: University of Edinburgh.

—— (2012). 'How is the Gospel Relevant to Sports?', *Sports Spectrum* (Summer): 20.

10 Reformation pastoral care in the Olympic Village

Ashley Null

Introduction

When a chaplain has long-standing relationships with participants, to be working in the Athletes' Village during the Olympic Games is like attending ten funerals and one wedding every day. Many more sportspersons bury their dreams during the course of those 17 days than achieve them. Of course, chaplains have the unique opportunity to share the indescribable joy of a participant who has just fulfilled a life-long quest to attain the ultimate sporting achievement. However, chaplains also have the even greater privilege of standing-by and supporting the many more athletes who have just seen their life's dream shattered before their eyes and lying now in jumbled, jagged pieces at their feet. For in sport, every person's thrill of victory comes at the cost of many, many other people's agony of defeat. That is the nature of competition.

'It was the best of times; it was the worst of times'

Nothing made this harsh reality clearer to me than US Swimming's Olympic trials for Sydney 2000 in the 200m men's freestyle. The meet was in Indianapolis, and I had flown in to help with the daily 'Swimmers' Chapel', a programme led by Josh Davis, a three-time Olympic gold medallist at Atlanta – the most of any male athlete at those games. Despite such success, however, Josh had yet to achieve his life-long goal of breaking the American record in the men's 200m freestyle set by his childhood hero, Matt Biondi. His goal at these trials was to win a second trip to the Olympics with a time that established a new record in his signature event.

Davis' roommate in Indianapolis was Ugur Taner. Their stories could not have been more different. At 13, Davis was told by his coach to find another sport because he lacked promise. By 14, Taner had become the fastest American swimmer for his age ever. In 1992 Davis watched the Barcelona Games on television. Taner competed in them for Turkey as a dual citizen. But in 1996 the roles were reversed. Taner tried and just missed making the US team with Josh. This time it was Taner who was forced to follow the fortunes of his friends on television, while Davis went on to Olympic glory. Four years later, at 26, the 2000 trials were Taner's last chance to fulfil all those expectations that came from his incredible success as a high school student – the expectations of his coaches, of his family and of himself. As Taner (2008: 69) described it, 'less than 1 percent of all swimmers at the Trials actually make the team, so you can imagine the level of stress I felt preparing for competition'.

As was our usual routine at a major event, I went to Josh's hotel room at 4:00 pm to pray with him before the finals in the 200m freestyle that evening. Six months earlier, Ugur had become a Christian. As a Turkish American with a decidedly non-Christian family background, his decision to follow Christ had naturally been a great surprise to everyone. But Josh was overjoyed to have a fellow born-again believer on the US National Team, even if they were direct competitors in the 200m freestyle. So Ugur was invited to join our prayer session. I prayed with each swimmer individually, and then we all prayed together. We asked that God would enable both Josh and Ugur to fulfil their calling and have the peace, power and sense of God's presence to perform at their very best.

The race was very fast and heart-breakingly close. In less than two minutes it was all over. Josh had at long-last broken the American record. But Ugur had missed the Olympic team once again: this time by 1/100th of a second. Both felt a degree of emotional intensity neither had ever known before. For Josh it was joy and the hope of better things to come. For Ugur it was the bitter pain of the things deeply hoped for that could now never be. We three had dinner together afterwards – a simultaneous toasting of Josh's new record and a eulogy for Ugur's long-held athletic dream. I can only describe the meal as surreal. Josh tried desperately to be sensitive to Ugur; Ugur tried desperately to be happy for Josh; I tried desperately to help both sense God's presence with them at this equally momentous, but vastly different moment in their lives. Sitting at that table, I was confronted with hope and heartache, cheek-by-jowl, the epitome of life as an Olympic chaplain.

What should a chaplain say in such circumstances? How can anyone explain such a turn-of-events? Was 2/100ths of a second too much to ask from God Almighty? Did the Heavenly Watchman who promises neither to slumber nor sleep blink for a mere instant? Or did God just love Josh more? Was Ugur guilty of some secret moral failure, some deep hidden sin that made God think he did not deserve to make the team? Was Josh just more humble and Ugur too proud? Such questions may sound foolish, but not to a grieving sportsperson. When the sting of defeat is still white hot, the human heart cries out for answers. Even years later, when a person least expects it, something can trigger that old memory. Then, with breathtaking speed the pain rushes back in a moment, and the hunger for an explanation roars back to life all over again. As a common locker-room wall poster warns: 'defeat is worse than death because you have to live with defeat' (Hoffman, 2010: 152).

In the face of failure, it is all too easy for Christian athletes to see God as their ultimate coach. Those who feel they have made good spiritual choices often expect to be included on God's winning team and be blessed with athletic success. Those who have made bad choices can easily fear they will be left off the roster and cut out of any reward, at least until they can prove themselves to be better spiritually again. When Christian athletes lose, they cannot help but wonder what failure of regular Christian duty, what recent bad moral choice, or even what on-going inner unworthiness made God decide they were not good enough to have their best efforts blessed with success this time. As a result, in the very moment these athletes need help from their relationship with God the most, their faith can easily become just another reason to feel ashamed for being a loser. In the final analysis, the only thing worse at that moment for a competitor than feeling that they let their country, their coach, their teammates, their family, their friends and themselves down is thinking the reason for all this pain is that they have let God down, too.

Even winning is not without its emotional hazards. After years spent dreaming of how wonderful an Olympic victory is going to be, the thrill, as incredible as it is, fades so very quickly. And the next morning comes with its own fresh set of problems. Success in sport does not insulate winners from all the stresses and strains of normal life, including relationship problems. Indeed, with the elite status of being a world champion comes a whole new set of special problems: 'Who are my real friends? Does that person care about me, or just want to brag about knowing an Olympic gold medallist? How come everybody always expects something from me? How do I squeeze in all these appearances for my new sponsors while still training to stay on top? Isn't there any time any more just for me? What if I lose now? How long can I ride this wave? What happens to me when my body finally gives out? Why am I still not satisfied? If winning a gold medal didn't satisfy me, what will?'

An Olympic chaplain must understand the heart of all those who long to become champions, even when they achieve their goals as well as when they do not. In the face of all of the intense aspirations and anxieties that elite sports people encounter, chaplains must be convincing witnesses to the truth of God's enduring love and the power of his promises to deliver a peace and purpose that passes all human understanding. Indeed, this is the reason why chaplains are given access to the Olympic Village: to be at the side of those competitors who wish to turn to God in preparation for their events and then to help them make spiritual sense of the results afterwards.

Yet, Shirl Hoffman has suggested that special chaplains for elite sportspersons is fundamentally inappropriate:

> Chaplain ministries in hospitals, retirement centers, the military and even on college campuses are easily understood, but the rush to minister to the needs of an outrageously paid and catered-to group of elite entertainers who choose to participate in an enterprise that exacts heavy tolls on life, limb, and Christian witness is not. Usual justifications point to the peculiar pressures that face the athletic star: vulnerabilities brought on by instant riches, the demands of the press, the threat of injury, the dangers posed by sycophants, and the lure of inviting women. But unlike patients in hospitals and nursing homes who struggle with difficult circumstances beyond

their control, athletes struggle with pressures, anxieties, injuries, and emotional ups and downs brought on by circumstances of their own choosing. These are part of the bargain struck when they sign a contract or accept a scholarship.

(Hoffman, 2010: 235)

Of course, Hoffman's argument that people should be expected to lie alone in an uncomfortable bed of their own choosing equally applies to America's all-volunteer military, for whom he, as a US citizen, readily concedes the appropriateness of a chaplaincy ministry. The only difference between the two groups would seem to be Hoffman's implicit respect for soldiers who wage war and his evident disdain for the enterprise of elite sports and especially for those who engage in them. Yet a more impartial commentator would surely agree that the Olympic authorities would, in fact, be remiss in their duty of care for their participants should they fail to provide chaplains to offer professional support for competitors of faith. Despite Hoffman's objection, such a task is as crucial for these participants as it is complicated. What then should be a chaplain's approach to ministry to the sporting elite?

The Gospel as the antidote to the shame culture of elite sports

The greatest pastoral need for any overachiever is to understand that the gospel is the antidote to performance-based identity. Olympians are no exception. So many factors in competitive sports encourage athletes to base their self-worth on what they are able to prove they can do. More often than not, they are trained to feel good about themselves only when they are winning. As one athlete told a researcher, 'if you lose, you're nothing' (Hoffman, 2010: 210). When they do lose, they are expected to internalize a deep personal dissatisfaction with themselves. For only if their emotional experience of losing is sufficiently horrendous will they find the willpower to make every sacrifice necessary to claw their way back to self-respect by winning the next time. Current research only confirms how common amongst perfectionist sportspersons is the fear of failure with its attendant sense of worthlessness and shame (Sagar and Stoeber, 2009; Sagar, Boardely and Kavussanu, 2011).

According to Andre Agassi's (2009) lyrical and deeply illuminating autobiography *Open*, by the age of 7 he associated winning tennis tournaments with emotional safety: safety from his father's rage at his not being good enough, safety from his own sense of shame at failing to prove he was good enough, safety from his consequent deep self-loathing – a self-imposed emotional abuse which the mature Agassi labelled 'torture'. At age 10, a well-meaning coach told Agassi how to harness his shame for success:

You're hurting right now, hurting like heck, but that just means you care. Means you want to win. You can *use* that. Remember this day. Try to use this day as motivation. If you don't want to feel this hurt again, good, do everything you can to avoid it. Are you ready to do everything? I nod.

(Agassi, 2009: 55)

At 22, Agassi discovered that even achieving a Grand Slam was not enough to heal the wounds from all the self-torture which he had inflicted upon himself to gain such rewards. After his victory at Wimbledon, he realized that 'winning changes nothing . . . . A win doesn't feel as good as a loss feels bad, and the good feeling doesn't last as long as the bad. Not even close' (Agassi, 2009: 167). Because so many elite sportspersons instinctively shame themselves as the price of, and power for, excellence, most champions compete not to win, since the thrill of victory is so short-lived, but rather compete not to lose, so as to avoid the bitter sting of their own deeply cutting emotional self-flagellation.

Therefore, the first task of any chaplain to elite athletes is to help them learn to separate their personal identity from their athletic performance. For only love has the power to make human beings feel truly significant, not achievement. Only knowing that they are loved, regardless of their current performance, has the power to make Olympians feel emotionally whole.

Failure to make the crucial distinction between significance and achievement will forever hold the self-esteem of athletes hostage to all the ups and downs of competitive life. Like all human beings, elite athletes need to know that they are valued not for what they have or have done or what they may still do, but for who they are, with both their good points and their bad. Only really being loved, continuously, as they are, deep down inside, with all their fears and failures, with all their deeds and dreams, only that kind of love will give them a sense of worth and value that will not go away, even when their athletic prowess does.

Of course, the only source for an assured, steadfast, unconditional love is God himself. Christian sportspeople, therefore, have a wonderfully clear opportunity for a different source of identity. According to the Bible, their worth and value is to be found solely in the love God proved he has for them by dying for them on the cross. Such was the clear message of the Protestant Reformation's recovery of the Pauline doctrine of solifidianism (Null, forthcoming). While we were yet enemies, Christ died to reconcile us to God (Rom. 5:8–10), and, through the gift of personal faith (Rom. 3:23–4), sinners are reckoned righteous, despite their evident shortcomings (Rom. 4:5). There is now no condemnation for those in Christ Jesus (Rom. 8:1). They are adopted as God's own children forever (Rom. 8:15–17). Nothing in all creation can ever separate believers from the love of God as revealed in Jesus Christ (Rom. 8:31–9).

In the Reformation tradition, Christians do not merit either their justification or their sanctification, neither wholly by their own efforts nor in part by their cooperation with God's grace. Both right-standing with God and loving right afterwards like God are the work of God himself within the hearts of his children. Individuals must certainly make choices in the Christian life, but good choices are always and only the fruit of God's promise to be at work in believers, drawing them ever closer into fellowship with himself so that they may become more like him. Once again, Paul summed up this aspect of Reformation spirituality the best:

> Therefore, my dear friends, as you have always obeyed – not only in my presence, but now much more in my absence – continue to work out your salvation with fear and trembling, for it is God who works in you to will and to act according to his good purpose.
>
> (Phil. 2:12–13)

Naturally, obedience to the ways of God is an essential part of being a member of His family. However, in the end even obedience itself is a gift that comes to Christians because of God's faithfulness to bring them into full relationship with him. After all, if nothing will separate believers from the love of God in Christ Jesus, then the love of God must seek to drive out, little by little, although never fully in this life, the self-centeredness of their hearts which naturally shies away from divine intimacy. Only the power of divine love can allure human beings to learn to love serving God and others more than sin and selfishness.

Here is the true nature of God's unconditional love for his children. Implicit within the gift of love is a calling of another into relationship. And any relationship requires both individuals to give up some measure of autonomy so as to think of the other's needs and desires, at least a little. For sinners to accept the gift of God's love is to admit into their hearts a power from outside themselves that then tugs at their very self-centeredness, seeking to draw them out of themselves into relationship with him. Consequently, divine perfect love must seek to stir up in believers an equally full, unreserved selfless self-giving of all of themselves to their God. Therein lies the gospel's power as the greatest antidote to performance-based identity. For God himself has promised to keep loving sinners until his love makes them as lovely as he himself is. In the age to come they will be eternal splendours, shining brighter than the Milky Way, for they will be radiated by, and radiating to, the Trinity as well as one another the transforming unconditional love of God, forever.

Why is the Reformation's teaching about obedience as a gift such an important principle for chaplains to communicate to elite athletes? Only a proper understanding of sanctification by grace will save Christian athletes from seeing God as the ultimate 'bad dad' sports coach who cuts them from the team in the face of spiritual failure. Only knowing that personal holiness is God's gift, not another achievement they have to earn, will save elite sportspersons from fearing that God's love is as contingent on their performance as every affirmation in the Olympic world. Only knowing the true nature of grace will save Christian athletes from spiritual shame at the very moment they need to turn to God for help in fighting off sporting shame for failing to reach their competitive goals. Only knowing the alluring power of God's unconditional love will save elite sportspersons from turning to the treadmill of self-loathing, where they look to self-hatred as the best motivation for fighting sin harder so that they can win back divine approval to ensure that God will bless them with victory the next time. Only knowing the gospel will foster emotional wholeness in Christian athletes facing the immense pressures of Olympic competition (Null, 2008; for Roman Catholic perspectives, see Mazza, 2008; Novak, 1976).

Three Reformation pastoral questions

Once elite sportspersons have come to identify the love of God revealed in Jesus Christ as their enduring source of worth and value, they need learn how to apply this truth practically to their competitive life – especially during such an emotionally intense event as the Olympic Games. Once again, the insights of the Reformation prove helpful. According to the English Reformer Thomas Cranmer, grace produces gratitude; gratitude engenders love; love births repentance; repentance leads to good works: good works bring about a better society (Null, 2004). Christian athletes must first focus on what God has done for them through sport before they can seek to do something for God through sport. Three questions are particularly useful in enabling Christian athletes to experience the Reformation's integration of their faith and their sport: (1) How has God's gift of sport enabled you to experience joy? (2) How has God's gift of sport drawn you closer to Him? (3) How has God's gift of sport drawn you closer to others in His service?

How has God's gift of sport enabled you to experience joy?

Most evangelical sports theology begins with Jesus' parable of the talents (Matt. 25:14–30). Christian athletes are told that they have a responsibility to be good stewards of the gifts which God has given them: consequently, they need to honour God through developing their athletic talent (e.g. Athletes in Action, 1994: 13–15). While such an appeal to duty and obligation fits perfectly with the sporting world's expectation of performance-based affirmation, a Reformation understanding of Christian vocation does not begin with what believers must do for God but with what God has already done for them and not merely in justification but in sanctification as well. As the Apostle Paul taught, even the good works Christians do for God are actually God's gifts to them which he has carefully prepared in advance to give to them at the *kairos* moment (Eph. 2:10).

Of course, God ultimately intends his gifts to be used to build up the body (Eph. 4:12) and to promote unity with himself (Eph. 4:13). However, the first reason He gives good gifts to human beings is the evangelism of joy. As a witness to his providential care for humankind, God gives the people of the earth sun and rain, plenty of food to eat and the opportunity to turn their hand to a variety of activities in order that they may have joy (Deut. 16:16; Matt. 5:45; Acts 14:17). The Psalmist recognized sport as one of these joy-giving activities: 'In the heavens [God] has pitched a tent for the sun which is like a bridegroom coming forth from his pavilion, like a champion rejoicing to run his course' (19:4–5). By comparing the feeling champions experience when performing their sport to a honeymoon – intense physical satisfaction and emotional contentment all at the same time – the Bible could not offer much higher praise for the joy of sport. As a God-given gift, every race, every game, every performance is an opportunity to experience afresh the thrill that comes from doing something God designed the heart of every sportsperson to love. In the film *Chariots of Fire*, Eric Liddell aptly expressed this Reformation approach to sport: 'I believe God made me for a purpose, but he also made me fast, and when I run I feel his pleasure.'

The Bible teaches that such joy is essential for enduring the hardships of life. Paul noted that because of their former abundance of joy, the Galatians would have gladly plucked out their own eyes, if it would have relieved Paul of the suffering his own caused him (Gal. 4:15). Hebrews says that Jesus ignored the shame and endured the cross because of 'the joy set before him' (Heb. 12:2). Little wonder, then, that Nehemiah told the people of Jerusalem that 'the joy of the Lord is your strength' (Neh. 8:10).

Some Christian coaches today seek to harness joy, in particular the joy of relationships forged under fire, as a healthy alternative for motivating their athletes through the stress and strain of competition. Coach Biff Poggi of the Gilman, Maryland, High School football team, begins each new season with this pep talk:

> We're gonna go through this whole thing as a team. We are the Gilman football community. A *community*. This is the only place probably in your whole life where you're gonna be together and work together with a group as diverse as this – racially, socially, economically, you name it. It's a beautiful thing to be together like this. You'll never find anything else like it in the world – simply won't happen. So enjoy it. Make the most of this. It's yours . . . . The relationships you make here . . . you will always have them . . . for the rest of your life, the rest of your life. Cherish this, boys, cherish this.
>
> (cited in Marx, 2003: 44; cf. Ehrmann, 2011; Drape, 2009: 45–6)

Coach Poggi is a wise man. Despite the ups and downs of life in competitive sports, there is so much to cherish as part of that experience, especially the relationships formed along the way.

Now what is true for a high-school football season is so much more true of the privilege to be competing in the Olympic Games. As a result, the first task of a chaplain in the Olympic Village is to help participants savour the sheer joy of being an Olympian. One of the best ways to do so is to ask participants to reflect on all the blessings they have received from God through sport over the years – counting them one by one, as the old hymn says: all the people who have invested in them; all the friends they have made; all the places they have seen; all the maturity in Christ they have gained; all the love they have experienced. Nothing pushes back Olympic anxieties like realizing that nothing which will happen during the Games can ever take away the joys of the athletic journey that brought them there. Then, of course, there are all the wonderful experiences of Village life to relish while they last. For example, Josh Davis has famously compared worship in the Olympic religious services centre to a fore-taste of heaven; people from all lands and languages gathered together, acknowledging the goodness of God and his lordship over all, regardless of the results of their competition. Counting it all joy is the best way for participants to prepare for their competition and to take in stride the results when they come.

How has God's gift of sport drawn you closer to him?

The second reason God gives gifts to people is to draw them into ever deeper personal fellowship with him (Eph. 4:13). Martin Luther understood this principle and argued that a person's vocation was a divinely devised school of discipleship (see Wingren, 1957: 28–38). Consequently, God has equipped all vocations with 'trouble and toil' to confront Christians with their need to turn to Him in prayer to be changed according to his Word. Here is the practical arena where God acts on his promise to turn His children inside out, enabling them to learn to die daily to ego and reorienting them toward loving service to Him as well as others. By leaning on the promises of God and asking His Spirit to write them on their hearts daily, Christian athletes have a never-ending stream of opportunities to grow in living out the truths of their faith:

> that their identity is based on the cross, not on today's success or failure;
> that their power to give their all during competition comes not from their own willpower, but from Christ who is at work in them to strengthen and draw their wills to his, for discipline and endurance are the fruit of the Spirit (Gal. 5:22);
> that their right-standing with God stays constant because of God's grace, regardless of all chances and changes of the world of sport, even regardless of all the vagaries of their own faithfulness to him, in sorrow and in joy;
> that living by faith means to trust that the value of all the struggle, sweat and self-investment to become an Olympian is not ultimately determined by their results during the games but by God's faithfulness to use everything for his eternal purposes;
> that if their day of competition turns out to be Good Friday, just because they are Christians does not mean that the nails will not hurt; however, God is a good steward of pain. The stinging bitterness of defeat will not have the last word. Easter will come. It may take three days, three years or even three decades, but Easter will come. God is faithful to work all things together for good (Rom. 8:28).

For so many Christian competitors in the Olympic Village, the games become the school of discipleship where they face the crucifixion of their deepest held aspirations as part of a divine plan to enable them to experience first-hand an even deeper joy of seeing God's love work all things together for good at the *kairos* moment.

How has God's gift of sport drawn you closer to others in his service?

If Luther emphasized vocation as a divine means to deepen individual faith, Calvin emphasized vocation as the divine call to take that deepened faith and work to restore human beings and their life together to God's intention in creation (Niebuhr, 1951). Once sportspeople have reflected on the joy God has given them through sport and the intimacy they have gained with Jesus as a result, they are equipped to make a difference for Christ. For now they have more joy and more of Jesus to share.

The Olympic Games offer so many opportunities to restore both sport and the people of sport to God's purposes. By how they participate in the games (Weir and Daniels, 2004), Christian athletes can witness to sport as something other than overly commercialized entertainment whose stars believe that 'you ain't trying if you ain't cheating' (Hoffman, 2010: 210). They can compete drug-free and in the spirit of the rules, not just by the letter, thus showing a credible alternative to the win-at-all-cost mentality that so pervades the Olympics. They can reject treating their opponent as an adversary who threatens their identity, but rather value them as a co-worker whose achievement and active resistance will call forth in the Christian a higher standard of sporting excellence which could not be achieved alone (Weir and Daniels, 2004). They can give their all during competition, expecting to sense Jesus' presence within them, since when they are in motion they are in harmony with the purpose for which Christ created them. When fear of failure whispers in their ear that they are going to lose, they can refuse to pull back, even though giving less than their best would make defeat easier to bear. For, ironically, it is easier psychologically to feel guilty for not having tried hard enough, than to feel powerless to have changed the situation. Consequently, Christian athletes can give everything they have to the very last moment of their competition, despite knowing that to do so will only intensify their emotional pain should they, in the end, fail. In victory, they can exhibit humility and gratitude, realizing that most other Christian athletes have worked just as hard and prayed as much, but God had set aside other gifts than Olympic success for them. In defeat, they can refuse to torture themselves with self-loathing or shame those on their team whose failures may have contributed to their own disappointment. They can rejoice for those who win and weep with those who have not, regardless of their own situation. They can, in short, bring the joy and hope of Jesus to all they meet which, of course, is the very best form of evangelism.

When God allows Olympians to see the difference their life and witness to Jesus have made in other people's lives – whether over a conversation in the locker room after a game in the Olympic stadium, over a cappuccino in the Village McCafe or in front of a bank of cameras before a televised audience of billions – that joy, that real joy, abides long after the Closing Ceremonies are over, even long after their physical prowess is gone. In the light of that joy, all the heart-ache along the way will seem as mere mosquito bites, real but only momentary pains of no lasting significance (2 Cor. 4:17).

Conclusion: God's redeeming love

In the Christian life, God takes all of his children on journeys they do not wish to go. He makes them travel by roads they do not wish to use. All so that he can bring them to places they never wish to leave. With Jesus, pain, no matter how great – even when of Olympic proportions – never has the last word. Nothing has made this hopeful reality clearer to me as an Olympic chaplain than watching God's pastoral care of Josh Davis and Ugur Taner since the 2000 Trials.

In 2004 Davis himself tasted the bitter disappointment of not qualifying for another Olympics. He would eventually retire to concentrate on his great love – motivating people to dream great dreams and achieve their best. In the intervening years, he has had the joy of speaking to literally hundreds of thousands of people. Today, amongst many other activities, he leads the Mutual of Omaha Breakout Swim Clinics, dispensing advice on technique, motivation and a healthy spiritual life to age-group swimmers all around the US.

And Taner? Faced with the death of his life-long ambition so shortly after he became a Christian, Ugur had to immediately wrestle deep within his soul as to why he had turned away from his family background to come to Jesus. Had he in reality just tried to take out an 'insurance policy'? Was he merely hoping to get the Christian God on his side so he would surely win his place on the Olympic team like Josh? If so, now was the time to admit his mistake, move on and move away from the Christian lies he had so foolishly listened to. Or were the claims of Christ true? Was Jesus' love in his heart more than enough to make life worth living, regardless of his loss? If so, now Ugur needed to lean on the grace of God to sustain him through all his doubts and despair until God made clear to him a new, deeply satisfying direction for his future.

In the end, Taner discovered that Jesus' love would not let him go. Despite the ups and downs of coming to terms with never being a US Olympian, Ugur found his trust, hope, love and even, yes, gratitude towards his saviour growing little by little with every passing day. And Ugur was not the only person to notice the deepening, maturing faith at work in him. Liesl, his not-yet-Christian wife, was too close not to see the changes happening to this man she loved so much. She had wanted nothing else but to heal her husband's broken heart, but her own heart broke when she discovered she could not. Then, when she saw Jesus doing for her husband what she longed to see, she found herself slowly falling in love with a saviour who so clearly loved her husband as deeply as she did. Four years later, Ugur's long-standing prayers were answered. At the *kairos* moment, Liesl became a Christian, and together they began to build a new family heritage – a Christian heritage – that they now share with six wonderful children. Today, they manage a large swimming school in California, and their lives continue to focus on the joy of serving Jesus, not because he made Ugur's Olympic dreams come true, but because Christ fulfilled an even deeper desire in Ugur's heart – to have a family knit close together in Christ – and Jesus did it in a completely unexpected but fully effective way. In the end, Christian Olympians, regardless of their performance during the Games, will find their 'mouths filled with laughter and their tongues with songs of joy'. For with Jesus all God's children will one day be able to say: 'The Lord has done great things for us, and we are filled with joy' (Ps. 126: 2–3).

References

Agassi, A. (2009). *Open: An Autobiography*, New York: A.A. Knopf.

Athletes in Action (1994). *The Total Athlete*, Lebanon, OH: Campus Crusade for Christ.

Drape, J. (2009). *Our Boys: A Perfect Season on the Plains with the Smith Center Redmen*, New York: Times Books.

Ehrmann, J. (2011). *Inside Out Coaching: How Sports Can Transform Lives*, New York: Simon & Schuster.

Hoffman, S. (2010). *Good Game: Christianity and the Culture of Sports*, Waco, TX: Baylor University Press.

Marx, J. (2003). *Season of Life: A Football Star, a Boy, a Journey to Manhood*, New York: Simon & Schuster.

Mazza, C. (2008). 'The Pastoral Ministry of Sport: Taking Stock and Looking Ahead', in *Sport: An Educational and Pastoral Challenge*, Vatican City: Liberia Editrice Vaticana, 31–59.

Niebuhr, H.R. (1951). *Christ and Culture*, New York: Harper & Brothers.

Novak, M. (1976). *The Joy of Sports: End Zones, Bases, Baskets, Balls, and the Consecration of the American Spirit*, New York: Basic Books.

Null, A. (2004). 'Thomas Cranmer's Theology of the Heart', *Trinity Journal for Theology and Ministry*, 1: 18–34.

—— (2008). '"Finding the Right Place": Professional Sport as a Christian Vocation', in Donald Deardorff and John White (eds), *The Image of God in the Human Body: Essays on Christianity and Sports*, Lewiston, NY: Edwin Mellen, 313–66.

—— (forthcoming). 'Cranmer and Paul', in J. Linebaugh and M. Allen (eds), *Reformation Readings of Paul*, Downers Grove, IL: InterVarsity Press.

Sagar, S.S., and J. Stoeber (2009). 'Perfectionism, Fear of Failure, and Affective Responses to Success and Failure: The Central Role of Fear Experiencing Shame and Embarrassment', *Journal of Sport and Exercise Psychology*, 31: 602–27.

Sagar, S.S., I.D. Boardly and M. Kavussanu (2011). 'Failure and Student Athletes' Interpersonal Antisocial Behaviour in Education and Sport', *British Journal of Educational Psychology*, 81: 391–408.

Taner, U. (2008). 'Pursuing God', in J. Davis (ed.), *The Goal and the Glory*, Ventura, CA: Regal Books, 68–9.

Weir, J.S., and G. Daniels (2004). *Born to Play!*, Bicester, Oxon: Frampton House.

Wingren, G. (1957). *Luther on Vocation*, trans. Carl C. Rasmussen, Philadelphia: Muhlenberg Press.

Part III

Sports chaplaincy

Practice and praxis

11 Beyond praying for players

An exploration of the
responsibilities and practices
of sports chaplains

Anthony M.J. Maranise

Introduction

In September 2007 the Pontifical Council for the Laity's Church and Sport section of the Roman Catholic Church convened an international seminar on the theme of sports chaplains in Vatican City. Cardinal Stanislaw Rylko (2008: 7) suggested that sport inherently contains 'extraordinary educational potential' and that sports chaplains 'play a decisive role in helping people to find a greater sense of meaning in a life subject to moral and physical challenges'. Though sports chaplains were in existence long before 2007, the fact that the emergence of such a ministry, pedagogy and profession captured the interest of the world's largest religious denomination speaks volumes about the need for further academic study, spiritual formation and professionalization in this rapidly expanding field.

Today, sports chaplaincy is no longer an 'abstract profession': that is, one that individuals are sceptical about in terms of academic training or rigour. Several institutions throughout the world now offer academic courses of study in sports chaplaincy such as Baylor University (US) and the University of Gloucestershire (UK). In this chapter, I describe and discuss six primary responsibilities and practices common to all sports chaplains, regardless of their country of origin and service, including: fostering inclusion among all religious traditions, recognizing the abilities and limitations of chaplaincy within sports, balancing both a ministerial and academic role, and serving with a sense of 'mission-mindedness'. This discussion leads to the conclusion that sports chaplains provide a valuable resource – both to athletes and to the people they regularly encounter – by assisting in the holistic growth and development of each person entrusted to their care.

What a sports chaplain expects and what to expect from a sports chaplain

The sports chaplain is 'a lay or ordained member of the clergy who provides spiritual care for athletes' (Waller, Dzikus, and Hardin, 2010). Speaking about the kinds of care and support that athletes might need, Francesco (2008) argues that it is useful for sports chaplains to have an understanding of the various challenges which sports performers may face in their everyday lives. For example, one of the most common challenges that a sports chaplain is likely to encounter is that of an athlete suffering from spiritual and emotional trauma following a major or career ending injury. According to a recently compiled list of frequently overlooked causes of emotional and psychological trauma, sports injuries ranks number 1 (Robinson, Segal and Smith, 2013). The fact that this challenge is commonly overlooked simply provides more evidence to illustrate that there is a need for athlete-specific intervention and training through chaplaincy. Also appearing on this list are recovery from surgery (which many athletes undergo to correct previous injuries), the breakup of a significant relationship (which is often a very personal and private matter and deeply masked – causing more emotional self-injury – and which could include the breaking off of a relationship with a team) and humiliating or deeply disappointing experiences (which, for many athletes, may simply constitute performing below their own self-imposed levels of expectation or the expectations of coaches, parents and spectators). These are but a few of the challenges in the lives of athletes wherein sports chaplains can be of assistance. Many such scenarios are highly superficial or exterior (things that first happen in the public eye but then become an internalized personal issue). However, athletes also experience interior struggles that may never become public but which may affect their performance levels – for example, relationships with teammates and family – and even their physical health. That said, athletes can sometimes face added responsibilities in their lives. While the general population may be responsible for their spouse, their work, their home, their children and their social and religious livelihood, athletes often concern themselves with practice, exercise and dietary regimen, as well as performance-skill maintenance and improvement. Stress levels may be magnified by the expectations of those who watch their every move and by a series of self-imposed expectations ('self-magnification'), which are based on the premise that improvement in performance will diminish exterior stressors. In this case, athletes might begin to participate in sport for reasons other than entertainment, leisure, camaraderie or enjoyment (the healthy reasons for competition) and may instead 'seek to unload their frustrations via sport making it an escape valve for social disorder' (Nanni, 2008: 15). Sports chaplains must be prepared to respond quickly to these types of emotional/spiritual/existential crises which, if left unattended, can become crises of faith with far-reaching and chronic negative effects in other areas and aspects of life.

Sports chaplains, regardless of their own religious denominational or organizational affiliation, fulfil their share of responsibility in the institutional settings which they frequent, many of which, like counselling and responding to spiritual and emotional crises, comprise the mainstay of their role. However, there are some responsibilities that are specific to sports chaplains alone. According to Johnson (2008), sports chaplains have six distinct responsibilities both to the individual athletes and to the teams with which they work. These include: (1) displaying and maintaining a spirit of inclusivity for all religious traditions, beliefs and spiritual practices: that is, making sure that no athlete in need is excluded because of personal indifference to religious or spiritual belief or practice; (2) balancing the requirements to be both 'clerical' or 'ministerial' in style as well as academic in educational standards and technique; (3) cultivating relationships which are trustworthy and non-judgemental while maintaining a professional attitude and respecting athlete confidentiality; (4) encouraging introspection and reflection based on 'big-picture thinking' or the idea that an athlete ought to view themselves, their performance, and their team as parts of an integrated whole; (5) serving with a 'mission-mindedness': that is, realizing that as a chaplain, one's services are provided at no cost therefore sports chaplains should not expect regular pay (however, if the team which they work for is large enough, they may obtain travel expenses and have use of office space); and, finally, (6) recognizing the limitations of their role as a chaplain, namely, that they are 'not in a position to "run the show" [at an athletic event, practice, or otherwise] but to help coordinate the spiritual care and in many cases the psychological support' of the athletes entrusted to them (Fair and Warden, 2012: 29).

All are welcome

Of the first responsibility of sports chaplains – that of inclusivity – a fascinating critique is commonly put forward by opponents of the idea that there is any common ground between (or any benefit in the combination of) sport and the spiritual life. Why so much talk of inclusion if sport is inherently exclusive? In this view, critics fail to acknowledge the needs of the people who animate and give life to sport itself, focusing instead on the nature of the game. Granted, sports are inherently competitive; where there is a competitive game, there must be a winner and a loser (Maranise, 2013). However, there could be no game at all if there first were not athletes to animate the sport and these athletes – human beings that they are – need spiritual and emotional support from time to time. Therefore, in order to ensure that no athlete is excluded from being able to speak to a chaplain openly and receive the appropriate care due to them, they must feel accepted and welcomed for who they already are rather than for who anyone else (coach, parent, chaplain) might wish them to be. While a sports chaplain may be of a specific religious affiliation, he or she is only permitted to discuss, preach, counsel or teach within that faith tradition to athletes who share that same faith. However, the chaplain ought not to be afraid 'to engage even with players who are atheist or agnostic' (Johnson, 2008).

Sports chaplains as academics and ministers

Performing a successful 'balancing act' is the second key responsibility of sports chaplains. At any time, the chaplain must be able to switch back and forth between the utilization of their academic training (for purposes of explanation, counselling or spiritual assessment) and their clerical responsibilities. The academic body of knowledge often covered by sports chaplains will naturally include their chaplaincy training but would usually also include a thorough knowledge of some field within religious studies, be it theology, ministry, comparative religion, biblical studies or even spirituality. Within these studies, typically, the sports chaplain will focus – whether known or unknown to them – on an emerging academic field known as 'sport spirituality', the study, integration, comprehension and application of which is vital to the success of their ministry to and workings with athletes. Sport spirituality, as an academic pursuit, has a variety of course descriptions; however, one seems to have become widely accepted within literature on the subject. Mazza (2008: 48) states that 'a spirituality of sport tends to form athletes in sensitivity towards what is of real and endless value, namely the recognition of "the divine" in sport, gratitude to "the divine" and the building of solidarity and fraternity'. Without question, athletes cannot be athletes forever for eventually age or infirmity weakens all. However, through academic study and careful application of sport spirituality, chaplains can convey the 'everlasting value' of sports participation to athletes which has the potential to reach far beyond their active sporting careers. In this way, 'sport unites people in a common goal' (Clemens, 2008: 57) and actually becomes a school of life teaching athletes by experience a plethora of socio-spiritual growth opportunities. For example, when an athlete faces a disappointing loss against an opponent, they must internalize the errors which led to the loss whether those errors be their own or those of their teammates. From that internalization, they must learn the means of correcting those errors. This process of 'skill improvement' teaches athletes something valuable in relation to the skills and attributes of social life, namely, that when faced with a difficult loss (such as that of a loved one), one must internalize this loss, regroup and move forward. Although this is only one isolated example, there exist numerous socio-spiritual growth opportunities in sport (see Clemens, 2008; Maranise, 2009; Parry et al., 2007) which, if properly studied, taught and utilized, allow chaplains to develop 'a pro-educational stance and an ongoing spiritual cultivation' within the lives of those with whom they work (Mazza, 2008: 59). Within the 'balancing act' of sports chaplaincy is also the non-academic side of their work: that of their clerical or ministerial responsibilities. Johnson (2008) describes the clerical aspects of sports chaplaincy, highlighting the need for the chaplain to be ever-ready and always 'available for pastoral care – baptisms, wedding preparations, deaths – and . . . a variety of Bible studies'. This ministerial role is often the most common, as it includes their service as spiritual counsellors and advisors. It is vital to remember that the sporting competitions viewed annually by so many in the US whether on television, in-person or even practised in their own lives 'magnifies only a corner of the sports world; there is also real life' (Carter, 1996: 157). That said, athletes inevitably face similar life circumstances as those of the general population which require the assistance of a lay minister or member of the clergy.

Building and maintaining appropriate relationships

Cultivating unique relationships with athletes is of paramount importance if a sports chaplain wishes to be successful in ministry. This is their third primary responsibility. What makes these relationships unique is that the sports chaplain must, at all times, be (or at least be viewed by athletes) as trustworthy, non-judgemental and able to keep the contents of personal conversations confidential. While it is common knowledge that people are most open, honest and comfortable around those whom they can both relate to and trust, several studies also evidence this fact. For example, Axner and Nagy (2013: 3) argue that 'in a climate of trust, people are a whole lot more likely to tell you what is on their mind'. In a similar vein, when an athlete seeks spiritual counsel from a chaplain, they may often be seeking guidance related to deeply personal matters of faith (such as actions committed which they may consider sinful and for which they often may feel ashamed). In such instances, the athlete needs to know that the chaplain will not judge them for their actions nor will the contents of their private consultations be disclosed. To that end, this area of sports chaplaincy has raised many eyebrows in the academic community regarding whether or not chaplains should be able to administer any sort of counselling to athletes should they not possess licensure for professional or pastoral counselling. Despite these concerns, an important distinction must be made between legal confidentiality in counselling (such as conversations in which one might engage with a licensed professional counsellor, a masters' level practitioner who uses 'talk therapy' and 'coping skills', or a psychologist, a doctoral level clinician, who may diagnose disorders and seek to offer cognitive behavioural therapy or refer individuals to a psychiatrist from whom they could obtain medication to aid in treating their conditions) and privileged communication. Confidentiality may best be described as an ethical decision not to reveal what is learned in the context of a professional relationship without the consent of the counselee unless statements made during a session indicate a credible threat to the safety of others (Fair and Warden, 2012). On the other hand, privileged communication 'is the same as confidentiality but is codified in law' (Levicoff, 1991: 141). Levicoff goes on to elaborate: 'Under a privileged communication statute, a minister [or chaplain] acting in his professional capacity as a spiritual advisor cannot be forced to reveal the content of confidential communications to any outside party, including a court of law' (ibid).

In the US, 'privileged communication is a legally defined class of confidential communication which is immune from court testimony' (Lyons, 2001: 34) through which an individual can discuss concerns, personal issues or actions which they consider sinful with either a lay minister or clergyperson, either of whom may serve in the role of chaplain. Current legal regulations in-place in the US extend the protected status of privileged communication to any lifestyle coach, counsellor or lay-chaplain so long as they 'first agree or contract with the client not to discuss the contents of the meeting with any third-parties unless appropriately referred' (Lyons, 2001: 96) when the situations expressed by the client are beyond the reach of competence of the person performing the counselling.

Only lay-persons serving as sports chaplains in the US would be required to agree or contract with the client in writing in order to ensure the protected status of privileged communication. Ordained members of the clergy are exempt from having to do this and are still guaranteed such protected communication 'based on the premises that free, honest, uninhibited communication between certain parties creates healing' which is a primary or expected role of a clergy person 'serving in the capacity as a spiritual advisor or confessor' (Lyons, 2001: 96).

Having the assurance of privileged communication would undoubtedly provide an athlete seeking the assistance of a chaplain with the sense of a more significant 'climate of trust' thereby allowing the athlete to feel more comfortable discussing vulnerable issues with the chaplain concerned. For their spiritual, emotional and existential needs, 'athletes also place tremendous trust in their chaplains' (Waller, Dzikus and Hardin, 2008: 119), finding in them people who are simultaneously 'readily approachable and totally trustworthy' (Moore, 2007). In these arguments, it is clearly illustrated 'that sport chaplains may serve as spiritual leaders, counselors, mentors or any combination of the three' (Dzikus, Hardin and Waller, 2012: 288) and can be most successful in those functions by cultivating a 'climate of trust' with the athletes who seek their pastoral care.

To inform but never with intention to conform

Fourth in the list of key responsibilities for nearly all sports chaplains is never to proselytize or to inform the athlete about how they might think or feel but to guide them to make such discoveries about themselves for themselves. Through encouraging introspection, the sports chaplain serves as a guide to help the athlete navigate the significance of their own thoughts and feelings as they pertain to their personal and professional lives. This responsibility is certainly one which is critical to the role of the sports chaplain because, as previously mentioned; sport is a human activity (Mazza, 2008) and to that end, is never played out in a social vacuum. Sporting activities – even those which are seemingly (and are argued by many to be) individual sports such as golf, wrestling, swimming or weight-training – are, in fact, collective in the sense that, although the individual competes on their own, others still compete with them, against them as their opponents, they have families and friends who support their efforts and, lest we forget, spectators, who constantly critique their performance for good or for ill. Because sport is a collective enterprise, it becomes the charge of the chaplain to guide the athlete in their processes of introspection into a realization that their participation in sport is always part of an integrated whole. Kerrigan (2008: 25) argues that 'rather than individual success, the importance of contributing to a group effort is emphasized'. In this sense, an athlete's realization that his or her individual success contributes to the success of an entire club, family or social unit can magnify the joy they experience in such successes. Further, when an athlete is unsuccessful, the stressors or burden of guilt that they may experience from the loss may be mitigated by the realization that their club, family, or social unit is a sort of 'de facto support system'. This responsibility of the chaplain becomes vital as he or she prepares athletes for successful contributions to society beyond merely those of entertainment. Through guided interior reflection of an athlete's performance, personal life, spirituality, morality, work ethic, weaknesses and strengths, the chaplain serves to reveal to the athlete their 'potential for positive formation of life skills in other areas such as family, community, and work' (ibid) thereby allowing them to see their sports participation as part of life's much 'bigger picture'.

A 'call' to service, not simply a job

Common to all chaplains, regardless of their area of specialization, whether it be military, hospital, school, law enforcement or even sport, must be the ever-present awareness of their 'mission-mindedness': that is, the fact that chaplains serve at the request and needs of others. Johnson (2008) explains of sports chaplains specifically that, 'none of us [chaplains] are paid by the teams' they serve, but rather are 'on-staff' through chaplain organizations and are 'attached' to a particular team in which their services are requested, invited or needed. That said, many sports chaplains 'are responsible for developing their own funding base' (see Fellowship of Christian Athletes, 2009: 59). Fundraising is important to the non-profit, mission-minded, nature of the chaplain's work. Though some sports chaplains may travel with their teams for free (on-invitation by coaching staff) and may be offered other perks for their work including free meals and team apparel, chaplains must never neglect their mission of service to all athletes in need (even if these are athletes on an opposing team), nor must the chaplain develop any attitudes or expectations which might otherwise be deemed unethical. Although different sports chaplaincy organizations may hold their chaplains to separate, yet carefully regulated and supervised, standards of accountability and ethics, each club or sporting institution may also 'establish limits on what a chaplain should be doing in association with the team' (Waller, Dzikus and Hardin, 2008: 115). These limits, standards of professionalization and lines of accountability reinforce the reality of a chaplain's duties and responsibilities in service to others rather than for the benefit of self. It can be argued that the results of a sports chaplain's work and ministry is, in itself, its own form of payment and reward. Constantini (2008: 94) argues that the work of the chaplain 'is that of accompanying, orienting, coaching [athletes, coaches, and spectators alike] in sacrifice, giving them hope, and helping them to constructively build their life project'. For the chaplain, knowing that they may have in any way positively contributed to the course and direction of one of their athletes' lives becomes not only their motivation to continue in their service but simultaneously allows for the enrichment and improvement of their own lives (Holm, 2009). While it is of great importance that a chaplain never neglects their mission and service, it is equally important that they do not allow themselves to become 'enslaved' to or by any athlete, coach or (club) staff member or that a state of dependency is created between themselves and their athlete(s). Chaplains may voluntarily assist other support staff such as managers, equipment distributors and the like, however, while being humble and genuine in one's endeavours, a sports chaplain must also be realistic. The sports chaplain provides a service, not a right or entitlement. Therefore, if the service of the chaplain is being abused or distorted by any athlete(s), coach or member of staff at the institution concerned, the chaplain ought to declare this conflict with their organizational authority as well as with the head coach so that the issue might be resolved. Service must at all times remain voluntary – both for the chaplain and those who seek, genuinely, the chaplain's assistance.

Serving in and out of bounds

The final of the six major responsibilities of sports chaplains is a clearly defined understanding of their own limitations. Chaplains, of any service coverage, are 'not in a position to "run the show"' (Fair and Warden, 2012: 29). In the context of sport, this means that a chaplain ought not to overstep his or her boundaries and attempt to assert, for example, their coaching insights or opinions on player performance but should be, most of all, a sure, strong, steady and resolute presence. While it may seem as if the chaplain is merely an isolated figure or one that should fade into the background until called upon, the exact opposite is true. The presence of the chaplain at all or at least many of their team's events (practices, meals, games) 'will create an identity among the coaches and the players' (Fellowship of Christian Athletes, 2013: 9; see also Lipe, 2006, 2013). Once the chaplain has established a reliable, trustworthy and credible identity within the context of the team, they can maintain a presence without necessarily being present physically or visibly. In other words, over time the team members and coaching staff will become aware that they have a resource at their service should the need arise. Finally, while there is certainly something substantial to be said about the importance of a chaplain being present for those they serve, it is also true that a chaplain ought to be active in their service and ministry even when not actively called upon by an individual athlete or team of athletes or coach, so long as this is clearly within their limitations.

The continuation of sports chaplaincy

Before concluding, it is important that a call be made for further research into this sorely neglected field. To date, there has been some work carried out around the vitality and usefulness of sports chaplaincy (cf. Dzikus, Hardin and Waller, 2012; Gamble, Hill and Parker, 2013; Waller, Dzikus and Hardin, 2008, 2010). However, given the rapid rate of growth in the number of both professional and volunteer sports chaplains and the formation of host agencies and organizations, more research is necessary. As previously discussed, the realm of sport provides numerous opportunities to bring together for the common good individuals within our own nations. This coming together to participate or to witness at various sporting events has become a phenomenon throughout the world, especially as it pertains to soccer, which is the sport with the largest international following. In an increasingly unpredictable economic, political, social and cultural climate, maintaining normalcy in life is crucial to positive holistic health and human well-being. Because sport is not automatically generated for our entertainment but is done so by human beings, it stands to reason that those who animate and give life to this form of normalcy (in that it brings people together for a common purpose and, in many cases, has a sort of cathartic effect), also need the support of others to ensure their own sense of normalcy. To this end, sports chaplains serve in a foundational way to enhance the world of sport in all its various guises.

Conclusion

In conclusion, though the idea may seem farfetched to many, if athletes were to become so overburdened by the stresses of their performance (and related lifestyle factors) that they became a threat to themselves and others, what would become of sport in our own nations and throughout the world? What would become of this unifying force that brings so many people together? Imagine if multiple or all major sports organizations went on strike (or were punished for unethical behaviour by sanctions, as they have been in the past) simultaneously. Already, the world of sport, while incredibly valuable in terms of economic and social stature, stands in need of special attention as Kerrigan (2008: 25) notes:

> The temptation to 'win at all costs' dominates sports, as evidenced by the current scandals of athletes fixing results for gambling purposes, using steroids and other performance enhancing substances, and the temptation to beyond commercialize sports so that athletes and spectators alike are seemingly reduced to commodities and exploited for financial gain.

Alongside such issues, reports of athlete lifestyle behaviours which appear in the media can, if allowed to go unchecked, pose threats to common civility and morality. The use of sports chaplains could certainly be instrumental in the resolution of such concerns as well as the maintenance of normalcy in the lives of athletes themselves. In turn, sports chaplains may well serve a vital role as first responders to any emergency which may take place at an athletic institution or event. While such occurrences are rare, the greater role of sports chaplains within both the emerging interest and practice of holistic care would certainly be the implementation and continual maintenance of 'an "ethical mentality" in sport that is capable of producing coherent acts and positive and virtuous dispositions' (Mazza, 2008: 43). In this way, the sense of normalcy which sport as a whole provides to the international community is able to remain free from disruption.

References

Axner, M., and J. Nagy (2013). 'Understanding People', in B. Berkowitz and K. Nagy (eds), *The Community Toolbox: Core Functions in Leadership*, Lawrence, KS: University of Kansas Work Group for Community Health and Development.

Carter, S. (1996). *Integrity*, New York: Harper Perennial.

Clemens, J. (2008). 'The Sport Chaplain and the Work of Youth Formation', in *Sport: An Educational and Pastoral Challenge*, Vatican City: Libreria Editrice Vaticana, 83–9.

Constantini, E. (2008). 'What Athletes Look For in a Sport Chaplain', in *Sport: An Educational and Pastoral Challenge*, Vatican City: Libreria Editrice Vaticana, 93–4.

Dzikus, L., R. Hardin and S. Waller (2012). 'Case Studies of Collegiate Sport Chaplains', *Journal of Sport and Social Issues*, 36/3: 268–94.

Fair, D., and L. Warden (2012). 'Certified Master Chaplain', online course content: American Board for Certification in Homeland Security, CMC101. Available at <www.abchs.com>.

Fellowship of Christian Athletes (FCA) (2009). 'Raising Support for the Ministry', in *Chaplain's Training Playbook: Training Excellence in Sports Ministry: 2009*, Kansas City, MO: FCA, 59–66.

—— (2013). 'A Ministry of Presence', in *Chaplain's Training Playbook: Training Excellence in Sports Ministry: 2013*, Kansas City, MO: FCA, 9–14.

Francesco, E. (2008). 'What Athletes Look for in a Sport Chaplain', in *Sport: An Educational and Pastoral Challenge*, Vatican City: Libreria Editrice Vaticana, 95–7.

Gamble, R., D.M. Hill and A. Parker (2013). '"Revs and Psychos": Impact and Interaction of Sport Chaplains and Sport Psychologists within English Premiership Soccer', *Journal of Applied Sport Psychology*, 25: 249–64.

Holm, N. (2009). 'Toward a Theology of the Ministry of Presence in Chaplaincy', *Journal of Christian Education*, 52/1: 7–22.

Johnson, A. (2008). '6 Things You Should Know . . . about Being a Team Chaplain', interview by A.K. Clemmons (23 Oct.). Available at <http://sports.espn.go.com/espn/print?id=3659969&type=story>.

Kerrigan, M. (2008). 'Sports in the Christian Life', in Center for Christian Ethics at Baylor University (ed.), *Sports*, Waco, TX: Baylor University Press, 19–27.

Levicoff, S. (1991). *Christian Counseling and the Law*, Chicago: Moody Press.

Lipe, R.D. (2006). *Transforming Lives in Sport: A Guide for Sports Chaplains and Sports Mentors*, Kearney, NE: Cross Training Publishing.

—— (2013). *Free to Compete: Reflections on Sport from a Christian Perspective*, Kearney, NE: Cross Training Publishing.

Lyons, R. (2001). 'A Chaplain's Guide to Privileged Communication', PhD thesis, Duke University.

Maranise, A. (2009). 'Practice makes Perfect: Growing Spiritually through Sports Participation', *Catholic World: A Journal at the Intersection of Faith and Culture*, 243/1453: 1–4.

—— (2013). 'Superstition and Religious Ritual: An Examination of their Effects and Utilization in Sport', *Sport Psychologist*, 27: 83–91.

Mazza, C. (2008). 'The Pastoral Ministry of Sport: Taking Stock and Looking Ahead', in *Sport: An Educational and Pastoral Challenge*, Vatican City: Libreria Editrice Vaticana, 31–59.

Moore, R. (2007). 'The Gospel according to James', *fca.org*. Available at <http://www.webfca.com/national/vsItemDisplay.lsp&objectID=0CA08459–4C7F–49C5–8AB406DBE60D7BAB&method=display>.

Nanni, C. (2008). 'Sport and the Educational Emergency', in *Sport: An Educational and Pastoral Challenge*, Vatican City: Libreria Editrice Vaticana, 13–29.

Parry, J. et al. (eds) (2007). *Sport and Spirituality: An Introduction*, New York: Routledge.

Robinson, L., J. Segal and M. Smith (2013). 'Emotional and Psychological Trauma: Symptoms, Treatment, and Recovery', *HelpGuide*. Available at <http://www.helpguide.org/articles/ptsd-trauma/emotional-and-psychological-trauma.htm>.

Rylko, S. (2008). 'Preface', in *Sport: An Educational and Pastoral Challenge*, Vatican City: Libreria Editrice Vaticana, 5–11.

Waller, S., L. Dzikus and R. Hardin (2008). 'Collegiate Sport Chaplaincy: Problems and Promise', *Journal of Issues in Intercollegiate Athletics*, 1: 107–23.

Waller, S., L. Dzikus and R. Hardin (2010). 'The Collegiate Sport Chaplain: Kindred or Alien?', *Chaplaincy Today*, 26/1: 16–26.

12 Finding the right key

An examination of global sports chaplaincy credentialing models and their implications for credentialing sports chaplains in the United States

Steven N. Waller, Lars Dzikus, Robin L. Hardin and James H. Bemiller

Introduction

Recently, there has been an upsurge in interest in chaplaincy as a vocation globally. The typology of professional chaplaincy has broadened during the past two decades to include corporate, retail, sport, travel and emergency services chaplains as well as those that are employed in institutional settings such as hospitals and prisons. Moreover, chaplaincy activity now attracts a wider theological spectrum than has formerly been the case. A growing number of clergy and laypersons, in a variety of settings, are engaged in part-time work as chaplains. As we examine the evolution of chaplaincy in contemporary times, there are clear signs of an emerging theological and academic interest in the field, both generically and within specializations (Ballard, 2009). These 'emergent ministries' or 'strands of chaplaincy' are commonly viewed as 'sector ministries', indicating that chaplaincies only address a particular (narrow) facet of society, in contrast to the normative ministry of the congregation or parish (ibid. 18). If, however, chaplaincy is of growing importance then it needs to be understood as having normative status and to be more firmly grounded both theologically and structurally.

The work of chaplains varies greatly across regions, localities, institutions and areas of specialization. One common thread is that all chaplains seek to understand the whole person and frequently engage in interdisciplinary, team-oriented holistic care of the individual. For example, in the case of sports personnel – athletes, coaches and families – the sports chaplain may work in tandem with sport medicine professionals and sport psychology consultants to assist a player and their families to overcome the impact of catastrophic injury. Moreover, chaplains offer a supportive presence that reminds recipients of care and care-givers that people are more than just their current human condition or their current collection of concerns.

This chapter examines efforts to credential sports chaplains in the United Kingdom, Australia, New Zealand and the United States. The vast majority of mainstream, traditional chaplains (institutional) and pastoral counsellors in the US are credentialed through their respective professional associations. In the majority of US states, after appropriate academic and professional training and board certification, chaplains and counsellors are eligible to pursue state licensure. Moreover, in the US, the process of certifying chaplains includes passing an examination and demonstrating the ability to meet the standards of a practice established by a professional organization (for example, the Association of Professional Chaplains) which represents chaplains. As both anecdotal evidence and scholarly research indicates, the majority of chaplains working in sports environments do not pursue either form of credential (Dzikus, Waller and Hardin, 2010; Waller, Dzikus and Hardin, 2008, 2010).

This topic is important for several reasons. First, on a global basis, there is no single organization that serves as a 'clearinghouse' for credentialing sports chaplains. Second, in light of the fact that the majority of sports chaplains are not credentialed, there are a myriad of administrative, theological, ethical and legal challenges that surface. Finally, research supports the fact that as long as sports chaplains remain uncertified and operate outside the professional sphere of mainstream chaplaincy they will be considered as 'aliens', if they are acknowledged at all by other professional chaplains (Waller, Dzikus and Hardin, 2010). Professional status and acceptance among their professional peers remains an issue for sports chaplains.

Chaplaincy as a vocation

In a classical sense, Kurian (2005: 148) defines a chaplain as a 'priest or minister in charge of a chapel . . . serving dignitaries'. Lay and ordained chaplains work in a variety of contexts (military, prisons, hospitals, schools and parliaments). The earliest chaplains served in military units and then later in hospitals, prisons, schools and diplomatic faculties (Bergen, 2004; Smith, 1990). Regardless of which faith group they serve, today's US armed forces refer to any of their officially assigned religious leaders as 'chaplains' (Bokhari, 1999).

Chaplains are pastoral care specialists who attend to the spiritual needs of people in distress (Handzo and Koenig, 2004). They may be employed on a full-time, part-time or volunteer basis. If paid, they may be compensated by their institution, by a denomination, church or synagogue, by a separate funding organization or may contract their services individually or through a contracting organization. In the case of those working as sports chaplains in the US, funding may come from organizations such as the Fellowship of Christian Athletes (FCA) or from private donors (Dzikus, Waller and Hardin, 2010; Paget and McCormack, 2006). Since the 1920s many chaplains have been clinically trained to function in their particular type of facility. In the early 1940s chaplaincy organizations in the US such as the Association of Protestant Hospital Chaplains began certifying chaplains for competency to function in specialized ministries (Smith, 1990).

The evolution of sports chaplaincy

Sports chaplaincy as a professional and volunteer endeavour has evolved over the past half century in the United States. Indeed, chaplaincy to sports communities has grown significantly in the past 20 years. The US, Canada, the UK,

Australia and New Zealand have well-established Christian sports chaplaincy ministries. Sports chaplains include people from many different walks of life. Most commonly, chaplains are ministers or full-time Christian workers but occasionally chaplaincy work is done without charge or any financial remuneration. Often, sports chaplains are former participants of the sport they now serve as chaplains. Practising sports chaplains frequently contend that having been a participant in the sport which they are assigned to serves a dual purpose: it helps the chaplain to provide contextualized spiritual support and guidance to athletes, and playing or coaching experience in the sport gives the chaplain the ability to empathize and relate to some of the challenges facing the athletes (Blackburn, 2010; Bonham, 2012; Conner, 2003; Lipe, 2006; Null, 2008).

Currently, a number of colleges and universities in the US with athletic departments use the services of team chaplains across various sports. Generally, in such contexts, the individual responsible for the spiritual care of a team is referred to as the 'chaplain' or 'sports chaplain'. Sports chaplaincy is typically an unpaid, appointed position that allows the chaplain to remain neutral while serving administrators, coaches and players (Fellowship of Christian Athletes, 2007). Scholarly sources trace the involvement of chaplains in sport back to the early 1900s at both the collegiate and professional level and at major events, such as the Olympics (Blackburn, 2010; Smith, 1988; Woods, 2011).

Definitions and titles

The term 'sports chaplain' (or sport chaplain) is commonly used to define the role and function of a lay or ordained member of the clergy that provides spiritual care for athletes. Despite the common understanding of the label 'sports chaplain', Lipe (2006) argues that the term is losing its usefulness in light of the many different approaches used to serve athletes. He goes on to offer a more definitive range of titles for Christian sports chaplains in line with their associated duties and responsibilities. These include: (1) evangelistic chaplains, whose goal is the conversion to Christ of people in sport and the proclamation of the gospel through people of influence in the world of sport; (2) pastoral chaplains, who advocate personal piety (Christ-like behaviour) and spiritual growth in people of sport; and (3) sports mentors who seek to bring about a more wholehearted, Christ-honouring life both in sport (relationships with the sport, teammates, coaches, support staff and officials) and outside sport (relationships with spouse, family, friends and the Church). Additionally, the International Sports Professionals Association (ISPA), an organization which advocates for sports counselling, uses the term 'sports pastoral counsellor' to describe individuals that counsel and provide spiritual care for athletes. The FCA, a broad-based, US para-church organization labels those that serve players and coaches in a spiritual capacity as 'character coaches/chaplains'. In summary, there is no firm agreement on a definitive title, but the name 'sports chaplain' appears to be the most commonly adopted term. Regardless of the title used by chaplains, what is of primary importance is their charge – to provide pastoral and spiritual care for the athletes, coaches, their families and, in a broader sense, the sporting community. Moreover, it is critically important that sports chaplains exercise this charge with the utmost competence, compassion and respect for the religious or spiritual position of the people they serve.

Sports chaplaincy in the United States

A large number of practising sports chaplains in the US are affiliated with college athletics programmes (Hastings et al., 2006; Waller, Dzikus and Hardin, 2008). According to the FCA, these individuals are typically in unpaid, appointed positions that allow them to remain religiously neutral while serving the needs of administrators, coaches and players (Fellowship of Christian Athletes, 2007). Anecdotal evidence and related scholarship suggests that the key duties and responsibilities of collegiate sports chaplains are: (1) praying for and encouraging athletes, coaches, their families and support staff; (2) being available and equipped to assist in crisis situations; (3) alerting coaches, administration and tour staff to critical issues that might affect a team, programme or tour; (4) providing training and resources for character development and life management skills; (5) coordinating and leading chapel services; (6) coordinating special ministry and outreach events; (7) setting a positive example; (8) emphasizing how spiritual development can help in sports; (9) emphasizing the experience of playing sports rather than winning or losing; and (10) attending practices (Fellowship of Christian Athletes, 2011; Waller, Dzikus and Hardin, 2008). Moreover, there appears to be a movement afoot to care for college athletes in a more holistic sense: that is, making concerted efforts to promote the academic, physical, social and spiritual well-being of student athletes (Waller, Dzikus and Hardin, 2008).

In the US, very little is known about chaplains who serve professional sports franchises. Periodically, there are stories in trade publications, textbooks and the popular press that allude to the work of sports chaplains. Of particular interest are chaplains that are affiliated with athletes and teams within the Association of Tennis Professionals, the Ladies Professional Golf Association, Major League Baseball, Major League Soccer, Major League Lacrosse, the National Basketball Association, National Football League, National Hockey League, the National Association of Stock Car Automobile Racing, Professional Golf Association and the Women's National Basketball Association. Very little is mentioned about their qualifications to serve as a chaplain.

The work of chaplains in professional sports in the US is very similar to that of those working with collegiate teams. Common duties and responsibilities include: conducting Bible studies, chapel services, being available on games days and, perhaps more importantly, developing relationships with players and owners that are grounded in trust (Ferrin, 2008; Kelber, 2009). The overwhelming majority of chaplains in US professional sports are Protestant (Ferrin, 2008; Hardy, 2007; Kelber, 2009) and typically will seek help in ministering to players that practise Judaism, Islam, Buddhism or other faith traditions. Observing how National Football League (NFL) teams handle religious diversity among players, Kelber (2009) has stated that 'the NFL is overwhelmingly Christian; when the occasional Jewish or Muslim player requires counsel, the teams generally outsource'. Invariably, this may speak to the need to train sports chaplains to minister in a multi-faith perspective.

Finally, in the US, 'club chaplains' support individual athletes and teams ranging from swimming and diving to rugby. It is not uncommon to find chaplains that are associated with track and field, cycling, baseball, basketball, American football, soccer, car racing, rowing, ice-hockey and other sport clubs. Moreover, many are appointed as volunteer chaplains by the management of the club concerned or simply offer to serve under their own volition. The use of club chaplains to support sports teams is also common in countries such as Australia, New Zealand and the UK.

Credentialing sports chaplains

Chaplaincy as a professional vocation has an extended history of credentialing its incumbents, especially those that work in institutional, military and public service environments. Currently, there is no single organization serving as a clearinghouse for training and credentialing sports chaplains in the US (Waller, Dzikus and Hardin, 2008). The ISPA, based in Chicago, does provide an international registry of sports professionals which includes sports chaplains. This organization also offers a certificate programme by which one can be certified as a sport pastoral counsellor subsequent to the evaluation of the training and applied experience of the applicant by a panel of experts.

Unlike credentialing organizations in the UK, Australia or New Zealand, leading national chaplaincy organizations in the US generally do not recognize sports chaplaincy as a sub-discipline within the profession. Among such organizations are the Association for Professional Chaplains (APC), the American Association of Pastoral Counselors (AAPC), and the Association for Clinical Pastoral Education (ACPE) (Waller, Dzikus and Hardin, 2008). Only recently has the APC begun to consider sports chaplaincy as a viable strand of chaplaincy per se (Waller, Dzikus and Hardin, 2010). Moreover, organizations such as the National Association of Catholic Chaplains (NACC), the National Association of Jewish Chaplains (NAJC) and the International Fellowship of Chaplains all play major roles in establishing standards for the training, practice and certification of institutional and sports chaplains.

Further research on the qualifications of sports chaplains is critical, since the quality of training 'will have a direct bearing on the quality of ministry' (Conner, 2003: 23). Some collegiate institutions, para-church organizations and non-profit faith-based organizations do offer sports chaplaincy training programmes. However, at present, there are no organizations that establish criteria and competencies for certification as a sports chaplain in the United States (Waller, Dzikus and Hardin, 2008). The majority of people practising sports chaplaincy may be ordained within a religious denomination or have some level of theological training or a seminary degree, but chaplains potentially perform duties other than providing spiritual care. It seems that the area of training and credentialing is being neglected. As is the case with other groups of professionals who work with athletes such as sports coaches, trainers and nutritionists, an important issue that athletic directors and university administrators need to consider is how they assess the competence of chaplains to perform their duties.

The importance of credentialing sports chaplains

It is important to distinguish between credentialing, certification, licensure and registry. Credentialing is a general term that may refer to both certification and licensure. Certification is typically a non-statutory process, whereas licensure is a statutory process through which states or provinces regulate the professional standards and conduct in certain professions. Licensure is required for the use of professional titles that are legally protected (for example, psychologists) as well as certain professional services, like pressure welding (Zaichkowski and Perna, 1992). Certifications are recognitions by professional organizations and are typically non-statutory designations (that is, not protected by law), but certifications can also be statutory as is the case for teachers in state schools (ibid.).

Credentialing has the potential to be a major victory for sports chaplains for several reasons. First, it would allow for the standardization of training and development of those aspiring to work in this particular field of ministry. Second, it would help to create the parameters for work and continued professional development. Third, it would serve to delineate where the boundaries for practice lie. For example, there is a difference between spiritual encouragement and counselling, the former requiring a willing spirit and hopeful disposition while the latter in most US states requires specialized training and licensure. Fourth, the willingness to participate in a meaningful credentialing programme would create a sense of solidarity and *esprit de corps* with chaplains working across various sub-fields. Moreover, it would provide an opportunity to enlighten and engage mainstream chaplaincy organizations about the breadth and depth of sports chaplaincy. Finally, access to a meaningful credentialing programme is a natural 'next step' for students matriculating through sports ministry/sports chaplaincy at Association of Theological Schools sanctioned programmes such as Baylor University's Truett Theological Seminary and United Theological Seminary. Seminarians who aspire to be chaplains follow the pathway for board certification, which typically means matriculation through a graduate theological education, a year's clinical training and 1,600 hours of clinical pastoral education. Since 2009 approximately 74 per cent of the members of the NACC who were functioning as chaplains have received board certification from their association (Lichter and O'Gorman, 2009).

Similarly, in the UK, the programmes of study related to sports chaplaincy operated by the University of Gloucestershire receive a comparable level of scrutiny by the British equivalent of the Association of Theological Schools. On the surface, there appears to be a litany of affirming reasons to encourage credentialing among practising and future sports chaplains. In theory, the standards set by organizations such as the APC, NACC and NAJC should both guide and govern the manner in which all chaplains in the US are credentialed. This would include practising sports chaplains. There remains an uncomfortable silence as to why sports chaplains have been resistant to adherence to these standards of training and competency in order to enhance the quality of ministry to people of sport. In part, this silence may be attributed to a lack of awareness about these standards and the rigour associated with attaining them. Likewise, credentialing may simply seem unnecessary to some. Yet it must also be recognized that progress relating to the credentialing of sports chaplains has not come without its challenges.

Challenges to credentialing sports chaplains

One of the great challenges to credentialing sports chaplains is determining standards for training and practice. Globally, this matter remains an area of on-going discussion among leading sports chaplains. Despite the fact that viable certificate programmes exist (Sports Chaplaincy Australia [SCA], Sports Chaplaincy New Zealand [SCNZ]) there remains the issue of agreement on whether training and credentialing are necessary for sports chaplains. Some resist the movement toward training and subsequent credentialing. It has been noted in wider circles that those who prefer the status quo or who feel threatened by the progression toward professional status can weaken efforts by the occupational group to professionalize (DeVries, Berlinger and Cadge, 2008).

A second challenge emanates from the fact that sports chaplaincy is not yet broadly recognized as a distinct sub-field of chaplaincy per se (Waller, Dzikus and Hardin, 2010; Paget and McCormack, 2006). For example, in the US, some clergy who minister to others in the name of their local church or parish claim the title 'chaplain'. Volunteers in institutional chaplaincy departments and trained 'lay persons' associated with college athletic departments are frequently called 'chaplain' by the people they serve. These realities compete against efforts to distinguish the work of professional chaplains and make it difficult for other professional groups and the public to see chaplaincy as a distinct profession with a number of 'emerging' facets such as sports chaplaincy. A patient in a hospital is unlikely to encounter a 'volunteer' physician simply because the category of 'physician' is understood to be a professional category. Similarly, if an individual becomes closely associated with a sports performer or a team they are commonly referred to as a 'chaplain' with little or no regard for their training or experience. The pivotal question for the profession of chaplaincy as a whole and within the sub-field of sports chaplaincy is who should be called 'chaplain' and by what means does the individual earn that title.

International models of certifying sports chaplains: laying the foundation

In order for the credentialing movement in the US to continue to move forward, perhaps a crucial next step is to closely examine what has been successfully achieved in other countries. Initiatives in the UK, Australia and New

Zealand have already generated momentum, thus making them excellent points of departure. The following section provides examples from each of these countries that may be used in the construction of a US credentialing initiative.

In the UK, Sports Chaplaincy UK (SCUK) provides sport-specific initial training and continuing professional development for practising sports chaplains in the UK and Ireland. The target audiences are those chaplains that seek to practise at the local level and perhaps beyond. An examination of the information placed on the SCUK website does not reveal a curriculum of training nor a plan for the issuance of certificates for courses or training completed. Moreover, in 2010 SCUK collaborated with the University of Gloucestershire to create a suite of postgraduate courses in sports chaplaincy. Designed for those new to or with prior experience of sports chaplaincy, these courses comprise the following part-time or full-time pathways: Postgraduate Certificate in Sports Chaplaincy, Postgraduate Diploma in Sports Chaplaincy, and Master of Sports Chaplaincy. These courses target the training needs of ordained clergy, church leaders or lay workers that aspire to work in sports as a chaplain. The programme is the only one of its kind in the UK and Europe and provides students with an opportunity to understand, critique and develop practice in the realm of sport and spiritual development within chaplaincy roles and settings (Sports Chaplaincy UK, n.d.).

Sports Chaplaincy Australia offers an array of courses within their training scheme that accommodate new and experienced chaplains. These training courses are offered at two levels and are certificated programmes. The Level 1 course provides a basic introduction to sports chaplaincy and is designed to familiarize students with the basic responsibilities of such a role. The Level 2 certificate programme is disseminated over three days and provides a range of more detailed subject matter. The courses offered at Level 2 include: Foundations of Sports Chaplaincy, Fundamentals of Sports Chaplaincy, Serving and Working with Athletes, Anatomy of an Athlete, Introduction to Grief and Loss in Sports, Introduction to Critical Incident and First Response, Introduction to Life Care and Preservation (Suicide Awareness), Working with Sports Management, Relationships and the Sports Person, Pastoral Care Skills of Sports Chaplains, and Professional Conduct. Additionally, specialty training courses are offered that include an Advanced Sports Chaplaincy Certificate, Critical Incident Stress Management/Debriefing, Full Suicide Awareness and First Aid Adrenaline and Stress in Sports to assist chaplains (Sports Chaplaincy Australia, n.d.). Similarly, Sports Chaplaincy New Zealand offers a 30-hour certificate course in sports chaplaincy that is completed in four phases. This programme provides a basic foundation in sports chaplaincy. The courses included in the SCNZ training programme are the same as those offered by SCA (Sports Chaplaincy New Zealand, n.d.).

Credentialing sports chaplains in the United States: the maiden voyage

Efforts to credential sports chaplains in the US lag behind those in the UK, Australia and New Zealand. In 2011 work began on developing a three-tiered certification programme for sports chaplains in the US. The primary aim of this initiative is to afford all practising and future US sports chaplains the opportunity to be certified to practise. To date there have been no related (formal/structured) documents released for public consumption:

Gold

The focus is on credentialing Olympic-calibre chaplains or those who seek professional sports chaplaincy as a paid vocation. A Master of Divinity degree or the equivalent of educational training and at least one basic unit of contextualized clinical pastoral education will be required for this level of certification.

Silver

This band of certification is for those that aspire to work in a number of areas in sports chaplaincy, especially as a chaplain to a professional, semi-professional or college sports team. Some theological training and contextualized experience in sports chaplaincy will be required for this level of certification.

Bronze

This band of certification is for those that aspire to work in a volunteer capacity in some area of sport at the local level. The context may be high school, club or semi-professional sports. Some theological training and contextualized experience in sports chaplaincy will be required for this level of certification.

As this certification programme evolves, the hope is that the successful courses presently hosted in the UK, Australia and New Zealand will be replicated and applied within the US context. The work on this project is still in its early stages, but shows promise. Optimally, if the efforts persist at a reasonable pace, the launch of a pilot programme may be feasible in the near future.

Where do we go from here?

Notwithstanding what we know about sports chaplaincy through the available historical and anecdotal evidence, scholarship and practice, where should proponents of this strand of chaplaincy begin to address the credentialing question? Perhaps the most appropriate place to begin is for all of the global stakeholders to agree that credentialing in some form is necessary to legitimize the vocation of sports chaplaincy, to ensure minimum levels of education and practical ministry training in-context and to facilitate the professional status that allows for the successful pastoral and spiritual care of players, coaches and families. Organizations such as International Sport Chaplains, APC, AAPC, FCA, Athletes in Action, ACPE and academic institutions such as Baylor and Neumann Universities, the University of Tennessee and seminaries such as Denver, Truett, United, the University of Gloucestershire and others that provide curriculum and training in the area of sports chaplaincy must help to catalyse this conversation. Without question when we view the issue from a global perspective, the efforts of the International Sports Coalition, SCUK, SCA and SCNZ offer a solid foundation for the construction of a global training initiative that, with the aid of technology, has the potential to be disseminated worldwide.

Second, there needs to be a continuing examination of existing models of credentialing in order to facilitate the development and refinement of such a programme for sports chaplains globally. The credentialing programmes of SCUK, SCA and SCNZ have proven standards and metrics that may be replicated. An examination of these three models might be the point of confluence for organizations such as APC and ISPA and the US Collegiate Sports Council to continue deliberations over certification.

Finally, sports chaplains must rationally embrace the movement toward professionalizing, institutionalizing and legitimizing their work within the overall schema of chaplaincy. Being labelled as the 'other' or 'alien' among credentialed practising chaplains potentially undermines all that sports chaplaincy represents – the ability to care for the souls of those that are sportspersons (Null, 2008; Paget and McCormack, 2006; Waller, Dzikus and Hardin 2010). Indeed, it is essential that we realize that the legitimization of sports chaplaincy as a strand of professional chaplaincy is contingent upon how we view training (theological and experiential), praxis (conducting ministry by proven standards, guidelines and best practices) and movement toward the mainstream of chaplaincy. This is not to say that in countries like the US the very 'roots' of sports chaplaincy (which are anchored in long-term involvement with organizations such as FCA and Athletes in Action) should be abandoned, rather that existing practice should be used to bring new perspectives on sports chaplaincy to mainstream organizations like APC, NAJC and NACC.

Conclusions

As this important conversation about sports chaplaincy credentialing unfolds, one of the requisite items is to see with full clarity the greater good that will emanate from a well-thought through and collaboratively constructed credentialing initiative. Inclusiveness – extending an invitation to all the key stakeholders that have a vested interest in the continued evolution of this facet of sport ministry – will be a key.

Defining exactly what chaplains do within sporting organizations and claiming their role as collaborative organizational leaders committed to quality individual and team-centred care has previously been an elusive challenge. As a result, questions have emerged regarding the contribution of sports chaplains to professional chaplaincy. These questions are especially pressing in today's sporting environment, in which administrators are pressured to evaluate resources, including the investment in holistic care for athletes, coaches and their families (Seifart, 1984). The need to set clear standards for sports chaplains has contributed to an international dialogue related to credentialing. The progress that has been made in the UK, Australia, New Zealand and the US in relation to certifying such a role is laudable and exhilarating. With the advent of the academic programmes offered at Truett and United Theological Seminaries and the cutting edge educational programme at the University of Gloucestershire, the training and placement of professional chaplains lays a great foundation to normalize the professionalization of sports chaplaincy but, more importantly, to cement their rightful place among chaplains globally. This is especially significant as efforts to train sports chaplains in nations like China continue to emerge. Speaking of the excitement behind this training momentum, sport chaplain Revd Brad Kenney (2012) stated:

> I do believe that we are seeing movement in a positive direction . . . . I am thankful for having a broader understanding and training as a chaplain which allowed me flexibility to be a chaplain in a hospice and to translate much of my training into the professional sports environment. I am looking forward to seeing how education for sports chaplains develops in the coming years and I think that it speaks well for the future of sports chaplaincy to see some education and accreditation structure and standards being developed.
>
> (Kenney, 2012)

Despite the issues presented in this chapter about credentialing sports chaplains there is reason for optimism. The forward progress seen in current credentialing initiatives and those in progress is a positive indicator that sports chaplains are prepared to take their esteemed place among the wider community of chaplains.

References

Ballard, P. (2009). 'Locating Chaplaincy: A Theological Note', *Crucible*, July/September, pp.18–24.

Bergen, D.L. (ed.) (2004). *The Sword of the Lord: Military Chaplains from the First to the Twenty-First Century*, Notre Dame, IN: University of Notre Dame Press.

Blackburn, R.R. (2010). 'An Olympic Chaplain', *Christianity Today*, 15 Feb. Available at <http://www.christianitytoday.com/ct/2010/februaryweb-only/17.12.0.html>.

Bokhari, E.A.S. (1999). 'Religious Orientation of Muslim Soldiers in the United States Armed Forces', *Defence Journal*, 3/5. Available at <http://defencejournal.com/jun99/orientation.htm>.

Bonham, C. (2012). 'Chaplains Minister Motivation to Olympic Athletes', *Charisma News*. Available at <http://www.charismanews.com/world/33794-chaplains-minister-motivation-to-olympic-athletes>.

Conner, S. (2003). *Sports Outreach: Principles and Practice for Successful Sports Ministry*, Tain, Ross-shire: Christian Focus Publications.

DeVries, R., N. Berlinger and W. Cadge (2008). 'Lost in Translation: The Chaplain's Role in Health Care', *Hastings Center Report*, 38/1: 23–7.

Dzikus, L., S. Waller and R. Hardin (2010). 'Collegiate Sport Chaplaincy: Exploration of an Emerging Profession', *Journal of Contemporary Athletics*, 5/1: 21–41.

Fellowship of Christian Athletes (2007). *Chaplain Training Manual*, Kansas City, MO: FCA.

—— (2011). 'What do Chaplains Do?' Available at <http://www.fcachaplains.org/>.

Ferrin, R.P. (2008). 'The NFL Chaplaincy: Duties, Expectations and Perceived Accomplishments', MA thesis: Bemidji State University.

Handzo, G., and H.G. Koenig (2004). 'Spiritual Care: Whose Job is it Anyway?', *Southern Medical Journal*, 97/12: 1242–44.

Hardy, D. (2007). 'NFL Chaplains: Unique Access Brings Unique Problems', *Multnomah Message*, 9/1: 2–3, 9.

Hastings, E.T. et al. (2006). *Mission Integration in Athletic Departments of Catholic Colleges and Universities*. Retrieved from <http://www.neumann.edu/mission/center/ACCU_Study_Report_Color.pdf>.

Kelber, M. (2009). 'God and Football: The NFL's Chaplains give Advice', *Time*, 30 Oct. Available at <http://www.time.com/time/arts/article/0,8599,1933406,00.html>.

Kenney, B. (2012). 'From the Rev: The Future of Sport Chaplaincy', *Cross Training*. Available at <http://crosstraining-us.org/from-the-rev-the-future-of-sport-chaplaincy/>.

Kurian, G.T. (2005). *Nelson's Dictionary of Christianity*, Nashville, TN: Thomas Nelson.

Lichter, D., and M.L. O'Gorman (2009). 'Establishing a Chaplain's Value', *Health Progress*, 90/3: 30–3.

Lipe, R.D. (2006). *Transforming Lives in Sport: A Guide for Sport Chaplains and Sport Mentors*, Kearney, NE: Cross Training Publishing.

Null, J.A. (2008). 'Some Preliminary Thoughts on Philosophies of Sports Ministries and their Literature', in D. Deardorff II and J.B. White (eds), *The Image of God in the Human Body: Essays on Christianity and Sports*, Lewiston, NY: Edwin Mellen.

Paget, N.K., and J.R. McCormack (2006). *The Work of the Chaplain*, Valley Forge, PA: Judson Press.

Seifart, H. (1984). 'Forum Sport and Economy: The Commercialization of Olympic Sport by the Media', *International Review for the Sociology of Sport*, 19/3–4: 305.

Smith, K.W. (1990). 'Chaplain/Chaplaincy', in R.J. Hunter (ed.), *The Dictionary of Pastoral Care and Counseling*, Nashville, TN: Abingdon Press, 136.

Smith, R. (1988). *Sports and Freedom: The Rise of Big-Time College Athletics*, New York: Oxford University Press.

Sports Chaplaincy Australia (n.d.). *Prepared for Service: Sports Chaplaincy Training*. Available at <http://sportschaplaincy.com.au/training/>.

Sports Chaplaincy New Zealand (n.d.). *Sports Chaplaincy Training*. Available at <http://www.nz.sportschaplaincy.com/SportsChaplaincyTraining.html>.

Sports Chaplaincy UK (n.d.). *Sports Chaplaincy Training*. Available at <http://www.sportschaplaincy.org.uk/training/>.

Waller, S., L. Dzikus and R. Hardin (2008). 'Collegiate Sport Chaplaincy: Problems and Promise', *Journal of Issues in Intercollegiate Athletics*, 1: 107–23.

Waller, S., L. Dzikus and R. Hardin (2010). 'The Collegiate Sports Chaplain: Kindred or Alien?', *Chaplaincy Today*, 26/1: 16–26.

Woods, R.B. (2011). *Social Issues in Sport*, 2nd edn, Champaign, IL: Human Kinetics.

Zaichkowski, L.D., and F.M. Perna (1992). 'Certification of Consultants in Sport Psychology: A Rebuttal to Anshel', *Sport Psychologist*, 6/3: 287–96.

13 Serving the spirit?

The sport psychologist and the chaplain in English Premiership Football

Mark Nesti

Introduction

Despite considerable efforts by academics, practitioners and professional bodies, sport psychology and sport psychologists have long struggled for acceptance in the world of professional sport. One of the reasons for this is the perception surrounding psychology, namely that it is only for those suffering from problems or for weak individuals (Fifer et al., 2008). Other obstacles relate to beliefs about the value of sport psychology work and that many coaches, especially at the elite level, think of themselves as very competent applied psychologists, albeit without formal qualifications in the discipline. These and similar challenges are commonly experienced in professional football. Describing my experiences as a sport psychologist inside several English Premier League clubs, I have argued elsewhere that the culture of professional football is particularly difficult for sport psychologists to operate within because top-level managers and their players often view themselves as highly knowledgeable about psychological factors and performance (Nesti, 2011a). They maintain this opinion, quite reasonably some would suggest, because they know that to achieve and survive at the highest levels of the game requires outstanding psychological qualities and skills (Brown and Potarc, 2009).

In contrast to the task facing the sport psychologist, the chaplain working in professional football is rarely seen as someone whose role and function is already catered for inside the club. Few coaches and managers would make any public claims to the type of expertise possessed by the chaplain but they may suggest that they also provide some form of pastoral support for players and staff. However, most would be quick to acknowledge that this type of activity is not their primary function and, unlike the chaplain, such provision is not normally guided by a specific theological orientation or system of religious belief. Interestingly, a close examination of various autobiographies of successful coaches and managers in a range of professional sports reveals that a significant number are strongly influenced by their own personal religious beliefs or faith in how they view their job and how they work with the teams: for example, Vince Lombardi and Sir Matt Busby. Nevertheless, this is not the main source of difficulty that a chaplain may face in providing a service within professional football or in professional sport in general. A more common problem is that chaplains are often seen as people lacking any real, in-depth understanding of the demands of elite level performance sport. They could be viewed as a rather whimsical figure who is hoping to find converts, someone, who, despite a low-key and friendly demeanour, is really engaged in a surreptitious programme of religious evangelization. In contrast, the sport psychologist may be seen more positively at times, despite concerns over their value and effectiveness, because they are supposed to be engaged in enhancing performance and helping players maximize their talents. In an environment where continual failure to win games almost invariably results in the removal of the manager and accompanying staff (Nesti, 2010), the chaplain may be seen as someone with a different focus because the security of their position does not depend on match-day results. Because of this, the chaplain might be perceived as one whose sole concern is with spiritual life and the redemption of souls, someone whose interest does not lie in helping footballers to play better but rather in supporting them to become better people.

In this chapter, I look more closely at the roles of both the sport psychologist and the chaplain to reveal that the stereotypes and limited viewpoints outlined above do not fully represent the realities of high-level professional footballing environments. Although I will partly draw on my experiences working inside a number of English Premier League clubs, my main focus is to more closely examine the theoretical and philosophical problems which sport psychologists may encounter when working alongside club chaplains in professional football at the highest level. To achieve this we will look at four key issues: (1) the underlying approach to the science of psychology and sport psychology; (2) the so-called 'performance or care' debate; (3) the place of spiritual belief and religious faith in the lives of professional footballers and coaches in the English Premier League context; and (4) the impact of the sport psychologist's personal religious beliefs on their applied work. Given my own background in the Catholic faith, this final section will highlight how two specific beliefs and practices from this tradition have had an impact on my work with players, staff and football chaplains, and influenced the approach I have taken in my role as a sport psychologist in English Premier League football.

The science of sport psychology

In this section I will discuss the underlying philosophy of science that has influenced the dominant approach to sport psychology since its inception. This is important because it is one of the clearest reasons why many sport psychologists feel they should have little to do with the work of chaplains. That is, psychology as an academic discipline has been almost neurotic in seeking to establish its distance from theology and philosophy, despite critics like Vitz (1997) accusing psychology of becoming a new secular religion. In sum, the clash is essentially at the level of presuppositions which govern sport psychology's theoretical commitments (and all reflection and deliberation for that matter): that is, fundamental beliefs, epistemology and hermeneutics.

The academic discipline of sport psychology is still in its infancy. It is approximately 50 years old. Most of the subject matter in terms of theories, research paradigms, methods and epistemological foundations has been borrowed from the parent discipline of psychology (Vealey, 2006). Psychology is in some ways unique in that it can be approached as a branch of the physical sciences – for example, psychophysics – or from a more philosophical base as is found in much counselling psychology (Maslow, 1962). In its attempts to establish its credibility as an academic discipline, early sport psychology positioned itself firmly at the experimental, natural scientific and empiricist end of the spectrum. Several voices have tried to point out that by doing this, sport psychology has restricted the types of subject matter and topics that can be studied and discussed within the context of the discipline (e.g. Ryba and Wright, 2005). Cartesian dualism and the desire to measure, predict and control, dominates thinking. This has led to opposition, with some in the discipline adopting a radical postmodern perspective and suggesting that the future lies in an almost total dismantling of all preconceived ideas and methods in order to reach a new, emancipatory situation.

Unfortunately, the epistemological positioning of sport psychology makes it difficult to study a number of psychological concepts that are not easily measured, including hope, humility, sacrifice and courage. Other rarely encountered terms in sport psychology such as spirit, spirituality and personal meaning are denied existence (Crust, 2006) or seen as inappropriate for the discipline to consider. Cognitive sport psychology (the dominant approach), grounded as it is in the philosophy of scientism, has nothing to offer on spirit and spirituality since in this view they cannot be measured, quantified or understood purely objectively. Meanwhile, the postmodernist viewpoint in academic sport psychology tends to reduce everything to discourses and feelings. Ideas like religious belief become stripped of any substance, understood only as an epiphenomenon, an irrational set of thoughts that bring emotional comfort. There is much to object to about this kind of argument, but one of the most amusing objections for religious believers is the common failing of postmodern critics to overlook the fact that almost all religions include ideas concerning punishment in this life or after death. All of which represents quite a challenge to the idea that religious faith is merely some sort of pleasant emotional crutch.

Spirituality and sport psychology

In examining sport psychology literature on spirituality, Watson and Nesti (2005) identified at least two major obstacles to further study and consideration. The first is the scientific and philosophical basis of sport psychology outlined above. The second is the tendency to see spirituality as only related to religion. However, the majority of literature in psychology and related fields differentiates between spirituality and religion, conceptualizing the former as a broader phenomenon including also humanistic perspectives (Pargament, 1999). The situation in the academic literature in sport is less well developed, although in recent years a small number of sport philosophers and theologians have begun to address this topic, leading to the publication of books and articles on sport and religion (Ladd and Mathisen, 1999) and sport and spirituality (Parry, Nesti and Watson, 2011; Robinson, 2007).

For the sport psychologist hoping to explore how spirituality could be important in their applied work or research, one avenue is to draw on the ideas of the Thomist philosopher Josef Pieper, who has distinguished between religious spirituality and human spirituality. As a Catholic philosopher, Pieper (1998) argues that while these two ways of understanding spirituality and the idea of spirit itself are fundamentally related, it is also possible to make distinctions. Human spirit refers to our capacity for free will. Pieper further argues that we use the word 'spirit' to describe human agency articulating this in terms of a belief in our ability to act beyond the limitations arising from our inherited characteristics or influence of the environment. As a result, words like 'courage' – such an important term in sport – can be understood, to some extent, as a psycho-spiritual idea. Indeed, Corlett (1996a) has suggested that 'courage' means to choose a course of action that may result in a morally good and desirable outcome in the face of considerable uncertainty. Both Pieper and Corlett are postulating that courage cannot be viewed as merely a psychological skill. Rather, they want us to conceive of it as something that is evidence of our free will, in this case our freedom to choose a course of action that in certain situations could even lead to our death or serious injury. This term can be differentiated from the semantically similar, yet quite different, word 'bravery', which means to do something instinctively, to act without carefully thinking through the risks involved. According to Aristotle and Aquinas, acting courageously involves doing something (or not doing something) to achieve a moral good after careful consideration of the risks involved and possible outcomes. It is for this reason that many sports coaches and managers value courage in their players, well above psychological skills and emotional control (Nesti, 2011a).

Another important and frequently used term in professional sport, including football, is 'spirit' (Nesti, 2011b). Coaching staff and players often talk about the need to show spirit in times of adversity. Teams call on spirit when they are stuck in the relegation zone, when they find themselves 3–0 down at half time, or when players experience long-term injury or do not get selected for the team on match days. Of course, not all sport psychologists see things this way, and some have explained notions of 'courage' and 'spirit' by reference to psychological skills (Crust, 2006). However, it is clear that this is not necessarily how things are interpreted and understood by those inside elite sporting organizations. In the environment of professional football, spirit is seen as a quality of the person, something intangible yet real, that reveals the inadequacy of describing human actions only in terms of behavioural or cognitive processes (Pieper, 1995).

Sport psychologists who wish to deal with spiritual ideas and concepts in their work will have to look for alternative theoretical foundations for their practice. Examining the theoretical spectrum within psychology and sport psychology, we find that it is only those adopting person-centred approaches that take terms like 'courage', 'spirit' and 'spirituality' seriously (Ravizza, 2002). Humanistic, phenomenological, existential and some forms of Jungian psychology recognize that the philosophical concept of free will must be part of an empirically sound definition of human being. In contrast, mainstream sport psychology, both in its academic form and professional practice, is derived from behaviourist, trait and cognitive psychological approaches. These are all, consciously or unconsciously, based on natural scientific foundations involving a complete rejection of the idea of human free will and associated terms. It is for this reason that, despite being mentioned daily at training grounds in the English Premier League, words like 'hope', 'courage' and 'faith' are very rarely found in the mainstream academic sport psychology literature. This is especially the case in English-speaking countries compared to places where an orthodox Christian or Catholic anthropology of the human person has a greater influence on theorizing and practice in the human and social sciences. In those countries a greater number of philosophers (Marcel, 1948) and psychologists (Caruso, 1964) have based their work on the idea that the human person is made up of mind, body and soul. Where the sport psychologist acknowledges this idea of the human person, the psychological understanding of human being should be much closer to that of the chaplain regardless of their religious or faith tradition. In addition, if the sport psychologist's work is also guided by approaches such as those strands of existential psychology that place an emphasis on meaning (Frankl, 1984), or on spirit (Kierkegaard, 1980), one will have the reassurance of knowing one's professional philosophy and practice is based on a coherent theoretical position (Slife, Hope and Nebeker, 1999). This shared theology of the person should make fruitful cooperation between the psychologist and chaplain a viable reality. This is especially true if the chaplain is an adherent of one of the majority monotheistic religions where considerable agreement exists concerning definitions of the human person.

Performance or care?

One of the most important recent debates in applied sport psychology centres on whether work should be exclusively directed at performance enhancement or more focused on athlete care. Within the literature, the dominant view is that sport psychologists must attend only to performance-related matters. The reasoning behind this position is that sport psychology theory and research is aimed at helping athletes to improve, to develop better psychological skills and achieve their goals. According to Brady and Maynard (2010), clubs, teams and individual sports performers expect these improvements from their work with sport psychologists, and it is through serving in this capacity that psychologists can offer an effective professional and ethical service. Opposing this view, Andersen (2009) claims that applied practice should focus on athlete care alone. The rationale for this position is based upon arguments surrounding measurement and the needs of individuals operating in competitive sport. Andersen suggests that because it is impossible to reliably identify and measure the impact a sport psychologist can have on athlete performance, we must abandon our interest in this factor and instead address ourselves to supporting the athlete as they experience the rigours of performance sport. It could be argued that sport psychologists who adopt this kind of practice and professional philosophy would be better placed working constructively with and alongside sports chaplains. Indeed, a focus on the ordinary human needs of the athlete rather than simply their sporting performance, especially when delivered through a pastorally oriented approach, is very close to the working practices of the club chaplain.

In my previous work, I have suggested that although the 'care only' perspective might appeal to some chaplains, it is highly unlikely that it would be welcomed by those within elite level professional sports where performance and winning are central concerns for all (Nesti, 2011b). Based on my experiences of delivering sport psychology inside a number of English Premier League clubs over several seasons, I have observed that almost everyone at those clubs (including the club chaplain) sees themselves as helping the team to become more successful. While the coaches might do this through their tactical acumen, the medical team via their skilled application of injury prevention programmes, and the fitness staff by the design of scientifically supported strength and conditioning interventions, the sport psychologist and chaplain are not exempt in this respect. It is very difficult to imagine why an organization operating at the highest level in professional sport would hire a sport psychologist with no interest in helping the team, staff and athletes to perform better. Of course, this does not mean that it is impossible for the psychologist to demonstrate a caring approach to those with whom he or she works, but it highlights the need to strike a balance in intensely competitive sporting cultures between meeting individual human need and offering support for performance enhancement. It is the sport psychologist adopting this type of perspective who will be the one hired by the clubs and who will be most able to work creatively and positively with the club chaplain. In addition, it is highly likely that most chaplains in professional football clubs feel that they also contribute in subtle and less explicit ways to team and individual performance. After all, providing care and support for someone usually enhances their general psychological, physical and spiritual health, which, in turn, may have a positive impact upon their performance of professional roles.

Spirituality and religious belief

English Premier League football is a global phenomenon. At the start of the 2013/14 footballing season over 70 per cent of first team players at the 20 Premier League clubs were non-UK citizens. At the top clubs this figure is even higher, and it is common to see starting line-ups containing no UK-based players at all. This level of international diversity is not as marked amongst support staff where the majority of managers, coaches, sports science and medical personnel are from the UK. These are very important issues for sport psychologists and chaplains for a number of reasons. First, it means that there are usually a significant number of players professing an allegiance to one faith tradition or another. Second, given that support staff come mainly from the UK, it is often the case that significantly fewer of these individuals possess an active religious faith. In this sense, levels of religiosity and belief amongst support staff broadly reflect the societal backdrop from which they emanate. In common with most other Western countries, the UK has become a largely secular culture and one that has increasingly turned away from an affinity with organized religion (Voas and Crockett, 2005; Theos, 2013). Thirdly, it is common to find chaplains working with players from a variety of faiths, the largest being Catholic Christianity and Islam. Indeed, it is entirely possible that a chaplain could work in a club where no co-religionists exist amongst the playing staff, although there may be individuals in senior management positions or on the commercial side of the club, who share the chaplain's religious affiliations. This unusual situation will bring many challenges and opportunities for the chaplain as they fulfil their role. The chaplain will be in a very privileged position to help the coaching and sports science staff to understand the demands placed upon players on account of the various religious obligations and practices to which they may adhere. For example, there is little to guide clubs in terms of how they might manage the dietary and other demands a player may encounter during Ramadan. The chaplain can be an important conduit between the players and the staff to ensure that the dictates and demands of particular religious beliefs are respected and accommodated in a way that does not undermine performance and competitive edge. The chaplain may be invited to events like staff away-days to help the coaching team understand more about the central role of religious belief and practice in the lives of players. This type of activity is something that occurs in high-level, professional football and is welcomed at some clubs (Nesti, 2010). In my experience, the sport psychologist can play an important role in facilitating this type of information exchange and educational opportunity by inviting the chaplain to attend and speak at away-days or to take part in smaller, more focused meetings with key first team staff.

Common ground in adversity

The sport psychologist can become an important ally in the work of the chaplain in a number of practical ways. Where the psychologist conceives of their work as being both about player performance and caring for the person, it is much easier for them to develop a close working relationship with the chaplain. Again, to return to an earlier discussion, this becomes altogether more feasible – and indeed professionally consistent – if the psychologist is guided in their activity by human science conceptualizations of psychology (Van Deurzen and Arnold-Baker, 2005) and uses models derived from humanistic and other person-centred approaches. The sport psychologist who uses one-to-one confidential counselling sessions as part of their work should discover that they share much common ground with the chaplain. This will also be apparent if the sport psychologist is interested equally in football-related matters and the player's life beyond the training ground. And finally, greater professional respect and mutual sharing of important information will increase if the sport psychologist is committed to carrying out longer-term developmental work rather than using 'quick-fix' mental training interventions to remove or alleviate symptoms (Corlett, 1996b).

During those inevitable periods when a team or club is facing crisis the chaplain could benefit considerably from the visible and active support of the sport psychologist. It is not uncommon for some staff to see the chaplain as someone whose interests are very different from their own. At such times there may even be attempts to keep the chaplain away from the training ground or to make him or her feel less welcome than they would during more fruitful periods. This tension is unavoidable when one group of people is under intense pressure in relation to their performance and the inability to improve club circumstance quickly may result in job loses. However, paradoxically, it is in these frequently encountered moments that the chaplain may find that they are most in demand by players if not staff. When clubs and teams are facing adversity, players in particular can be placed under intense scrutiny. Passions run high, communication commonly becomes abrasive, scapegoating takes place and team spirit is strained (Nesti & Littlewood, 2011). The pastoral care offered to players in these arduous situations is important at a human level, and may even go some way to helping indirectly with performance enhancement.

There will be many occasions when players and staff seek support from the chaplain because of hardship in their personal lives. For example, the chaplain may be key to helping a player's family deal with the illness of a child, the death of a close relative, or the consequences of an accident. Sometimes when new players join a club, especially if they come from a different culture, they might encounter social dislocation, severe homesickness and disorientation. At Premier League level, this can be experienced even more acutely because of a range of unique factors such as the levels of media interest in players' lives and the accompanying lack of privacy, language and communication problems and unfamiliar cultural practices. On top of this, players might have to quickly adjust to new ways of playing and training and to winning over teammates and fans. In these situations, the chaplain, may be viewed by the troubled player as someone who is prepared to approach them as a fellow human being rather than a highly paid, elite professional footballer. This type of support from the chaplain and the sport psychologist working in partnership can be highly beneficial to the team and can help individual players settle in more easily and contribute more fully (see Gamble, Hill and Parker, 2013).

Catholic perspectives

Where the sport psychologist is a Catholic working in English Premier League football, there are some opportunities that may be more easily afforded them than may be the case with a practitioner of another faith tradition or secular belief. Given the large numbers of Spanish, French, South American, Italian,

Irish, Polish and Dutch players in the English Premier League, the sport psychologist will find that many of these individuals are practising Catholics or have some understanding of this religion having lived in traditionally Catholic cultures. It is not uncommon for these players to ask the sport psychologist as well as the chaplain for information about Mass times, locations of churches and, if they have children, access to local Catholic schools. These can be very powerful ways for both the chaplain and the sport psychologist to build relationships with and to begin to support players. Many clubs have a comprehensive induction process in place for new players and their families; this may involve the chaplain and the sport psychologist as well as other specialist staff like liaison officers and coaches.

The famous psychotherapist Carl Gustav Jung (1963) claimed that throughout his professional life, he very rarely worked with any Catholic patients in his clinic despite this group representing around 40 per cent of the Swiss population at that time. He suggested that this was not necessarily a comment on the mental health of this section of Swiss society, but was likely due to the psychological benefits associated with the sacrament of confession. In commenting on the psychotherapeutic value of engaging in a confidential and private encounter where the believer speaks about their failures to another trusted figure, Jung pointed out that the unburdening of guilt resulting from this type of dialogue in confession can have a profound and positive impact on an individual's psychological state. The Catholic sport psychologist guided by a personalist perspective in their work and with personal experience of the encounter that takes place in confession and reconciliation, may draw on this experience. This knowledge, working in a subtle and implicit way, may then influence the approach taken to dialogue in one-to-one sessions with players. This can help to reassure the player that no matter what is discussed, complete confidentiality will be maintained, something that they have encountered when attending confession or by knowing about the seal of the confessional. This is especially important given that it is quite common for players to want to discuss a number of delicate and very sensitive matters. These might include feeling anger and frustration at not being selected for the team, objecting to how the manager and coaches are treating them, doubting their own ability to consistently meet expectations concerning performance and a range of non-football related, broader life challenges that they would rather keep completely private from management, support staff and teammates.

Sometimes the sport psychologist and the chaplain can work together to provide players with opportunities to meet their spiritual and religious needs that are not attached to any one specific faith tradition. For example, some clubs are beginning to establish prayer rooms and private spaces where players and staff, regardless of their religious affiliation, can find a place for quiet reflection and prayer. Again, this is something that the sport psychologist following a person-centred and holistic working philosophy can help to create alongside the club chaplain. This type of fruitful partnership between the chaplain and the sport psychologist can be a highly visible way to demonstrate that the club is committed to meeting the deepest, most personal needs of their players and supporting their quest for performance excellence. This level of cooperation between chaplain and sport psychologist can encourage players and staff to reflect on their own identity and represent a gentle but persuasive reminder that there are more important things than winning football matches and succeeding as a professional footballer. I would respectfully suggest that some of those things are health, family, love and finding meaning in one's life.

Concluding comments

Sport psychologists operating inside professional football clubs have much to gain from developing strong and close professional relationships with club chaplains. If this means that the academic discipline of sport psychology needs to confront the limitations of its underlying scientific foundations and recognize its philosophical antecedents, then this should be welcomed. If this were to happen, chaplains operating in professional football would have provided a great service to those sport psychologists who conceive their role as helpers of persons who just happen to be professional sports performers. The chaplain's pastoral role and care for souls extends to everyone at the club; staff and players alike. Best practice for sport psychologists must follow this lead from chaplains, not only because it is ethically sound to do so, but because it is the optimum way to support performance enhancement.

As I have argued previously, there is much resistance from within academic quarters to sport psychologists being involved in matters spiritual and religious (Nesti, 2011b). However, these issues are very important for some players and staff (Nesti, 2011a) and therefore should not be ignored by sport psychologists just because they lack a religious faith or feel uncomfortable about people with a spiritual outlook on life (see Sarkar, Hill and Parker, 2014). This is not consistent with the importance of toleration and inclusivity that we hear about so often from psychologists and other social scientists. Sport psychologists are not being asked to provide a religious or spiritual answer to the problems faced by their clients; this would require them to go beyond their professional role. However, it could be considered a missed opportunity if the psychologist does not fully support the work of the chaplain in professional football. Not only will this assist the sport psychologist to understand the players and staff team in a more rounded way, but it might also cause them to reflect more deeply on their own philosophy of practice and to examine the sources of meaning that guide them both personally and professionally.

References

Andersen, M.B. (2009). 'Performance Enhancement as a Bad Start and a Dead End: A Parenthetical Comment on Mellalieu and Lane', *Sport and Exercise Scientist*, 20: 12–14.

Brady, A., and I. Maynard (2010). 'At Elite Level the Role of the Sport Psychologist is Entirely about Performance Enhancement', *Sport and Exercise Psychology Review*, 6: 59–66.

Brown, G., and P. Potrac (2009). '"You've not made the grade son": De-Selection and Identity Disruption in Elite Level Youth Football', *Soccer and Society*, 10: 143–59.

Caruso, I.A. (1964). *Existential Psychology: From Analysis to Synthesis*, London: Darton, Longman & Todd.

Corlett, J. (1996a). 'Sophistry, Socrates and Sport Psychology', *Sport Psychologist*, 10: 84–94.

—— (1996b). 'Virtues Lost: Courage in Sport', *Journal of the Philosophy of Sport*, 23: 45–57.

Crust, L. (2006). 'The Myth of Spirituality in Sport', *Online Journal of Sport Psychology*, 8: 17–31.

Fifer, A., K. Henschen, D. Gould, and K. Ravizza (2008). 'What Works when Working with Athletes', *Sport Psychologist*, 22: 356–77.

Frankl, V. (1984). *Man's Search for Meaning: An Introduction to Logotherapy*, New York: Simon & Schuster.

Gamble, R., D.M. Hill and A. Parker (2013). '"Revs and Psychos": Impact and Interaction of Sport Chaplains and Sport Psychologists within English Premiership Soccer', *Journal of Applied Sport Psychology*, 25: 249–64.

Jung, C.G. (1963). *Modern Man in Search of a Soul*, London: Tan.

Kierkegaard, S. (1980). *The Concept of Anxiety*, Princeton. NJ: Princeton University Press.

Ladd, T., and J.A. Mathison (1999). *Muscular Christianity: Evangelical Protestants and the Development of American Sport*, Ada, MI: Baker Books.

Marcel, G. (1948). *The Philosophy of Existence*, London: Harvill.

Maslow, A.H. (1962). *Toward a Psychology of Being*, Princeton, NJ: D. van Nostrand.

Nesti, M. (2010). *Psychology in Football: Working with Elite and Professional Players*, London: Routledge.

—— (2011a). 'Phenomenology and Sport Psychology: Back to the Things Themselves!', *Sport, Ethics and Philosophy*, 5/3: 285–96.

—— (2011b). 'Sporting Recommendations for Spiritual Encounters: Delivering Sport Psychology inside the English Premier League', *Physical Culture, Sport Studies and Research*, 52/1: 14–21.

Nesti and M. Littlewood (2011). 'Making your Way in the Game: Boundary Situations within England's Professional Football World', in D. Gilbourne and M.B. Andersen (eds), *Critical Essays in Applied Sport Psychology*, Champaign, IL: Human Kinetics, 233–50.

Pargament, K.I. (1999). 'The Psychology of Religion and Spirituality? Yes and No', *International Journal for the Psychology of Religion*, 9/1: 3–16.

Parry, J., M. Nesti and N. Watson (2011). *Theology, Ethics and Transcendence in Sports*, London: Routledge.

Pieper, J. (1995). *Divine Madness: Plato's Case against Secular Humanism*, San Francisco: Ignatius Press.

—— (1998). *Leisure: The Basis of Culture*, South Bend, IN: St Augustine's Press.

Ravizza, K.H. (2002). 'A Philosophical Construct: A Framework for Performance Enhancement', *International Journal of Sport Psychology*, 33/1: 4–18.

Robinson, S. (2007). 'Spirituality: A Story so Far', in S.J. Parry et al. (eds), *Sport and Spirituality: An Introduction*, New York: Routledge, 7–21.

Ryba, T.V., and H.K. Wright (2005). 'From Mental Game to Cultural Praxis: A Cultural Studies Model's Implications for the Future of Sport Psychology', *Quest*, 57/2: 192–212.

Sarkar, M., D.M. Hill and A. Parker (2014). 'Working with Religious and Spiritual Athletes: Ethical Considerations for Sport Psychologists', *Psychology of Sport and Exercise*, 15: 580–7.

Slife, B.D., C. Hope and R.S. Nebeker (1999). 'Examining the Relationship between Religious Spirituality and Psychological Science', *Journal of Humanistic Psychology*, 39/2: 51–85.

Theos (2013). *The Spirit of Things Unseen: Belief in Post-Religious Britain*, London, Theos.

Van Deurzen, E., and C. Arnold-Baker (2005). *Existential Perspectives on Human Issues: A Handbook for Therapeutic Practice*, New York: Palgrave Macmillan

Vealey, R.S. (2006). 'Smocks and Jocks outside the Box: The Paradigmatic Evolution of Sport and Exercise Psychology', *Quest*, 58/1: 128–59.

Vitz, P. (1997). *Psychology as Religion: The Cult of Self-Worship*, Grand Rapids, MI: Eerdmans.

Voas, D., and A. Crockett (2005). 'Religion in Britain: Neither Believing nor Belonging', *Sociology*, 39/1: 11–28.

Watson, N.J., and M. Nesti (2005). 'The Role of Spirituality in Sport Psychology Consulting: An Analysis and Integrative Review of Literature', *Journal of Applied Sport Psychology*, 17: 228–39.

14 Moving toward a faithful relationship

Sport psychology consultants speak about the potential of engaging with spirituality in consultation

Trevor J. Egli and Leslee A. Fisher

Introduction

During my graduate work in sport psychology, I (Trevor, first author) consulted with an elite, Division I (collegiate) female, freshman volleyball athlete. From my initial ('intake') interview with her, I knew that she was struggling with a lack of confidence stemming mainly from her coach's negative behaviour related to her performance in practice. The intake interview also included questions regarding spirituality and religion and assessed whether the athlete wanted to include any discussion of such issues in our work together. She was a committed Christian and said that since being a Christian was a very important part of her identity, she would like Christianity to be part of our consultation process. She also mentioned that she saw Tim Tebow as a role model. At the time, Tebow was a successful collegiate American football player and renowned (outspoken) Christian. Given that I too am a committed Christian, I occasionally referred to Bible verses during our discussions and related these to her sporting performance.

After working with this athlete for several sessions, I felt like we were not moving forwards. This led me to ask her, 'What is it that you enjoy about what we have done together?' Her response changed my approach to the way that I worked with her for the rest of our time together (and with future consultees). She said, 'I loved it when you included the Bible verses.' From then on, we discussed a Bible verse in each of our consultation sessions and also reflected on her Christian identity and its role in her performance. She believed that including a Bible verse made consultations both more effective and more enjoyable. However, my peers expressed very different reactions after watching a video of me consulting with this athlete about a month into our work together. They made comments like, 'Why would you include direct discussions of faith in your sessions?' 'Tim Tebow doesn't even play that sport!' 'Where are you going with this?' 'Are you sure this isn't your own bias?' Only one peer believed that the way I was approaching this work – integrating an athlete's faith into performance consulting – made sense. He went so far as to speculate about his own lack of experience in this area: 'What if that had been me (a person who did not profess the Christian faith) working with that athlete – and she could have benefited from the inclusion of her faith in our work together? What would I have done?' Leslee (second author) has also encountered similar questions in her experience as an Association for Applied Sport Psychology (AASP) certified consultant and supervisor of sport psychology postgraduate students who are working toward their AASP certification but believe that faith has absolutely no place in sport psychology consultation.

To situate our discussion of how sport psychology consultants might engage with faith and spirituality issues in consultation, we first briefly define what the field of applied sport psychology is. We then discuss how applied sport psychology has engaged (or not) with concepts like faith, spirituality and religion. Next, we present a series of practical steps that sport psychology consultants might undertake before they work with athletes who consider spirituality a salient component of their identity. We end with a description of how we believe sport psychology consultants and sports chaplains might work together to better facilitate the needs of athletes. We believe that these kinds of discussions should be included in all sport psychology graduate training programmes as well as in requirements for sport psychology consultant certification.

Definitions

What is applied sport psychology, who can practise it and what do sport psychology practitioners call themselves? According to its website, the AASP (founded in 1986) is the largest applied sport and exercise psychology organization in the world (Association for Applied Sport Psychology, 2013). Beginning in 1989 AASP members developed and approved certification criteria for those who wished to consult with performers in a variety of contexts. These certification criteria include mandatory undergraduate and postgraduate coursework in sports science and psychology and counselling. In addition, AASP certified consultants must have at least 400 hours of supervised practicum to be considered for 'provisional' status (for example, practising with a master's degree).

Sport psychology

Sport psychology has been defined as 'the study of psychological principles aimed at enhancing sport performance' and 'the study of the psychological aspects of sport' (Andersen, 2000: xiii). For the purposes of this chapter, we adhere to the latter definition and broaden it to include consultation in a variety of sport and performance contexts (for example, children's sport, elite-level sport, military training, music performance). We believe that the practice of 'doing sport psychology' is inclusive of all applied sport psychological aspects: for us, this allows for a more holistic approach when working with performers (Andersen, 2000; Egli, Fisher, and Gentner, 2014a).

Sport psychology consultants

Weinberg and Gould (2011: 7) define a sport psychology consultant (SPC) as a psycho-educator who 'educates athletes and exercisers about psychological skills and their development'. SPCs focus their work on the kinds of performance-related issues that arise with athletes and exercisers such as performing under intense pressure, increasing confidence, lowering anxiety and concentrating on relevant cues. As previously noted, SPCs are required to successfully complete primary training coursework in the areas of sports science and psychology and counselling. In addition, unless they have specialized psychological licensure, they are not permitted to treat emotional and mental disorders. Sport psychology consultants may also be referred to as educational sport psychology specialists (Weinberg and Gould, 2011), mental coaches or performance enhancement consultants (Association for Applied Sport Psychology, 2013). In the US they work toward and receive certification through AASP. For the remainder of this chapter, we focus on professionals who use the title, sport psychology consultant.

Sport psychologists

The AASP defines a sport psychologist as one who is 'trained in clinical or counselling psychology to provide individual or group therapy relative to a broad range of behavioural and emotional issues' (Association for Applied Sport Psychology, 2013). This means that a sport psychologist can treat such issues as eating disorders and depression but also has training in sports and exercise psychology. In the United States, a sport psychologist – also referred to as a clinical psychologist – must pass an examination in the state in which they work in order to obtain a licence to practise (Weinberg and Gould, 2011).

Faith, spirituality, religion and sport

While not the specific focus of this chapter, it is also important for us to briefly define faith, spirituality and religion and the ways that these constructs have intersected in sporting discourse throughout history. It is worth noting at this stage that the terms 'faith', 'spirituality' and 'religion' have often been used interchangeably in academic literature (see Sarkar, Hill and Parker, 2014).

Faith

Finding meaning and purpose in life is a task that, it could be argued, is pertinent to everyone. However, living life with a sense of purpose, values or commitment may not necessarily be a conscious process. As Fowler (1981) suggests, when understood as a general human phenomenon, faith is a process by which individuals become devoted to something greater than themselves that they believe has an impact on their being. According to Fowler, this 'something' can come in the form of material possessions, relationships, traditions or a divine being. In addition, people may not initially think of sport as a place to reflect on faith; however, sport is a place where many individuals see their faith as inextricably intertwined with who they are. Therefore, helping-professionals such as sport psychology consultants and practitioners should be aware of how faith, spirituality and religion intersect with sport.

Spirituality

Referring to spirituality within the context of sports performance excellence, Ravizza (2002) suggests that there is a spiritual dimension achieved by athletes when their entire sporting experience comes together. He describes this phenomenon as multidimensional when athletes' mental, emotional and physical components intertwine to create an appreciation of something greater than themselves. Furthermore, Watson and Nesti (2005) state that when athletes achieve camaraderie in sport or in other success areas, such victories and individual accolades can be defined by them as spiritual experiences. Watson and Nesti accept spirituality as being individually defined suggesting that religion may or may not be included in athlete definitions of spirituality. Regardless, as Koenig (2008) argues, any definition of spirituality one chooses for oneself is positive in nature. For us, this means that spirituality – as a phenomenon which some people would like to have in their lives – may also be something that they would like to experience in their sporting lives.

Religion

In a formal sense, religion denotes social institutions that rely on specific doctrine (Robinson, 2007). Examples include Christianity, Islam, Buddhism and Taoism. This may be both public and private and often entails religious practices, such as reading scriptures or meditation (Koenig, 2008). Religion is also a place where faith and spirituality may be directed; however, faith and spirituality are 'not exclusive to religion' (Robinson, 2007: 34). Although faith, spirituality, religion and sport are relevant to many people in US society, they are no longer as intertwined as they once were (Mandelbaum, 2004). For example, the ancient cultures of the Central American Mayans and Aztecs as well as that of the native North Americans each blended religion and sport (Baker, 2007; Guttmann, 1992). More recently, US sport has become highly secular in nature and is more often a site of mass entertainment than anything else (Krattenmaker, 2010; Roberts and Yamane, 2012). Despite the growing disconnection between religion and North American culture, this has not stopped religious or spiritual athletes and coaches from participating in sport (Hoffman, 2010). That said, it would appear beneficial to athletes if helping-professionals could become more culturally competent and conversant about the ways that athletes incorporate faith, spirituality and religion into their sporting identities.

Sport psychology research

Most of the sport psychology research surrounding these constructs has highlighted the use of religion in sport, particularly Christianity. Researchers have focused on various facets of the sport–Christianity interface such as Christian athletes' experiences within sport (Stevenson, 1991, 1997), Christian coaches' experiences of sport (Bennett et al., 2005), the use of prayer by athletes (Czech et al., 2004) and coaches (Egli et al., 2014b). Watson and Nesti (2005) have also attempted to bring discussion of spirituality into sport psychology. They describe how spirituality can be understood within the context of sport, how it can be involved in mental-skills training and a counselling relationship and in relation to the 'flow' experience.

Recently, discussion of spirituality has also emerged within cultural sport psychology (Schinke and Hanrahan, 2009). Cultural sport psychology theorists place primary importance on seeing culture as an integral part of being able to understand athletes and other performers. Moreover, Schinke and Hanrahan have suggested that practitioners need to be aware of how their own experiences of 'race', ethnicity, gender, sexuality, geographic location, religion and spirituality might have an impact upon individual identity and sporting experience (see also Fisher, Butryn and Roper, 2003, 2005; Fisher, Roper and Butryn, 2009; Gill and Kamphoff, 2010). However, while the AASP includes statements about cultural competency within their ethical guidelines (Watson, Etzel and Loughran, 2012), there is still no formal requirement for sport psychology consultants to have training in cultural competence, including in matters related to spirituality. In addition, while some scholars have addressed specific aspects of culture within sport psychology research such as 'race' (Butryn, 2002; Duda and Allison, 1990), sexual orientation (Krane et al., 2010) and gender (McGannon and Busanich, 2010), spirituality has yet to feature to the same degree (Egli et al., 2014a). We believe that it is imperative that the development of culturally sensitive and competent sport psychology consultants should involve some consideration of how spirituality might be used in consultation settings.

Sport psychology consulting and spirituality

This brings us to a discussion of how sport psychology consultants might prepare themselves for a time when spirituality arises as an important component of identity for an athlete with whom they are working. In their review of spirituality in sport psychology consulting, Watson and Nesti (2005: 230) describe the potential of integrating spirituality into an athlete–consultant relationship through an athlete-centred model whereby 'performance excellence and personal excellence are viewed as equally important developmental outcomes'. Although some athlete-centred models do not incorporate spirituality (Miller and Kerr, 2002), we agree with Watson and Nesti that when spirituality is not incorporated sport psychology consultants may be neglecting an integral component of athlete identity. However, although the topic of spirituality has been addressed in sport psychology literature (Schinke and Hanrahan, 2009; Watson and Nesti, 2005), there is a lack of discussion about how applied consultants might handle spirituality when it is present in consulting relationships. One reason for this may be that within applied sport psychology spirituality is seen as something of a 'taboo' subject. Despite this perception, we believe that we cannot ignore the fact that spirituality may in fact be a central component of a working relationship between the athlete and consultant (Gamble, Hill and Parker, 2013; Nesti, 2007). To this end, we offer some practical steps which sport psychology consultants may consider prior to encountering spirituality in practice.

Step 1: Examining helpful theoretical frameworks

A helpful framework allowing for an athlete-centred and spiritual approach to consulting could begin with a humanistic philosophy. In this view, helping professionals are encouraged to see and understand their clients within context. Such a holistic approach also encourages consultants to be cognizant that each individual is unique (Hill, 2001; Patton, 2002). Corey (2008) has discussed five themes occurring within all humanistic approaches: (1) the importance of self-awareness; (2) commitment to a phenomenological approach; (3) self-actualization; (4) the belief that humans are free, self-determining beings; and (5) respect for the subjective experience of each person. Existential philosophy is one specific humanistic approach that sport psychology researchers and practitioners have successfully used in order to address spirituality (see e.g. Czech et al., 2004; Nesti, 2004). Egli and colleagues (2014a) have also noted how using a humanistic athlete-centred approach within applied sport psychology consulting relationships may be helpful when spirituality is relevant to athletes.

Step 2: Reflexivity

A second step that sport psychology consultants can take is to practise reflexivity. This entails reflecting on one's own personal beliefs and biases in relation to a particular topic. For the purposes of this chapter, this means reflecting on the role of faith, spirituality and religion in one's own life (McGannon and Johnson, 2009). The kinds of questions that one may ask oneself in this respect include: 'How do I define faith, spirituality, and religion?' 'How has my training prepared me to consult with athletes who incorporate religion into their sport performance?' 'Am I competent to handle spirituality issues?' 'How do I view others who hold belief systems different to my own?' Such questions and considerations appear to be absent from US sport psychology graduate training programmes. For example, in a study of practising sport psychology consultants, all participants alluded to the fact that spiritual considerations were not included in their graduate coursework (Egli et al., 2014a). We believe that consultants should regularly take time to reflect on spirituality and its potential for being a critical component of behaviour change in consulting relationships.

As recommended by Koenig (2008), regardless of how one addresses the above questions, it is important for practitioners to initially maintain a broad understanding of spirituality within consulting relationships.

Step 3: Intake interview questions

Another practical step for practitioners interested in pursuing a more holistic approach to consultation is to include questions pertaining to athletes' faith, spirituality and religion during intake interviews (Egli et al., 2014a). This does not mean that such issues will necessarily be important to every athlete or to individual athletes all of the time. However, such questions allow athletes to include this component in their conversations. Indeed, of critical importance is that the athlete determines the frequency and regularity of discussion surrounding spirituality during the consulting relationship (ibid.). Like all sport psychology consultants, we believe that imposing one's own beliefs onto one's clients represents unethical behaviour.

Step 4: Using the athlete's own language

When athletes bring spirituality language into consultation, sport psychology consultants should consider adopting the same language that athletes use. Egli and colleagues (2014a) found it common practice amongst their AASP certified consultant sample to incorporate the language of spirituality into mental skills training such as self-talk statements, imagery, routines and goal setting. Many participants spoke of the amalgamation of spirituality and mental-skills training as frequently occurring during times of adversity, especially in the case of injury. In using the athlete's own language, consultants described how they were better able to connect with their clients and build enhanced rapport when such issues were considered. As Ryba (2009) states, when a 'shared language' is developed this can become a meaningful form of communication, especially when cultural differences are present. Knowledge of the language that athletes use also allows sport psychology consultants to educate themselves in relation to certain cultural components with which they may be unfamiliar. This can facilitate a better understanding of the background of the athletes in question (see also Balague, 1999; Storch et al., 2001; Watson and Nesti, 2005).

Step 5: Caveat and referral

All of the steps above are predicated on the notion that the therapeutic relationship between athlete and consultant is more important than any of the techniques used: it is also vital if change is to occur (Corey, 2008). Therefore, while we believe that spirituality is a component of sport psychology practice, either seen or unseen, when spirituality becomes the central component of the sport psychology consulting relationship and extends the practitioner beyond their comfort or competency level, they should consider partnering with or referring to other helping professionals with appropriate expertise such as sports chaplains (Egli et al., 2014a; Storch et al., 2001).

Sport psychology consultants working with sports chaplains

When it comes to academic investigations into the interaction of sport psychology consultants and sports chaplains, there is little empirical evidence available. We know that the role of a sport psychology consultant is generally to handle performance issues, while sports chaplains primarily provide spiritual and pastoral care for athletes (Waller, Dzikus and Hardin, 2008). Yet, these two skill-sets may be more complementary than has been previously realized (Nesti, 2007).

For example, in a recent study, Gamble, Hill and Parker (2013) examined the relationship between sport psychologists and sports chaplains in English professional football (more specifically the English Premier League). The authors found that both psychologists and chaplains perceived their positions as not being fully integrated into the structure of the clubs with which they worked and described times when they felt decidedly limited in their roles. In addition, while both parties had an understanding of each other's role, little interaction (personal or professional) occurred between them. We believe that this may also be the case in many US sporting contexts where both sport psychology consultants and sports chaplains are present. For example, at our own institution (University of Tennessee, Knoxville), a network of helping-professionals was developed and asked to create a welfare model to best serve student athletes. Hosted by the Sports Medicine Department, the Health and Wellness Team is made up of physicians, psychiatrists, clinical psychologists, a clinical social worker, a nutritionist, academic personnel, head coaches, a director of mental training and a graduate student sport psychology consultant, a sports sociologist and a sports chaplain. Student athletes are encouraged to choose the services which they believe best suit their individual needs, a process which is based on the premise that this type of athlete self-selection offers the optimum chance of achieving successful outcomes. However, both the director of mental training and the sports chaplain are not considered to be part of the primary services on offer; instead, they are designated 'support services'. Although it is generally recognized that the director of mental training and the sports chaplain are an integral part of the Health and Wellness Team, one might conclude that these professionals are less valued than the primary service providers.

One positive aspect of this team approach is that there is a sound professional relationship in place between the director of mental training and the sports chaplain. Despite this, referrals in either direction have not necessarily occurred indicating a lack of professional networking (see Gamble, Hill and Parker, 2013). Although a sport psychology consultant may be aware of the existence of a sports chaplain in a particular sporting context, we believe that it would be mutually beneficial for the two parties to connect on a personal basis, regardless of the institutional structures within which they work.

Another issue for both sport psychology consultants and sports chaplains to become familiar with is the other's training and educational background. Sport psychology consultants may benefit from learning more about the role, credentials and professional associations of sports chaplains. Waller, Dzikus and Hardin (2008) have discussed the multiple titles and training programmes associated with sports chaplaincy in the United States, each of which represent different competencies. Likewise, sports chaplains may benefit from investigating the training and credentialing of sport psychology consultants (for example, in the US this may mean enquiring if they are currently a member of AASP, are AASP certified or are pursuing such certification) and the type of services which they provide for athletes. It is important to note, of course, that while credentialing can reflect the quality of service on offer, it is no guarantee of this.

Sport psychology consultants may also find it advantageous to refer athletes to sports chaplains because of their familiarity with both spirituality and the culture of sport. Like many sport psychology consultants, sports chaplains may have played sport at a similar level as the athletes with whom they are working and, as a consequence, may have spent a considerable amount of time processing the interaction between spirituality and sport. In turn, the personal experiences of sports chaplains may be especially helpful when athletes themselves struggle to make sense of sporting experience alongside their spiritual beliefs. For example, numerous scholars have suggested that the Christian ethic does not fit well with the culture of elite sport (Higgs, 1995; Higgs and Braswell, 2004; Hoffman, 2010). Indeed, Higgs and Braswell use the analogy of oil and water to represent this fit. Such tensions can cause sports performers to wrestle with their own identities both as athletes and as spiritual people (see Stevenson, 1991).

Prior to referring an athlete to a sports chaplain, sport psychology consultants should make it a priority to discuss the prospective referral with the athlete in question. In such situations, being knowledgeable about and familiar with the work of the sports chaplain may better help consultants explain why they believe that referral is the most appropriate course of action. In addition, it is possible that sport psychology consultants and sports chaplains could work together with athletes given that each has a unique perspective to bring to the table.

Conclusion

In this chapter we have primarily focused on engaging sport psychology consultants with notions of spirituality and with the work of sports chaplains. Ultimately, our goal is to better enhance athlete welfare, especially where elements of spirituality are present. We believe that spirituality is a phenomenon that can penetrate an athlete's sporting experience and performance (Robinson, 2007). We also believe that more needs to be done to better prepare sport psychology consultants in how to engage with these constructs during consultation. Despite the fact that there appears to be scope for sport psychology consultants and sports chaplains to work together, as yet this is not common practice. It has been our contention throughout that if we are to move towards an enhancement of the holistic support services available to athletes, then the encouragement of increased interaction between sport psychology consultants and sports chaplains is a useful place to start.

References

Andersen, M.B. (2000). 'Introduction', *Doing Sport Psychology*, Champaign, IL: Human Kinetics, xiii–xvii.

Association for Applied Sport Psychology (2013). *About Applied Sport and Exercise Psychology*. Available at <http://www.appliedsportpsych.org/about/about-applied-sport-and-exercise-psychology/>.

Baker, W.J. (2007). *Playing with God: Religion and Modern Sport*, Cambridge, MA: Harvard University Press.

Balague, G. (1999). 'Understanding Identity, Value, and Meaning when Working with Elite Athletes', *Sport Psychologist*, 13: 89–98.

Bennet, G., M. Sagas, and D. Fleming (2005). 'On Being a Living Contradiction: The Struggle of an Elite Intercollegiate Christian Coach', *Journal of Beliefs and Values*, 26/3: 289–300.

Butryn, T.M. (2002). 'Critically Examining White Racial Identity and Privilege in Sport Psychology Consulting', *Sport Psychologist*, 16: 316–36.

Corey, G. (2008). *Theory and Practice of Group Counseling*, 7th edn, Belmont, CA: Thomson Brooks/Cole.

Czech, D.R., et al. (2004). 'The Experience of Christian Prayer in Sport: An Existential Phenomenological Investigation', *Journal of Psychology and Christianity*, 2: 1–19.

Duda, J.L., and M.T. Allison (1990). 'Cross-Cultural Analysis in Exercise and Sport Psychology: A Void in the Field', *Journal of Sport and Exercise Psychology*, 12: 114–31.

Egli, T.J., L.A. Fisher and N. Gentner (2014a). 'AASP-Certified Consultants' Experiences of Spirituality within Sport Psychology Consultation', *The Sport Psychologist*, 28: 394–405.

Egli, T.J., D.R. Czech, S.Y. Todd, G.W. Shaver, N. Gentner, and D.D. Biber (2014b). 'The Experience of Christian Prayer in Coaching: A Qualitative Investigation', *Journal of Psychology and Christianity*, 33: 45–57.

Fisher, L.A., T.M. Butryn and E.A. Roper (2003). 'Diversifying (and Politicizing) Sport Psychology through Cultural Studies: A Promising Perspective', *The Sport Psychologist*, 17: 391–405.

Fisher, L.A., T.M. Butryn and E.A. Roper (2005). 'Diversifying (and Politicizing) Sport Psychology through Cultural Studies: A Promising Perspective Revisited', *Athletic Insight*, 7: 23–35.

—— E.A. Roper and T.M. Butryn (2009). 'Engaging Cultural Studies and Traditional Sport Psychology', in R.J. Schinke and S.J. Hanrahan (eds), *Cultural Sport Psychology*, Champaign, IL: Human Kinetics, 23–34.

Fowler, J.W. (1981). *Stages of Faith: The Psychology of Human Development and the Quest for Meaning*, San Francisco: Harper & Row.

Gamble, R., D.M. Hill and A. Parker (2013). '"Revs and Psychos": Role, Impact and Interaction of Sport Chaplains and Sport Psychologists within English Premiership Soccer', *The Sport Psychologist*, 25: 249–64.

Gill, D.L., and C.S. Kamphoff (2010). 'Sport Psychology and Representation', in T.V. Ryba, R.J. Schinke and G. Tenenbaum (eds), *The Cultural Turn in Sport Psychology*, Morgantown, WV: Fitness Information Technology, 53–74.

Guttmann, A. (1992). 'From Ritual to Record', in S.J. Hoffman (ed.), *Sport and Religion*, Champaign, IL: Human Kinetics, 143–52.

Higgs, R.J. (1995). *God in the Stadium: Sports and Religion in America*, Lexington: University Press of Kentucky.

—— and M.C. Braswell (2004). *An Unholy Alliance: The Sacred and Modern Sports*, Macon, GA: Mercer University Press.

Hill, K. (2001). *Frameworks for Sport Psychologists: Enhancing Sport Performance*, Champaign, IL: Human Kinetics.

Hoffman, S.J. (2010). *Good Game: Christianity and the Culture of Sports*, Waco, TX: Baylor University Press.

Koenig, H.G. (2008). *Medicine, Religion, and Health: Where Science and Spirituality Meet*, West Conshohocken, PA: Templeton Foundation Press.

Krane, V., et al. (2010). 'Queering Sport Psychology', in T.V. Ryba, R.J. Schinke and G. Tenenbaum (eds), *The Cultural Turn in Sport Psychology*, Morgantown, WV: Fitness Information Technology, 153–80.

Krattenmaker, T. (2010). *Onward Christian Athletes: Turning Ballparks into Pulpits and Players into Preachers*, Lanham, MD: Rowan & Littlefield.

McGannon, K.R., and R. Busanich (2010). 'Rethinking Subjectivity in Sport and Exercise Psychology: A Feminist Post-Structuralist Perspective on Women's Embodied Physical Activity', in T.V. Ryba, R.J. Schinke and G. Tenenbaum (eds), *The Cultural Turn in Sport Psychology*, Morgantown, WV: Fitness Information Technology, 127–52.

McGannon, K.R., and C.R. Johnson (2009). 'Strategies for Reflective Cultural Sport Psychology Research', in R.J. Schinke and S.J. Hanrahan (eds), *Cultural Sport Psychology*, Champaign, IL: Human Kinetics, 57–75.

Mandelbaum, M. (2004). *The Meaning of Sports: Why Americans watch Baseball, Football, and Basketball, and What They See When They Do*, New York: PublicAffairs.

Miller, P.S., and G.A. Kerr (2002). 'Conceptualizing Excellence: Past, Present, and Future', *Journal of Applied Sport Psychology*, 14: 140–53.

Nesti, M. (2004). *Existential Psychology and Sport: Implications for Research and Practice*, London: Routledge.

—— (2007). 'Person and Players', in J. Parry et al. (eds), *Sport and Spirituality: An Introduction*, London: Routledge, 135–50.

Patton, M. (2002). *Qualitative Research and Evaluation Methods*, 3rd edn, Thousand Oaks, CA: Sage.

Ravizza, K. (2002). 'A Philosophical Construct: A Framework for Performance Enhancement', *International Journal of Sport Psychology*, 33: 4–18.

Roberts, K.A., and D. Yamane (2012). *Religion in Sociological Perspective*, 5th edn. Thousand Oaks, CA: Pine Forge Press.

Robinson, S. (2007). 'Spirituality: A Working Definition', in J. Parry et al. (eds), *Sport and Spirituality: An Introduction*, London: Routledge, 22–37.

Ryba, T.V. (2009). 'Understanding your Role in Cultural Sport Psychology', in R.J. Schinke and S.J. Hanrahan (eds), *Cultural Sport Psychology*, Champaign, IL: Human Kinetics, 35–44.

Sarkar, M., D.M. Hill and A. Parker (2014). 'Working with Religious and Spiritual Athletes: Ethical Considerations for Sport Psychologists', *Psychology of Sport and Exercise*, 15: 580–7.

Schinke, R.J., and S.J. Hanrahan (2009). *Cultural Sport Psychology*, Champaign, IL: Human Kinetics.

Stevenson, C.L. (1991). 'The Christian Athlete: An Interactionist-Developmental Perspective', *Sociology of Sport Journal*, 8: 362–79.

—— (1997). 'Christian Athletes and the Culture of Elite Sport: Dilemmas and Solutions', *Sociology of Sport Journal*, 14: 241–62.

Storch, E.A., et al. (2001). 'Religiosity of Elite College Athletes', *Sport Psychologist*, 15: 346–51.

Waller, S., L. Dzikus and R. Hardin (2008). 'Collegiate Sport Chaplaincy: Problems and Promise', *Journal of Issues in Intercollegiate Athletics*, 1: 107–23.

Watson, J., E. Etzel and M.J. Loughran (2012). *Ethics and Cultural Competence*. Retrieved from <http://appliedsportpsych.org/resource-center/professionals/articles/competence>.

Watson, N.J., and M. Nesti (2005). 'The Role of Spirituality in Sport Psychology Consulting: An Analysis and Integrative Review of Literature', *Journal of Applied Sport Psychology*, 17: 228–39.

Weinberg, R.S., and D. Gould (2011). *Foundations of Sport and Exercise Psychology*, 5th edn, Champaign, IL: Human Kinetics.

15 Football, chaplaincy and sport psychology

Connections and possibilities

Richard Gamble, Andrew Parker and Denise M. Hill[1]

Introduction

Despite an increased focus on spirituality and wellbeing in sport in recent years (Watson, 2011; Sarkar, Hill and Parker, 2014), there remains a dearth of research regarding those who provide athlete support in these areas. The aim of this chapter is to explore the work of sports chaplains and sport psychologists within English professional (Premier League) football (soccer) and to identify the ways in which these two practitioner disciplines facilitate athlete wellbeing within this context. Drawing upon the findings of a small-scale, qualitative research project into the potential connections between those inhabiting these two distinct occupational roles, the chapter reveals the significant overlap between the work of sports chaplains and sport psychologists whilst, at the same time, identifying barriers that may restrict the kinds of support which they offer.

Football, wellbeing and holistic care

Like many professional sporting contexts, the English Premier League is one in which a win-at-all-costs mentality predominates, where the drive for success is paramount, and where players live out their everyday existence in the media spotlight. Professional football is often an abrasive, irrational and unpredictable setting, and thus the emphasis for both the sports chaplain and the sport psychologist is on the deployment of holistic approaches to player wellbeing in terms of resolving lifestyle or personal issues and in offering compassion and empathy towards the individual circumstances of those concerned (Nesti, 2010, 2011). Watson and Nesti (2005) have argued that if an athlete holds religious convictions, then the sport psychologist needs to understand those beliefs in order to support the athlete. However, it is acknowledged that the sport psychologist may not be best placed to address fully these specific needs and that on matters of faith the sports chaplain is the appropriate point of referral.

Sports chaplaincy provides holistic pastoral and spiritual care for the wellbeing of people in sport (athletes and non-athletes alike), and, to this end, the core responsibility of chaplains is to ensure athlete welfare (Hastings and Delle Monache, 2007; Heskins and Baker, 2006). The number of sports chaplains working within English professional football has grown significantly in recent years, alongside the evolution of working relations between Sports Chaplaincy UK (the leading national agency in the field), the English Premier League, the Professional Footballers Association and the Football League Trust – an alliance which witnessed the emergence of a pastoral support director in English professional football in 2009. The remit of this role is to oversee the provision and development of chaplaincy within English professional clubs in accordance with a non-proselytizing ethos.

Nesti (2011; see also this volume) has argued that because of the rich diversity of player nationalities and cultures represented in the English Premier League, there is a necessity for each club to provide appropriate spiritual support. Yet the demands of high-profile, footballing lives and lifestyles are such that sports chaplains are often required to place emphasis on broader pastoral care, such as friendship, support, guidance and encouragement, the key aim being to enable players to cope with the extreme pressures of the professional game (Amos, 2006; Baker, 2006; Boyers, 2006).

Whilst academic literature surrounding the sport–Christianity interface continues to grow, (see Ellis, 2014; Harvey, 2014; Watson and Parker, 2014), relatively little has emerged on the specifics of sports chaplaincy in elite sport, which, at times, has led to misunderstandings about the chaplaincy role itself (Nesti, 2010; Waller, Dzikus and Hardin, 2008). Indeed, to date, the only real insight offered with regards to the work and impact of chaplaincy within professional sport has emerged from the biographical accounts of chaplains themselves (see e.g. Boyers, 2000, 2006, 2010, 2011; Chawner, 2009; Heskins and Baker, 2006; Wood, 2011). Accordingly, the nature and extent of the support provided by sports chaplains to professional football has yet to be explored empirically. Furthermore, the interaction of chaplains with other service providers, particularly sport psychologists, has yet to be examined to any significant degree.

As we have seen, the roles of the sport psychologist and sports chaplain are distinct in that the former are primarily required to focus on enhancing player performance and are therefore judged against performance-related outcomes (see Anderson et al., 2002). Conversely, sports chaplains deploy their spiritual expertise to respond specifically to issues of faith and religious belief and affiliation (Boyers, 2006; Watson and Czech, 2005). Nevertheless, Nesti (2007) speculates that given that the sport psychologist and sports chaplain have much in common and given that their skills are complementary, they might benefit from working collaboratively. Alongside their respective areas of expertise, both aim to provide holistic pastoral support to enhance athlete wellbeing. However, both roles have yet to be accepted fully as distinct disciplines within professional football and need to demonstrate their occupational worth. There is evidence from research completed within the health industry that psychologists and chaplains have become increasingly accepted, professionalized and accountable within this context by working cooperatively to improve healthcare provision (see Flannelly et al., 2003; Monod et al., 2010). Therefore, the argument that sport psychologists and sports chaplains should work together within sporting contexts appears to have foundation. That said, research has yet to examine the potential for such collaboration.

Accordingly, sports chaplains and sport psychologists appear to offer an important service within English professional football, but in order to discern their potential impact a further exploration of their respective roles – particularly with regards to their contribution to the support of players with faith – is required. Furthermore, there remains a need to investigate the level of cooperation that already exists between the two disciplines and to consider the potential for collaboration and partnership working within the professional football context. In the remainder of this chapter we seek to address this gap in the literature by presenting empirical findings concerning the experiences of sports chaplains and sport psychologists with regards to their individual and collective working lives.

Context and method

The research reported here was carried out between April and July 2011 at the end of the 2010/11 English Premier League season. Participants were selected using purposive sampling (Miles and Huberman, 1994) and were identified according to the experience that they had of working with elite athletes. The research sample consisted of seven participants: four sports chaplains and three sport psychologists, all of whom had experience of providing services in the English Premier League and one with international experience also. All participants were male. The four sports chaplains had practised at five different football clubs for a total of 36 years, 26 of these in the English Premier League serving under 23 different managers. Two of the chaplains came from the Anglican tradition, one was a Methodist and the other was from a more charismatic 'house church' background. Collectively, the three sport psychologists had a total of 19 years' experience of operating in the English Premier League and had served under seven managers at six different clubs. In addition, one had four years' experience in the lower football leagues and another had specific experience of working with young players. Whilst all of the sport psychologists interviewed were paid workers, they were employed largely on a part-time basis. Two attended their respective clubs for one day per week, the other having a more sporadic yet intensive presence. In contrast, the sports chaplains all operated in a voluntary capacity working in their respective clubs for one or two days a week on secondment from their home church. Such voluntary arrangements are the norm amongst sports chaplains in the UK.

Participants were contacted (by email or SMS) to arrange an interview, the venue for which was left for them to decide upon. All of the interviews with chaplains took place at professional football grounds. Two psychologists were interviewed away from the footballing environment in their private offices and the other by telephone. Participants were asked initially about how they came to be working within their respective professions. In turn, discussion turned to respondent perceptions of whether or not they had made an impact within their working environments. Finally, chaplains were asked about their interaction with sport psychologists and vice versa. Interview questions were open-ended and, where necessary, further probing took place to clarify participant responses (Bryman, 2015). Interviews lasted between 30 and 90 minutes and were recorded and transcribed verbatim.

Data were analysed in four stages (Giorgi and Giorgi, 2008). Firstly, the transcripts were read in full to gain an overview of the data. Secondly, each transcript was individually coded and indexed whereby a capturing of the different aspects of participant experience took place. Thirdly, these experiences were then categorized into a number of over-arching topics. The final stage of the analysis involved the formal organization of these topics into three generic themes in line with which the remainder of this chapter is structured. The first theme identifies the perceived impact and activity of the sport chaplaincy role. The second presents the perceived impact and activities of the sport psychologists. The third theme considers the levels of interaction between the two. We conclude by considering ways in which the culture of English professional football might serve to shape the contours of these distinctive roles and the potential relationship between them.

Sports chaplaincy in practice

Despite the range of backgrounds and differing theological stances of the respondent chaplains, there appeared to be no discernible difference in their day-to-day workplace behaviours. Indeed, there was a common perception amongst all chaplains that their core role was spiritual and pastoral care. To this end, the majority of their activities centred on supporting players (as opposed to managers, coaches or other auxiliary or administrative staff) in these areas.

All chaplains identified players for whom faith was an important issue, with three observing that players were significantly more open to embracing spirituality as part of their life and having a commitment to faith, than was evidenced in their everyday work in the community. One of the chaplains explained why he believed this to be the case:

> We found that there is a disproportionate passion for faith inside this club when compared to the rest of society and put that down to ... we have a lot of people from across the world coming in [to the club], so their passion for faith is much stronger than you find in the cultural norm of England .... And in this case ... our [club] Captain was a ... larger than life character ... a Christian ... and he was part of [others] becoming a Christian ... the knock on effects were huge.

Nor did chaplains see their spiritual expertise as being solely for the benefit of players or for those who demonstrated a faith. Rather, spiritual care was extended to all staff at their respective clubs, and this manifested itself in a variety of ways. Examples ranged from the everyday needs of people around the club to more formal situations, such as presiding over baptisms and memorial services (see Heskins and Baker, 2006). One chaplain's accommodation of the multi-faith ethos amidst which he found himself was to produce a calendar of key religious festivals to support club staff in relation to the particular faith-based requirements of individual players. Other examples of spiritual support included purchasing Bibles, Bible studies on faith and sport, the provision of daily devotionals designed for athletes and seeking out appropriate places of worship for players of all faiths.

A significant sub-theme to emerge from interviews with chaplains in relation to the provision of spiritual care was that of prayer. All of the chaplains interviewed invested some of their time in praying with players. For three of the four respondents this took place on match days in the form of what were termed 'pre-match prayers', with one chaplain holding prayer meetings for up to 15 players at a time (see also Boyers, 2010). Two of the chaplains highlighted instances where managers had attended pre-match prayers and one recounted a club where opposing players were also invited to take part. In addition, accounts were given of players with non-Christian beliefs attending prayers. One chaplain stated that he suspected that superstition was the main driver for the attendance of non-Christian players at such get-togethers (see Maranise, 2013).

Pre-match prayers typically lasted around 10 minutes and were not solely focused on the forthcoming game. Indeed, all chaplains stressed that they never prayed for teams to win. Chaplains noted that players mainly wanted to pray about family issues, friends or even world events. Where prayers did relate to the forthcoming game they were offered around personal matters such as protection against injury and playing to the best of one's abilities. One chaplain admitted that there was sometimes a 'fine line' between praying for performance and praying for victory. Prayers occasionally took place in club dressing rooms (with non-participating players being asked to leave) or in other rooms in and around clubs, this with the full cooperation of the managers concerned. Chaplains described pre-match prayers as something that were very much part of the match day experience for those players involved. There was a sense from one chaplain that such practice had become an embedded aspect of club culture:

> [The players] started pre-match prayer . . . . The team led that, and they were getting up to 15 players . . . even Jonesy[2] [an international player] used to come to it. It was the most remarkable thing. They used to go into the kit room . . . . The Kit Man had this sign on the door saying, 'Welcome to . . . the Chapel. If you want to pray, come in. If you don't, ★★★★ off.' I thought that summed up football brilliantly.

It was around the specific area of prayer that three of the four chaplains believed they had the potential to impact player performance. One highlighted an instance where a player with no particular faith had witnessed a marked improvement in his game which he attributed to pre-match prayers:

> It was about six months down the line I said to him, 'You've had a good season. What's changed?' . . . He said: 'Coming along to prayer . . . . I go out now with a sense of peace when I go to play, so that whatever happens . . . I'm at peace in how I play . . . and that has enabled me to perform better.'

The chaplain went on to explain that for the player in question prayers served to provide a sense of personal perspective whereby there was a realization that there were more important things in life than football and this, in turn, helped him to relax when it came to playing.

Alongside spiritual care, pastoral care was identified as a key activity of chaplains and an area where they were able to evidence impact as a result of their role. In distinguishing pastoral care from spiritual care, chaplains pointed to the former as comprising a more general form of support for players rather than one which was specifically faith-based. Amidst such support chaplains placed great emphasis on simply listening (with an independent and non-judgmental ear) to the needs of those with whom they worked, thus providing an opportunity for players to 'sound off' and vent their frustrations. In this sense, confidentiality was sacrosanct. Most pastoral care was exercised through one-to-one meetings between chaplain and player the majority of which came about as a result of informal conversations around the club. Subsequent meetings generally took place away from the club and training ground and sometimes in hospitality suites at the stadium, in hotels or at players' homes in order to ensure confidentiality. Chaplains reported that these meetings mainly tended to cover bereavement and family issues. Indeed, all respondent chaplains had experience of handling instances of bereavement at their respective clubs. This might involve the organization of formal ceremonies, the 'scattering ashes for fans' or the undertaking of a memorial service for an ex-player. In this context the chaplain was usually involved in supporting players, staff and coaches/managers who had suffered the loss of a close friend or family member. As one chaplain recalled:

> I remember this lad whose Grandfather had died many years ago . . . . he still wasn't coping . . . got very angry. . . . it was because his Granddad . . . had actually brought him up . . . . I address that kind of thing a lot in my work.

Interestingly, it was revealed that bereavement was the only area in which managers were prepared to refer employees to the sports chaplain within the club. In terms of family matters, these were predominantly relationship issues concerning girlfriends and wives, infidelity and homesickness. The latter applying predominantly (yet not exclusively) to younger players:

> When he came into the [Youth] Academy he was very homesick . . . and cried himself to sleep every night. Now he is a bit of a hero in the Academy

because he made it to the first team and told the story in a national news-paper about it . . . and how the chaplain helped him.

The main restriction on the amount of time that chaplains spent providing spiritual and pastoral care was imposed upon them not by the clubs but by the demands of their own community and church-based commitments. Such time limitations restricted the ability of chaplains to have regular contact with all of the various facets of club life, with one participant actively choosing to concentrate only on the needs of players at the expense of other areas:

> My problem is I just don't have the time really to follow up on a lot of them [players] like I'd like to . . . . [My] biggest regret . . . is I have never done as much with the youth [players] as I could do because, again, it's a time issue really.

In addition, because chaplains were not integrated formally into the organizational structures of their respective clubs, they only worked with players when requested to do so. Hence, overall, chaplains perceived that they did not have as much impact within their clubs as they would have liked.

Sport psychology in practice

The focus for the sport psychologists interviewed was first team player performance. It was clear from the responses of all three that the majority of sports psychologists that they had encountered in English Premier League football were exclusively performance oriented (rather than having existential and holistic motives) and that most would not consider other elements of player make-up. Even those who believed that wellbeing may lead to improved personal outcomes were clear that their primary function was to concentrate on those areas that provided tangible results:

> As a sport psychologist we know that our prime function is, in some shape or form, to help performance . . . . The focus is definitely on football; that's where it starts . . . that's where it ends. How could you play better? Then, [the player] will, depending on their level of trust in me, open up on other 'life' things.

The respective club managers of the sport psychologists had made it clear to them that they should operate solely on a performance basis and care should be taken not to step outside of this designated role. As a result, psychologists suggested that they focused on helping players with confidence, concentration and attention. However, despite their primary aim and workplace focus being framed around player performance, it became apparent during interview that the sport psychologists had frequently become involved in providing pastoral care for players. All three practitioners operated largely through one-to-one meetings with players which were arranged formally as part of their club role. It was during these meetings that players discussed pastoral issues, either in their initial interactions with practitioners or once a level of trust had been established. Indeed, pastoral issues were perceived to arise because the sport psychologist had built a rapport with the client, who was therefore at ease to 'open up'. On other occasions it was the pastoral issue itself which was the catalyst for the practitioner's involvement. When asked about the perceived impact that they had had on the players with whom they had worked, all three psychologists gave examples of resolving or providing support on pastoral issues and were notably more at ease talking about the help they had provided for players who were struggling with non–footballing issues. As in the case of the sports chaplains, these largely related to relationship problems or issues surrounding bereavement:

> I've got a football client at the moment who is going through a very, very difficult relationship with his wife and his kids. The tools I'm using are not sport psychology . . . . I would say it was crisis management. And [I] would be operating . . . outside the scope of sport psychology but much more in a player care capacity.

Hence, whilst all three sport psychologists recognized that their focus and role primarily related to performance enhancement, they also acknowledged that in essence their activities and impact were centred on pastoral care. As one respondent noted: 'Well I suppose at the higher level, [the] issues we are talking about have nothing to do with [performance], because they were already doing these things brilliantly.'

Importantly, the psychologists felt that all pastoral issues fell firmly within their remit and expertise, as they perceived that they were in a position to offer a superior level of support to that provided by sports chaplains:

> Well, if there's been some long-term trauma within the family or family circumstances then I think there's a big difference between the pastoral listening ear and actually a psychologist being able to take that forward a bit further, and actually build that confidence in that person, or restore their confidence.

In the case of athletes with faith, all three sport psychologists were of the opinion that if a player had issues, concerns or questions regarding their religious beliefs which were affecting their performance, then they should be referred elsewhere given that this aspect of a player's life was considered to be outside of their expertise. Moreover, sport psychologists perceived that their role remained unaffected by a player's religious beliefs. As one explained: 'I know that [the player] is a very staunch Christian. But I haven't explored the dynamics of that and what it means to him and how that affects his life, impacts his thoughts or anything.' However, it could be argued that by failing to consider fully the spiritual needs of players, the sport psychologists may not have adequately addressed the holistic needs of these athletes and optimized wellbeing (see Egli and Fisher, this volume). This may particularly be the case when accounting for the importance of faith within the elite football population (Nesti, 2011).

It is also worth noting that all three psychologists observed that the managers of their respective clubs sometimes felt threatened when receiving advice from them about player welfare. This is likely to be a consequence of the general level of occupational and personal insecurity prevalent in the professional footballing environment (see Roderick, 2006). It was perceived by the sport psychologists that their impact on athlete welfare was restricted because players often avoided meeting with them, even after being instructed to do so by management. For all the psychologists interviewed, the importance of player approval was a prominent theme, with the acknowledgement that some players and managers were disinterested in the services that they had to offer and, in some instances, opposed to working with a sport psychologist because of the stigma attached to seeking this type of support. The respondents therefore suggested that to have an impact, they relied upon a snowball effect whereby once one player claimed to have been helped by the resident sport psychologist, others then followed. As one respondent recounted: 'By helping one player that just unlocked the door really in terms of people then making use of me.' Pain and Harwood (2004) argue that such evidence suggests that there remains a need to address player perceptions of sport psychology within football, given the potential of negative inferences to act as barriers to their work.

Alongside a host of other comments made by respondents from both practitioner disciplines throughout the course of interview discussion, what a number of the above extracts indicate is that there are clear similarities (and significant overlaps) between the roles of sports chaplains and sport psychologists in professional football. Indeed, it is to the interaction between the two that we now turn.

Sports chaplaincy and sport psychology: connections and possibilities?

All seven of the respondents in this study had found working within English professional football a difficult and unique experience. Neither the sport psychologists nor the sports chaplains were integrated into the formal structures of the clubs in which they worked, and because of this they were perceived generally as outsiders. This was seen by all participants as frustrating and for the most part disadvantageous.

Respondents also indicated that the role that they played within their respective clubs – and the impact that they had on players – was normally determined by the manager's attitude towards them. One respondent noted that the attitude of managers tended to fall into one of three categories. First, some managers advocated a holistic view of player care and, as a consequence, were positive towards the idea of chaplains and psychologists actively making use of both.

Second, managers adopted a position of indifference towards chaplaincy and psychology whereby practitioners were allowed to fulfil their respective roles but were not accepted as an embedded part of club culture. Thirdly, managers actively obstructed and restricted chaplains and psychologists in their roles, allocating little, if any, worth to the support services on offer. On this evidence, further collaborative and educational work with managers, coaches and players by sports chaplains and sport psychologists is required to highlight the critical contribution that such support can make to the personal and professional lives of elite performers.

Hence, despite a combined 55 years of experience within English professional football, and having collectively served under 30 different managers, the sports chaplains and sport psychologists identified only one instance where practitioners from these two occupational areas had worked together. Why, we might ask, was this the case?

Throughout the interview process, it became evident that the respondent psychologists had a broad understanding of the role of the chaplain and vice versa. However, two of the sport psychologists admitted to not knowing the sports chaplains based at the clubs in which they had practised. Similarly, the sports chaplains were not able to readily recall the names of the sport psychologists at the clubs where they had worked. Indeed, all three sport psychologists noted that the relationship between themselves and the resident sports chaplain had been largely non-existent. One of the sport psychologists stated that he was also aware of a number of fellow practitioners who would at best 'tolerate' the presence of a chaplain and would, more likely, become obstructive toward them. Another sport psychologist openly expressed concern over the presence of sports chaplains in professional football arguing that they may carry with them some kind of proselytizing ethos and an ulterior evangelistic motive (see Hoffman, 2010; Krattenmaker, 2010). As a result, two of the three sport psychologists interviewed admitted to never having referred their clients to a sports chaplain. Likewise, three of the sports chaplains had not referred players to a sport psychologist, this despite an acknowledgement that, at times, this may have been helpful to the players concerned.

In the one instance of collaboration between the two disciplines which was identified, the sports chaplain and sport psychologist (both of whom were respondents) had developed a strong working relationship, with the chaplain describing the sport psychologist as 'my biggest ally'. Both practitioners observed that because their roles had a number of practical similarities, particularly with regard to offering pastoral care and enhancing player wellbeing, a cooperative working relationship had proved both efficient and effective. According to these respondents, the success of this relationship was a result of the fact that the players with whom they had worked had a clear understanding (through communication from the management team concerned), of the different functions of their respective roles and that players were referred to the sport psychologist on matters of sport performance and to the sports chaplain on matters relating to religion and spirituality. Both parties contributed to the pastoral care of the players with the sports chaplain taking primary responsibility for this aspect of player support (Nesti, 2011). As a result of having an appreciation of each other's role and function, these respondents were enthusiastic about future interdisciplinary collaborations.

Conclusions

In this chapter we have set out to map the roles and responsibilities of sports chaplains and sport psychologists in English professional football in an attempt to discern the degree of synergy and compatibility between the two. Through interview discussion with practitioners working within the English Premier League, our findings suggest that both chaplains and psychologists play an important role within this context. Sport psychologist respondents primarily focused on performance enhancement within their day-to-day work whilst chaplains primarily offered spiritual care: both contributed to addressing the pastoral needs of players.

What these findings also suggest is that the impact of both disciplines may be restricted due to a number of factors. These include: (1) the lack of information which players, coaches and managers receive about the respective roles of chaplains and psychologists; (2) the kinds of attitudes, views and assumptions which managers might hold about these two distinct disciplines (some of which may be highly dismissive); and (3) the kinds of views that psychologists and chaplains may have about each other (which may be equally dismissive). It is suggested that in order to counter such restrictions and barriers, further collaborative and educational work should be carried out with managers, coaches and players in order to highlight the kind of contribution that such support can make to the overall well-being (and performance levels) of professional footballers. In turn, further research is necessary to explore the potential of collaborative relationships between sports chaplains and sport psychologists and how they might work alongside coaches and managers to provide better holistic support for players.

Notes

1 Sections of this chapter have previously been published elsewhere (see Gamble, Hill and Parker, 2013).
2 In the interests of anonymity, pseudonyms have been used throughout.

References

Amos, P. (2006). 'Who ate all the pies?', in J. Heskins and M. Baker (eds.), *Footballing Lives: As Seen by Chaplains of the Beautiful Game*, Norwich: Canterbury Press, 80–92.
Anderson, A.G., et al. (2002). 'Evaluating the Effectiveness of Applied Sport Psychology Practice: Making the Case for a Case Study Approach', *Sport Psychologist*, 16: 432–53.
Baker, M. (2006). 'You only sing when you're winning', in J. Heskins and M. Baker (eds), *Footballing Lives: As Seen by Chaplains of the Beautiful Game*, Norwich: Canterbury Press, 93–104.

Boyers, J. (2000). *Beyond the Final Whistle*, London: Hodder & Stoughton.

—— (2006). 'We can see you sneaking in', in J. Heskins and M. Baker (eds), *Footballing Lives: As Seen by Chaplains of the Beautiful Game*, Norwich: Canterbury Press, 14–24.

—— (2010). 'Prayers for the Players', *Thinking Faith*, June: 1–4. Available at <http://www.thinkingfaith.org/articles/20100630_1.htm>.

—— (2011). 'Manchester United F.C.', in M. Threlfall-Holmes and M. Newitt (eds), *Being a Chaplain*, London: SPCK, 81–4.

Bryman, A. (2015). *Social Research Methods*, Oxford, Oxford University Press.

Chawner, D. (2009). 'A Reflection on the Practice of Sports Chaplaincy', *Urban Theology*, 3/1: 75–80. Available at <http://www.urbantheology.org/journals/journal-3-1/a-reflection-on-the-practice-of-sports-chaplaincy>.

Ellis, R. (2014). *The Games People Play: Theology, Religion and Sport*, London: Wipf & Stock.

Flannelly, K.J., et al. (2003). 'Psychologists and Health Care Chaplains Doing Research Together', *Journal of Psychology and Christianity*, 22: 327–32.

Gamble, R., D.M. Hill and A. Parker (2013). '"Revs and Psychos": Impact and Interaction of Sport Chaplains and Sport Psychologists within English Premiership Soccer', *Journal of Applied Sport Psychology*, 25: 249–64.

Giorgi, A., and B. Giorgi (2008). 'Phenomenology', in J.A. Smith (ed.), *Qualitative Psychology: A Practical Guide to Research Methods*, London: Sage, 25–50.

Harvey, L. (2014). *A Brief Theology of Sport*, London: SCM Press.

Hastings, E., and L. DelleMonache (2007). 'Promoting the Spiritual Growth and Character Development of Student Athletes', paper presented to the Institute on College Student Values, Center for Sport, Spirituality and Character Development, Neumann College, Aston, PA, 9th Feb.

Heskins, J., and M. Baker, M. (eds) (2006). *Footballing Lives: As Seen by Chaplains of the Beautiful Game*, Norwich: Canterbury Press.

Hoffman, S.J. (2010). *Good Game: Christianity and the Culture of Sports*, Waco, TX: Baylor University Press.

Krattenmaker, T. (2010). *Onward Christian Athletes: Turning Ballparks into Pulpits and Players into Preachers*, Lanham, MD: Rowan & Littlefield.

Maranise, A.M.J. (2013). 'Superstition and Religious Ritual: An Examination of their Effects and Utilization in Sport', *Sport Psychologist*, 27: 83–91.

Miles, B.M., and A.M. Huberman (1994). *Qualitative Data Analysis: A Sourcebook of New Methods*, London: Sage.

Monod, S.M., et al. (2010). 'The Spiritual Distress Assessment Tool: An Instrument to Assess Spiritual Distress in Hospitalized Elderly Persons', *BMC Geriatrics*, 10: 1–32.

Nesti, M. (2007). 'Person and Players', in J. Parry et al., *Sport and Spirituality: An Introduction* London: Routledge, 135–50.

—— (2010). *Psychology in Football: Working with Elite and Professional Players*, London: Routledge.

—— (2011). 'Sport Psychology and Spirit in Professional Football', in J. Parry, M. Nesti and N. Watson (eds), *Theology, Ethics and Transcendence in Sports*, Abingdon: Routledge, 149–62.

Pain, M.A., and C.G. Harwood (2004). 'Knowledge and Perceptions of Sport Psychology within English Soccer', *Journal of Sports Sciences*, 22: 813–26.

Roderick, M. (2006). *A Labour of Love: Professional Football Careers*, London: Routledge.

Sarkar, M., D.M. Hill and A. Parker (2014). 'Working with Religious and Spiritual Athletes: Ethical Considerations for Sport Psychologists', *Psychology of Sport and Exercise*, 15: 580–7.

Waller, S., L. Dzikus and R. Hardin (2008). 'Collegiate Sport Chaplaincy: Problems and Promise', *Journal of Issues in Intercollegiate Athletics*, 1: 107–23.

Watson, N.J. (2011). 'Identity in Sport: A Psychological and Theological Analysis', in J. Parry, M. Nesti and N. Watson (eds), *Theology, Ethics and Transcendence in Sports*, London: Routledge, 107–48.

—— and D.R. Czech (2005). 'The Use of Prayer in Sport: Implications for Sport Psychology Consulting', *Athletic Insight: The Online Journal of Sport Psychology*, 7: 26–35. Available at <http://www.athleticinsight.com/Vol7Iss4/PrayerPDF.pdf>.

—— and M. Nesti (2005). 'The Role of Spirituality in Sport Psychology Consulting: An Analysis and Integrative Review of Literature', *Journal of Applied Sport Psychology*, 17: 228–334.

—— and A. Parker, (2014). *Sport and the Christian Religion: A Systematic Review of Literature*, Cambridge: Cambridge Scholars Press.

Wood, S. (2011). *Keeping Faith in the Team: The Chaplain's Story*. London: Darton, Longman & Todd.

Conclusion

Game over and rewind

John B. White, Nick J. Watson and Andrew Parker

In sport, the dramatic arc of every game eventually ends with a moment of resolution when tensions and anxieties are released and the game is over – at least for the time being. On the one hand, it is fitting to use the sporting metaphor 'game over' to conclude our discussions. On the other, the preceding chapters act simply as a starting point for practitioners and scholars to join the game of critical inquiry into the relationship between sport, chaplaincy, practical theology and ministry. Just as coaches and athletes learn by rewinding and reviewing their game film, we conclude our efforts by pulling together some of the key themes that have emerged in the different parts of this book.

As all of our contributors indicate, because sports chaplaincy is not a homogenous entity, what chaplaincy looks like and how it functions in different sporting contexts depends largely on the why, who and where of how chaplaincy roles originate and develop and the extent of working relationship between chaplains and other helping-professionals. Although sports chaplaincy is a relatively new concept, a range of methods and models witness to this growing field of pastoral and spiritual care, which over the last 40 years has endeavoured – through trial and error – to establish itself as a legitimate expression of ministry.

In Part I, J. Stuart Weir started us off with an overview of the values, models and issues which have shaped this practitioner field. What this overview provides is a sense that, in general, North American sports chaplaincy has been characterized by a 'great commission' model of evangelism and discipleship where chaplains act as chapel service leaders, whereas the customary pattern in the UK has been for a local minister to establish contact with a professional sports club or team and to request permission to serve as a pastoral care-giver and spiritual advisor. Other forms of chaplaincy, such as tour chaplaincy and major event chaplaincy, focus on nurturing and providing spiritual support to professional athletes whose multiple commitments and itinerant schedules bring added tensions and pressures.

Thereafter Part I concentrated on practitioner experiences of sports chaplaincy. In Chapter 2, John Boyers, a chaplain in the English Premier League, observed that, notwithstanding the extent to which the US context inspired his original vision for sports chaplaincy, UK chaplaincy has continued to emphasize the pastoral care and support of players and staff by way of a non-proselytizing approach to ministry. Another distinctive feature of Boyers' narrative is that all of the chaplaincy pioneers which he identifies were ordained clergyman who used this formal role to establish a presence in local sports club settings. This distinction also marks a cultural difference in that in the UK sport and religion do not have the perceived symbiotic relationship (for good or bad reasons) that they do in the US; and thus, UK sports chaplains cannot leverage this alliance when engaging with such institutions. Despite this, a specialized sports chaplaincy organization called SCORE (later Sports Chaplaincy UK) would eventually be formed in order to help standardize the work of sports chaplains. We pick up the point about credentialing and certification more explicitly in due course.

Greg Linville, in Chapter 3, aimed to redress the perceived problem of ineffective and inefficient sports outreach models in North America by sketching an alternative conceptualization of chaplaincy. Linville argues that what is missing from US sports chaplaincy is a robust ecclesiology where true disciples of Christ are made. In turn, he advocates a re-envisioning of sports chaplaincy practice in line with a biblical church-planting model that calls chaplains to encourage sportspersons to pursue congregational life. Such ideas raise questions about how we should regard the relationship between sport-based para-ministries and the local church and how the local church might re-configure their outreach programmes. This theme is subsequently taken up by Cameron Butler and Noel Mitaxa in their discussion of the origins and development of Sports Chaplaincy Australia (SCA), in Chapter 4. Amidst unprecedented demand for chaplaincy services in both amateur and professional sport, the history and success of SCA has been characterized by a necessity to equip the local church to meet the needs of the sporting communities with which they interact. As a consequence, SCA has become a recognized provider of pastoral care within and across sporting locales whilst at the same time providing training resources for those who are called to chaplaincy in sport.

Turning to major event chaplaincy, in the concluding chapter of Part I, Duncan Green discusses his role as the Church of England Olympics executive coordinator for the 2012 Olympic and Paralympic Games in London which positioned him as chaplain both to and within the power structures of LOCOG and local faith communities. Because of how broad-based this network of local organizations was in forming alliances with diverse religious and non-religious groups, attentions were turned away from the routine problems of major event chaplaincy and more towards chaplaincy as a demonstration of justice and care for every citizen. Green assumes a kind of political theology in demonstrating how a shared vision of the common good permits faith communities to enter the public space to promote and defend the interests of diverse groups, which for him, as a Christian minister, meant seeking human fulfilment for everyone. In turn, Green talks about how basic necessities, such as the preparing of food for the Games, had to be understood culturally and religiously so that the needs of different faith groups and communities were respected and sensitively met.

He also discusses how he liaised with the London 2012 Faith Reference Group to plan and deliver chaplaincy programmes for the Games. What became of these efforts were not only inclusive strategies which respected the different faith traditions concerned, but also ministry that went beyond the athletes to serve the various staff and personnel associated with London 2012. In particular, chaplains employed a 'ministry of presence' ethos which has long been identified as a hallmark of wider forms of chaplaincy (Paget and McCormack, 2006; Threlfall-Holmes and Newitt, 2011). In summary, because this level of care and concern is relationally determined, it defies programmatic strategies and raises questions as to how these kinds of practices might become formally adopted in the training and development of sports chaplains worldwide.

In Part II, we took a step back and used some conceptual tools to draw on different perspectives for doing critical reflection on the Christian tradition in sports chaplaincy. In Chapter 6, Nick J. Watson brought to our attention the pandemic of fatherlessness in the modern era which, as a social and moral ill, has affected people participating in sport. A particular interest for Watson is how certain initiatives might combat this problem and what kind of role sports chaplains might play in the soul care of those who lack a degree of love and affirmation because their fathers are absent physically or emotionally. An immediate implication of this chapter is how important it is for chaplains to be aware of such moral and social issues and, furthermore, how they need to be cognizant of the interplay between theory, practice and their own biographies given that these influence how we attend and relate to such experiences. This also means that as an aspect of pastoral care sports chaplaincy involves the learning cycle of 'see–reflect–act'.

In Chapter 7, Ed Uszynski unpacked how the seismic shift of modernity with its individualized notions of spirituality has come to dominate our consciousness, making religion into something consumed at will by individual egos. What this historic shift in understandings of religion and spirituality means – amongst other things – is that many people are now on a quest to construct their own identities having abandoned traditional communities of religious enquiry. Uszynski infers both opportunities and threats which chaplains must be aware of in order to disciple biblically the minds and imaginations of Christian sportspersons, for instance, to see how God's transcendence and immanence relate to the visible world of sports. This theological clarification was re-visited in Part III where we identified how sports psychologists might conceive spirituality and faith. Another particular theme which emerges in Part III is how sports are a site for constructing and reifying personal identity and therefore how important the role of chaplain as care-giver is to identity formation in the performance-driven world of modern-day sport.

In Chapter 8, Steven N. Waller and Harold Cottom explicitly contextualize discussions of sports chaplaincy within the discipline of pastoral theology by reclaiming the rich biblical metaphor of the shepherd. In many ways, this metaphor gives permission to sport chaplains to say 'Yes' to creating communities of care where pathologies of the soul are treated and diagnosed, for undoubtedly systemic pressures assail sportspersons as they are pushed and pulled to meet a plethora of performance goals and the varied expectations of management, agents and families. The presence of maladies such as fear, guilt and shame make soul care all the more important in the dual work of chaplains and sport psychologists as intimated in Chapters 13 to 15. Consequently, Waller and Cottom's ecclesial focus raises questions concerning the shepherd role of the Church in supporting chaplaincy and in encouraging chaplains to receive life from their own communities of care.

In Chapter 9, John B. White argued that the story of the gospel prophetically and pastorally answers the perennial existential question: Who are we while playing sport? An individual's personal identity in sport can be fraught with deception, doubt and competing voices for evaluating self-worth and meaning which chaplains have a theological responsibility to engage with. White spades the soil into which Uszynski (Chapter 7) plants a number of practical suggestions as to how chaplains can assist sportspersons to discover an identity fully realized in the story of Christ crucified and resurrected. Concluding proceedings in Part II, Ashley Null's sentiments resonate well with those of the previous two chapters in that all three offer theological paradigms and resources which serve to function as remedies to the vagaries of souls confused by and trapped in the sham that one's doing determines one's being according to the 'gospel of sports'. In particular, Null reinforces a Reformation belief that the good news resolves how God unties or releases the grip which false beliefs about identity (justification) and living (sanctification) can have. Null concludes with a series of questions which any chaplain worth their salt would be wise to consider.

In Part III, we made explicit what others should expect with regards to sports chaplaincy practices and how chaplains might seek to develop their skills and responsibilities. In Chapter 11, Anthony M.J. Maranise underscored how chaplains might habitually encounter challenges such as spiritual and emotional trauma in their ministries whether related to career-ending injuries, career transitions, or marital and familial breakups. Such encounters assume distinct practices which demand, for instance, fundamental listening and responding skills in order to inhabit others' pain hospitably. If chaplains enter this supportive, pastoral care role haphazardly with little or no training or restraint then this could be detrimental to the wellbeing of those with whom they engage. Moreover, this detriment, according to Waller and colleagues (Chapter 12), brings with it a number of legal, ethical and theological implications. This is sacred work where good intentions will not necessarily bring healing to those whom chaplains serve, and resistance to such professional standards would seem nothing short of irresponsible. If recognized as an aspirational benchmark within the sports chaplaincy fraternity, the high standard of training and accreditation evident across many other forms of chaplaincy may help legitimize this role and aid sports administrators in assessing the competencies of sports chaplains as they do for other staff. In short, such endeavours would help set institutional standards, parameters and boundaries for what meets the threshold of competency for the practice of sports chaplains.

In Part III, reciprocal relationships and joint endeavours between different helping-professionals (sport psychologists, chaplains, trainers) is repeatedly explored, with all of the authors concerned believing that these relationships could be corrective of (and instructive towards) some of the internal challenges surrounding why chaplains do not go through the kinds of credentialing which are common to other forms of chaplaincy. A point which comes across forcefully here is that such credentialing processes may hold benefits for sports chaplains in terms of role recognition, accountability, the addressing of shared responsibilities, standards and skills and also for mutually exploring other practical responsibilities, such as how to welcome and negotiate multi-faith and multi-cultural issues and how to increase awareness and respect from other chaplaincy organizations, the church and the wider sports community: helping people to see what sports chaplaincy is all about. In Chapter 15, Richard Gamble, Andrew Parker and Denise M. Hill argue from empirical evidence, that sports chaplains and sport psychologists share compatible roles, and, if the respective establishments and leaders are properly informed, there is potential for effective joint ventures within sports clubs and organizations.

Since the relationship between chaplaincy as pastoral care and psychology has had a long history of intersection, it makes sense for spiritual care-givers to have an awareness of the tools and ideas which psychologists use and vice-versa. Although historically many sport psychologists may have had something of an 'allergic reaction' to sports chaplains, Mark Nesti in Chapter 13 has demonstrated how a careful retrieval of certain psychological insights can aid the two in a broader exploration of human spirituality and sports. Because there is no necessary threat to each other, then as Gamble, Parker and Hill have argued, this dialectical relationship opens up a series of connections and possibilities. According to Nesti, Catholic spirituality combined with classic virtue theory can overcome perceived conflicts between the two when interpreting what is human flourishing and what virtues may enable sportspersons to realize excellence. This approach offers an angle that Protestant chaplains may wish to reflect on in their own ministry deliberations. Christian theology affirms this integrated method because general revelation is not ultimately in conflict with special revelation: God uses the media of both to disclose his truth about humans.

In Chapter 14, Egli and Fisher pointed to a constructive model which they use in their work at the University of Tennessee, Knoxville, where a team of helping-professionals cooperate and coordinate their respective services in order to best suit the individual (wellbeing) needs of athletes. These authors hold that, because spirituality can be a salient aspect of athlete identity, the psychologist and chaplain can work together to assist athletes in their journey of incorporating faith for the betterment of themselves.

Because the study of sports chaplaincy is an emergent area of research, there is much to learn from the way in which the social and human sciences (as interdisciplinary partners) might aid our understanding of sporting experience. We welcome this kind of research and its discoveries as added bonuses to the chaplain's toolbox, for we contend that integration should be an objective of chaplains, so that other voices may help with prayerfully attending to who God is and what he might be saying in the here and now of athlete experience. Additionally, because sports chaplaincy is, in itself, a relatively new venture when compared to many other kinds of chaplaincy, this interdisciplinary dialogue may serve to foster new working relationships, to balance sports chaplains' academic and ministerial responsibilities, to promote further points of collaboration and to encourage sport psychologists to explore faith and spirituality in their consulting relationships. However, we acknowledge a potential sticking point when employing various methods of interpretation for understanding the human condition. That is, theological proposals should not be jettisoned in favour of social and human science. Practical theology as a legitimate discipline should not indiscriminately follow the other sciences nor should all answers be reducible to 'nothing but' explanations, since each discipline has its limitations and blind spots.

As we stated at the outset of this book, our aim here has not simply been to reflect on the processes and practices of sports chaplaincy but to critically analyse and interrogate how and what sports chaplains do and to uncover more fully what the role of the sports chaplain looks like within specific geographical and cultural contexts. To this end, we have sought to mount a series of challenges to existing trends and ideas in the field and to further contribute to scholarly debate in this relatively under-researched area. Of course, it is only through a continuation of such challenges that sports chaplaincy will remain a vibrant area of ministry and an effective expression of faith within the context of modern-day sport and we trust that the chapters featured in this volume have gone some way to encouraging our readership to join us in the pursuit of these goals.

References

Paget, N.K., and J.R. McCormack (2006). *The Work of the Chaplain*, Valley Forge, PA: Judson Press.

Threlfall-Holmes, M., and M. Newitt (eds) (2011). *Being a Chaplain*, London: SPCK.

Index